Choices and Echoes in Presidential Elections

The University
of Chicago Press
Chicago
and London

Benjamin I. Page

Choices and Echoes in Presidential Elections

Rational Man and Electoral Democracy

Benjamin I. Page, associate professor of
political science at the University of Chicago,
has also taught at Dartmouth and the University
of Wisconsin. He is a coauthor of *The Politics
of Representation* (1974).

The University of Chicago Press, Chicago 60637
The University of Chicago Press, Ltd., London

Library of Congress Cataloging in Publication Data

Page, Benjamin I
   Choices and echoes in Presidential elections.

   Includes bibliographical references and index.
    1. Presidents—United States—Elections. 2. Voting
—United States. I. Title.
JK524.P33   329'.00973   78–4997
ISBN 0–226–64470–7

Photograph on title page by Ted Lacey.

A choice, not an echo
Barry Goldwater
campaign slogan, 1964

The voice of the people is but an
echo. The output of an echo
chamber bears an inevitable and
invariable relation to the input.
V. O. Key, Jr.

Contents

Figures

Tables

Preface

As perhaps befits an effort to bring together such diverse elements as economic reasoning, democratic theory, survey data, and campaign speeches, this book has been long in the making. In the course of writing it I have enjoyed several pleasant and stimulating environments, and have accumulated debts to a number of institutions and individuals.

At Stanford University I benefited especially from the advice and criticism of Richard Brody—with whom I have been privileged to work closely on a number of aspects of elections and voting behavior; Heinz Eulau; Alexander George; Sidney Verba; and Raymond Wolfinger, who introduced me to survey research and helped in many ways with this project.

I was fortunate to learn much from Denis Sullivan and other colleagues at Dartmouth College, and from Hayward Alker and several economists at MIT and Harvard, particularly Jerome Rothenberg.

Most of the writing was done at the University of Chicago, where Donald Wittman was especially helpful. In addition I want to thank several colleagues at Chicago and elsewhere who commented on one or another version of the manuscript—most notably Brian Barry, John Ferejohn, Ira Katznelson, and John Kessel; and those, including James David Barber and John Holum, who made suggestions about particular chapters. It is no idle gesture to say that none of the above is responsible for errors in the final product; indeed some of their advice was treated with cavalier disregard.

I am also grateful for the able research assistance of Calvin Jones, Carol Nackenoff, and Scott Milliman, and for support provided by the National Science Foundation, the Social Science Research Council, and the Social Science Divisional Research Committee of the University of Chicago.

Most of all, I want to thank my family for enduring absences and irritability and mysterious monologues about elections, both at home and in such unlikely settings as the Sawtooth Mountains of Idaho. The book was conceived before Alexandra or Timothy, so that only young Benjamin had the pleasure of observing the whole of the creative process, but there is no indication that the others felt deprived. Mary not only remained cheerful throughout, but worked her way numerous times through the rhetoric of Humphrey, Nixon, et al., and employed her acute editorial eye to spare the reader a good many barbarisms of style. For those that remain, I am solely responsible.

Benjamin I. Page
Madison, Wisconsin
February 1978

Choices and Echoes in Presidential Elections

1

Introduction

Elections are seen by some as harmless athletic contests, in which it's fun to root for a winning team; by others, as mass deceptions which pacify citizens by making them think they control government; and by still others as solemn events in which popular sovereignty is exercised and rulers are held accountable to the ruled. We are concerned with which of these views is most nearly correct—to what extent elections do or do not bring about popular control of government action.

In order to understand the workings or nonworkings of electoral democracy, we must know something about what voters do—how they make voting decisions. We must also know what parties and candidates do—what sorts of choices they offer the voters. Above all, we must know how voters and politicians influence each other, and how these interactions affect the outcome of elections and the making of policy.

Much has been written about how voters decide. This book is chiefly concerned with the more neglected side of elections, the behavior of political parties and candidates. Such questions as the following are explored: To what extent are there distinct choices between opponents' policy stands? To what extent do candidates echo each other and respond to public opinion? How specific or vague are issue stands? Are issue stands changed to appeal to different audiences? What part is played by incumbents' past performance or by proclamations of future goals? What sorts of personal characteristics do candidates present to voters? In each case we will consider how the politicians' behavior influences and is influenced by the voters, and how these processes affect electoral democracy.

Barry Goldwater's promise of a genuine "choice" (that is, a contrast between himself and his opponent) suggests one way in which the behavior of parties is directly relevant to democratic theory. "Responsible party" models of democratic control, in agreement with Goldwater, call for parties to take clear policy stands, distinct from each other, so that voters will have real grounds for choice between them. Certain economic theories, on the other hand, envision parties which compete for votes and take highly similar stands at the center of public opinion, so that the winner optimally sums up the policy preferences of the public. It is important to discover whether either of these theories of democratic control actually operates.

Other theories of democratic control, too—whether involving the past performance of incumbents or the character and personality of candidates—rely on particular sorts of behavior by parties and candidates. A scrutiny of the relevant behavior can help tell us whether electoral democracy is functioning as these theories describe or prescribe.

Further, as V. O. Key's analogy of the echo chamber reminds us (see above, p. v), there is every reason to expect that our understanding of individual political behavior—that is, the opinions, participation, and voting decisions of individual citizens—can be illuminated by knowledge of the behavior of politicians. Electoral politics do not take place entirely inside voters' heads; what choices are made depend largely upon what choices are offered.

The accuracy or inaccuracy of perceptions of parties' stands, for example, might be expected to vary with the clarity or ambiguity of the stands themselves. How much difference voters perceive between the stands of Republican and Democratic candidates might well depend on how much difference there actually is between them. The extent of policy voting, and variations from one issue to another or one election to another, presumably have something to do with the amount of difference between opposing candidates and the clarity of their positions.

Much the same is true of retrospective voting based on past government performance, or of voting based on the personal characteristics of candidates.

Thus politicians' behavior may affect the extent to which *voters'* behavior fits democratic theories. Some voters' attitudes and actions which early studies portrayed as "irrational," or as reflecting limited cognitive capacity, may have had more to do with features of the political environment than with individuals' limitations. If so, any analysis of impediments to democracy should look to parties and the electoral process itself, as well as to characteristics of the citizenry.

In exploring the reciprocal relations between voters and their political environment, we relied heavily on evidence from the campaign speeches, media advertisements, party platforms, and other public materials of presidential campaigns, as well as on political events such as wars and depressions. We employed survey data about public opinion in order to investigate the influence of public preferences upon candidates' issue stands. We also used survey data to provide some evidence on the ways in which public perceptions and voting decisions are affected by the behavior of parties and candidates. For this purpose it is often possible to draw upon (and explain) previous findings from the survey research literature, using our own survey data only for illustration.

Evidence is drawn from United States presidential elections, both because of the availability of data and because these elections are important: they determine who occupies the highest office in the world's most powerful nation. But this evidence can also tell us something about electoral processes more generally, at least with respect to two-party systems with similar economic and social characteristics, whether in the American states and localities or in other nations.

We deal with a number of elections from 1932 onward, all of which fall into the era of New Deal and post–New Deal political alignment. The best data concern the more recent elections—particularly those of 1968 and 1960, for which extensive collections of campaign materials were available, and those of 1964, 1972, and 1976, also with substantial materials. The elections of 1932, 1948, 1952, and 1956 are treated more briefly, and Franklin Roosevelt's three reelection efforts are scarcely dealt with at all. We would hope that the time span and the variety of elections covered are sufficient to give an accurate picture of this historical period in the United States, as well as indicating some regularities which should be found in other periods and in two-party elections generally.

The theoretical perspective throughout the book is derived from economics. This is not to say that our views are congenial to all economists; far from it. But most of the book involves testing or empirically exploring—and in some cases elaborating or developing—various spatial models and other election theories based on economic reasoning about rational man.

Economic theories seek to explain or predict man's behavior in terms of his purposes. They make explicit assumptions about people's goals and about their beliefs concerning how best to attain those goals. The theories then predict that people will behave in ways designed to achieve the assumed goals in the light of the beliefs.

The postulated goals are generally based on a conception of self-interest, but not necessarily of a purely material sort. The beliefs are often—but not always—assumed to reflect perfect information about reality. Often mathematics or logic is used to deduce the predictions about individual and collective behavior. Such formal methods have the advantage of ensuring consistency and precision in the theories. If the predictions prove to be empirically correct, a theory is deemed satisfactory.

It is useful to apply this economic method to understanding elections, because it is reasonable to assume that most presidential candidates and party leaders are consciously goal-oriented individuals. They want political power, which they can obtain by winning elections; they may also want to enact particular policies. Further, they are intelligent and well-informed, and have a good idea of how to compete against the other major party (and perhaps also against factions of their own party) for votes and power. It is appropriate to seek explanations of their behavior in terms of rational pursuit of their goals.

Similarly, voters can be assumed to seek some policy-related goals, among others; they may have limited information about how best to attain them, and may have to calculate and heed the costs in time, energy, and money of political information and political action, but again one can profitably try to understand their political behavior in terms of these goals and calculations.

Clearly a great variety of different assumptions could be made, and the precise assumptions which a theorist chooses determine what sort of theory he comes out with. Milton Friedman[1] is sometimes cited for

the proposition that the plausibility or implausibility of assumptions is
irrelevant, but this neither accords with what economic theorists do
nor follows from Friedman's methodology. True, to him the ultimate
test of a theory is its predictive power, and the theory which best and
most parsimoniously accounts for reality must be accepted even if its
underlying assumptions seem odd. But assumptions merit close attention, both a priori in the construction or critique of theories, and a
posteriori—after gathering empirical evidence—in order to understand
why predictions fail and how to improve the theory. We will attend
closely to the consequences of changing assumptions about political
parties and voters.

Changing assumptions, in fact, underlie the development of this
inquiry: it follows a theoretical progression similar to that pioneered
by Anthony Downs in his *Economic Theory of Democracy*.[2] It begins
with the simplest sort of theory, which assumes that politicians are
pure vote (or plurality) maximizers taking definite policy stands, and
that citizens have purely policy-oriented goals, fixed policy preferences,
no cost of participation, and perfect information about all aspects of
political reality including parties' stands. We ask how well the resulting
predictions accord with reality, and then examine a series of alternative theories, of which some vary assumptions about what sorts of
positions candidates have the option to take, while others consider
different goals and beliefs of politicians and citizens, and postulate
costs of voting or obtaining political information.

The effects of changing assumptions, especially those related to information and transaction costs, are enormous. The voters' sovereignty
and political equality of the simplest theories, for example, give way
to political inequality and to influence by political and economic elites
in theories of greater complexity. Even one of the most cherished
axioms of economic theory, the assumption that citizens have fixed
policy preferences, must be abandoned in the face of a full treatment
of information costs. Thus, while using economic reasoning, we are
ultimately led to consider such matters as the possible manipulation
of policy preferences by politicians, which (like the possibility of corporations' manipulating tastes through advertising) have been foreign
to the mainstream of economic theory.[3]

The plan of the book reflects this theoretical progression, introduc-
ing new substantive topics as they relate to successive elaborations of
theory. Always the question is, What actually happens? How does it

relate to alternative theories about the behavior of parties and candidates and voters? And, most important, How does it affect the workings of electoral democracy? First we ask what influences the locations of candidates' policy stands, conceived of as points on policy dimensions. We then move on to questions of inconsistency and change, and the emphasis and specificity of policy stands; then to nonpolicy matters like goals and past performance and candidates' personal characteristics; and finally to the question of manipulation or leadership of voters.

Chapter 2 discusses two normative schemes of how one might want elections to ensure democracy—the "economic" and the "responsible party" theories. At the same time, two types of positive theory are distinguished, two different kinds of spatial models which seek to explain where, on policy dimensions, parties and candidates actually take their stands. "Party cleavage" theories differ from the more common "public opinion" theories in terms of their underlying assumptions, their predictions, and the type of normative democratic theory they are associated with.

Chapter 3 brings some data to bear on a question which is central to economic theories of democracy and to spatial models, especially those we call public opinion theories: to what extent candidates take policy stands close to the midpoint of public opinion.

Chapter 4 examines the nature and magnitude of differences between the policy stands of opposing candidates. Are "genuine choices" offered to voters, as prescribed by responsible party notions? Certain conflicting predictions of public opinion and party cleavage theories are tested.

Chapter 5 addresses a new set of theoretical questions flowing from still other spatial models, which do not restrict candidates to single fixed policy stands: To what extent are there inconsistencies in candidates' stands, or changes over time, or appeals to special audiences which could upset democratic processes?

Chapter 6 assesses how specific or vague candidates are in advocating policy alternatives, identifies the forums they use for policy statements, and suggests ways they camouflage vagueness. Alternative theories of ambiguity are discussed, based on voters' risk acceptance or on limited information and variations in emphasis; and the consequences of ambiguity for voters' perceptions and voting decisions and for the educative role of parties are explored.

Next, in chapter 7, the rhetoric and reality of problems, past performance, and general goals for the future are examined. Such rhetoric falls outside the purview of spatial models, but it accords with models of rational man who has limited information and hierarchies of goals and beliefs, rather than sets of specific policy preferences. We outline normative and empirical aspects of a theory of electoral democracy which is quite distinct from those of chapter 2 but is compatible with limited information: the theory of electoral reward and punishment.

Chapter 8 considers what sorts of candidates, with what personal characteristics, are offered to the voters, and what techniques are used in personal image making. These topics, too, follow from limited-information theories of electoral competition. Still another variant of normative democratic theory is discussed, under the rubric of "selection of a benevolent leader."

Finally, chapter 9 offers an analysis of some ways in which the electoral process may give leeway to political leaders or permit them to influence voters, for good or ill. It considers what kinds of influence are attempted, and how they affect democracy.

2

Some Theories of Elections and Democracy

Democracy means rule by the people. In this book it is taken to imply complete political equality: equal influence by all citizens in the making of government decisions. From this perspective, principles of rule which impose limits on the scope of popular sovereignty (whether in the form of constitutional rights or separation of powers or requirements of extraordinary majorities), or which permit inequalities in influence (whether on grounds of superior wisdom or greater wealth), may or may not be commendable, but they should be recognized as restrictions on democracy.

This definition focuses on results rather than institutional arrangements. It differs markedly from the institutional definitions of Schumpeter[1] and others; we leave open for investigation the question of whether and how elections bring about democracy, and admit the possibility that they do not do so at all.

Our definition, which corresponds to what Dahl calls "populistic" democracy, is a sweeping one. It is important to recognize that neither democracy in this sense nor elections have won the enthusiasm of many political philosophers. Nearly all philosophers have cherished certain values, such as liberty, which may conflict with democracy. Of those maintaining that governments ought to act in the interest of their citizens, most have doubted either the wisdom of the people in discerning their own interests, or the capacity of the people for carrying interests into political action.

Even if we were to set aside the philosophers of antiquity and the Middle Ages, on the grounds that their views merely reflected the elitist societies in which they lived, it is not easy to unearth whole-hearted advocates of democracy. Hobbes rejected rule by divine right, but argued that once people accepted the social contract, government need not respond to their whims. Locke contributed to the foundations of democratic theory, espousing government by consent of the governed, but he was concerned chiefly with a right of revolution. He did not think much of popular meddling in the making of policy, and believed in natural-law limits on government. Rousseau too had reservations, arguing that the will of all would not always coincide with the true general will; in any case, he had no use for elections or representative government, but advocated direct democracy in small communities.

James Madison, theoretician of the American political system, was much concerned with restraining the popular will and hedging it about with constitutional limits. During and after the expansion of democratic forms of government, most theorists and practitioners of politics —from Jefferson to de Tocqueville, Lincoln, and Dahl—have withheld any commitment to complete democracy.[2]

Perhaps the most compelling arguments in favor of democracy follow from utilitarianism, with its individualistic view of society and its rationalistic model of man. Utilitarianism also provides the beginnings of empirical theory on how democracy could operate through elections and representative government. James Mill in the 1820s outlined the argument: the proper end of government is the greatest good for the greatest number. Government's business is to increase to the utmost the pleasures, and diminish to the utmost the pains, which men derive from one another. The people are the best judges of what would contribute to their own happiness, and the best guarantors of their will being implemented; neither monarchs nor aristocrats can be trusted. It is impractical in a large society, however, to assemble all the people to carry on the day-to-day business of government; power must be entrusted to a few representatives. But representatives, like all individuals, are apt to act selfishly. In order to control them and make their interests identified with those of the community, their tenure in office must be regulated by frequent elections.[3]

Not all utilitarians took this argument to its conclusion. Bentham at first hoped that aristocracy could promote the greatest happiness of the people, and only later in his career advocated democracy and worked for parliamentary reform and universal suffrage. John Stuart Mill, fearing that ignorant working class votes would overwhelm the greater wisdom of the middle class, came to favor substantial restrictions on the powers of representative bodies, and some inequalities in suffrage.[4] The main theme of utilitarian thinking, however, held that the aim of government is the happiness of the people; the people are the best judges of what will make them happy and the only ones who can be trusted to enforce their interests. A representative system, in which the rulers are made strictly accountable to the people through elections, is the best form of government.

Neoclassical economists (that is, most economists in the United States and many in the Western world) are intellectual heirs of the utilitarians. They share the beliefs in individualism and rationality and self-interested behavior. In principle, at least, they also share the approval of democracy and of elections as devices to control the self-interest of rulers.

As we will see in the following sections of this chapter, these economists have contributed some important ideas about how elections work and how they ought to work. But first we must take note of their contributions to social choice theory, a branch of welfare economics which deals with the meaning of democracy itself. Social choice theory greatly advances and complicates our understanding of democracy, and casts doubt upon the possibility either of defining or of realizing democratic outcomes.

At first glance the notion of democratic policy making seems intuitively clear: government ought to adopt that set of policies which most people (that is, at least a majority) prefer over any alternative set of policies. Democracy is simply majority rule. The problem, however—as noticed long ago by Charles-Jean de Borda, Lewis Carroll, and other mathematically oriented students of voting—is that under some circumstances no such preferred set may exist. That is, if each citizen has preference rankings among policy packages A, B, and C, it is possible that a majority of citizens will prefer A to B, and a majority will prefer B to C, but a majority will also prefer C to A. In such cases of cyclical majority, or the paradox of voting, no one alternative is a majority winner against all others, and the "popular will" is not easily defined.[5]

Kenneth Arrow took up this problem in a more thoroughgoing and formal way, and laid the foundations of modern social choice theory. Arrow proved, in what is known as his "possibility" or "impossibility" theorem, that it is impossible to formulate *any* rule, majority voting or any other, which will always aggregate individual preferences into a definitive "social choice" or popular will, unless the rule violates at least one of certain apparently desirable properties—nondictatorship, citizens' sovereignty, positive responsiveness, and the like—or unless individuals' preferences happen to fall into patterns where the paradox does not appear.[6] The impossibility result applies both in practice (to actual decision procedures) and in principle (to definitions of social welfare or popular will).

Further work on social choice has elaborated on the ways in which the paradox can be avoided. One involves preferences which happen to fall into restrictive patterns for which the paradox cannot arise, like Duncan Black's "single peakedness," in which alternatives can be arranged along a dimension in such a way that every citizen's preferences decline, without reversals (that is, additional "peaks"), as he moves away in either direction from his most preferred point. Other ways can be opened by discarding Arrow's condition of independence of irrelevant alternatives and taking account of the intensity of preferences; to do so requires making interpersonal comparisons and using cardinal rather than economists' favored ordinal measures of preference. Still other ways around the paradox involve varying the mixture of normative criteria which decision rules are required to meet.[7]

Social choice theory must be taken into account in thinking about democracy. It makes clear that majority rule is only one of a number of decision rules which might be identified with democracy. In addition, there are a number of sometimes conflicting normative criteria by which democracy can be characterized, ranging from nondictatorship to anonymity, nonnegative responsiveness, and Pareto optimality. Finally, not all technical variants of democracy can come up with definitive policy choices under all circumstances, either in principle or in practice.

We will encounter Arrow's paradox from time to time in this book, particularly as it relates to lack of equilibrium in spatial models. For the most part, however, we rely on a simple conception of democracy in terms of majority-preferred policy alternatives, and assume that it meets sufficient normative criteria and specifies a definitive outcome sufficiently often to be of interest. (Some later chapters touch upon other conceptions of democracy not dealt with in the social choice tradition.) Our theoretical concerns do not require, and available data on preferences do not permit, any more refined treatment. It is tempting to argue, in fact, that the paradox of voting should be the least of a democrat's worries. Mass elections are so far removed from the usual axiomatic social choice processes, and there are so many obstacles in the way of popular will, however defined, that we need not devote too much concern to the difficulty of definition.

Our discussion so far leaves open the question of precisely how elections could or should reveal the will of the people and translate it into public policy. This would seem to be straightforward enough if the citizenry could be assembled for referenda and reveal their preferences among all possible alternative policies. But such referenda are impractical. How, in a representative government, can the voice of the people be expressed and enforced? In particular, how can this come about in systems like the American, with two major political parties alternating in government? The early utilitarians barely hinted at answers, and it was left to modern economists and others to spell out theories of electoral democracy.

The following sections take up two types of normative theory concerning how two-party elections *ought* to work, each of which is associated with a type of empirical theory about how elections *do* work. Both types of empirical theory are most notably represented by spatial models of electoral competition, which rest upon a simple sort of economic reasoning. The theoretical categories used, and the relations among them, are summarized in table 1.

Later, especially in chapters 7 and 8, we will encounter some different—and perhaps superior—normative and empirical theories of elections and democracy, still within a broadly economic framework, but resting upon different assumptions about the behavior of parties and voters.

Table 1	Types of Electoral Theory Discussed in Chapter 2	
	Normative	Empirical (Spatial models; electoral competition theories)
No systematic party differences	The economic theory of democracy	Public opinion theories
Party differences	Responsible party theories	Party cleavage theories

The Economic Theory of Democracy and Public Opinion Theories of Electoral Competition

Many economists hold a particular normative view of how two-party elections ought to work. At the risk of some confusion, therefore, we will speak of it as "the" economic theory of democracy, recognizing that this is a special usage, to be distinguished from economic reasoning generally and from the title of Downs's book.

The economic theory of democracy calls for elections to bring forth representatives who enact the policies most desired by the public. In the two-party system *both* parties should take identical policy stands which echo the popular will. It then does not matter which party wins; the winning party, whichever it is, carries out the same, most popular policies.

A set of empirical theories which can be called public opinion theories suggest how this desired result could occur. If citizens vote on policy grounds, and both parties adjust their policy stands so as to win as many votes as possible, the result may be precisely the taking of identical party stands, with both parties advocating the most popular policies. Thus self-interested competition by the parties leads to an optimal outcome.

The first theory of this type was offered in 1929 by Harold Hotelling.[8] Hotelling was primarily concerned with the question of how two merchants, seeking to maximize their profits, would decide what prices to charge and where in geographical space to locate their stores. In passing, he considered the analogous case of two political parties, and laid the foundation for public opinion theories of electoral competition and for spatial models generally.

Hotelling set forth a number of assumptions which may seem obscure or technical but which had important effects on his conclusions. He postulated two merchants, A and B, with stores located somewhere on a line—"Main Street." He assumed that buyers were uniformly distributed along the same line (although he asserted that his analysis would apply equally well to locations on a plane—allowing for cross streets—and to any distribution of customers). He assumed, further, that A and B sold a particular good, which cost nothing to produce (or, more generally, cost a constant amount per unit); that buyers had to pay transportation costs, which depended directly upon the distance between themselves and the store they patronized; that demand was completely inelastic—each consumer bought the same amount of the good in each period of time, regardless of price; and that each buyer shopped at the store which—considering both price and transportation costs—was cheapest for him. Finally, Hotelling assumed that each seller, A and B, would adjust his price to maximize profits, at a given value of the other's price.

After exploring the results of price competition, Hotelling analyzed the way each merchant would decide where to locate his store. He showed that, if A's location were fixed, B could increase his profits by coming as close to A "as other conditions permit," staying on that side of him where the greatest number of customers was located. This result is intuitively sensible. As B moved toward A, B would keep all his old customers, for A was still farther away from them; and B would add some customers who had originally been closer to A.

Hotelling did not claim that there was an equilibrium set of optimal locations for the two stores—that is, locations which could not be improved upon, no matter what the other merchant did—for in the economic case price competition upsets locational equilibrium. But he left the impression that the most profitable location for each store would be as close as possible to the median of the distribution of customers, that is (assuming his uniform distribution), as close as possible to the center of Main Street. Only if a merchant located at the center could he be sure that his competitor would not steal away more than half the customers. According to Hotelling, Woolworth's and Kresge's should be found side by side, in the middle of town.

Hotelling claimed there was a direct political analogy: the Republican and Democratic parties, competing for votes, choose their locations in a "space" of possible issue positions. "Main Street" becomes a liberal-conservative continuum. The "buyers" are voters, who choose the party to which "transportation costs" are lower—the party which is closer to them in ideology. Under these conditions each "merchant" —each party—would have an incentive to make the "location" of its platform as much like the other's as possible. According to Hotelling, presidential candidates would take stands very close to each other, near the midpoint of public opinion (see figure 1).

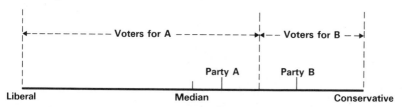

a. Party A, closer to the median, wins more votes.

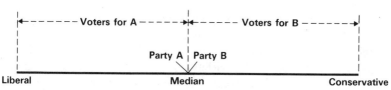

b. Neither party gains votes by moving away from the median.

Figure 1   **The Logic of Spatial Models**

Hotelling himself was not pleased with this outcome; he favored a more distinct choice between parties, so that more citizens could have a chance to vote for a party close to them, just as he wanted more dispersed store locations (so that customers wouldn't have to travel so far) and more variety in the quality of products.

But other economists would disagree, pointing out that in this case of unidimensional (single-peaked) preferences, the median policy is a majority winner against any other policy; it embodies the popular will. Thus most economists would approve the way in which the hidden hand of competition, in politics as in Adam Smith's economics, would produce a socially optimal result. Power-seeking, self-interested parties would have to embrace the most popular issue stands, promising to enact them into policy. Hotelling's model, in other words, suggests how the economic theory of democracy could be realized.

Many theorists have elaborated upon Hotelling's insight, and a whole literature of spatial models has blossomed forth. By all odds the most important advance came in the work of Otto Davis and Melvin Hinich, who—recognizing that a single "liberal-conservative" dimension offers only a crude approximation to political reality—introduced a model of electoral competition over a more complicated issue space with many policy dimensions.[9] Theorists have also considered the effects of variations in voter turnout due to alienation or indifference (first in the unidimensional and then in the multidimensional cases); differing shapes of opinion distributions, such as unimodality and bimodality; differences in the salience of issues to different voters; alternative candidate goals (vote maximizing as well as plurality maximizing); sequences of elections; collusion between parties; and other factors.

Unfortunately this progress has brought with it considerable confusion about exactly what, if anything, spatial models predict. Depending upon what assumptions are made concerning turnout, the shape of opinion distributions, the nature of voters' utility functions, and candidates' goals, a bewildering variety of contingent predictions can be made.[10] The hidden hand seems to have lost its touch; there is no assurance of an outcome of optimal or midpoint policies.

The confusion has been compounded by a tendency of theorists to use the axiomatic method in two different ways. Sometimes they choose and commit themselves to a set of assumptions, letting the theory stand or fall in terms of its predictive power. At other times they apparently regard some of their assumptions as boundary conditions or empirical parameters, intending the theory to apply only when those assumptions are met. Either approach can be proper, but failure to make clear which is intended blurs the meaning of predictions. Then too, in the latter approach the relation between theory and reality is sometimes left problematic because key assumptions—those concerning candidate goals, for example—are almost impossible to validate empirically.

The clearest theoretical result is a discouraging one. Once we abandon the unidimensional spatial model, under most plausible circum-

stances *no* definite prediction about parties' or candidates' stands can
be made. There does not exist any single set of positions which wins
more votes than all others. That is generally the case, for example, if
voters differ in nonrandom ways concerning the salience of issues, or
if probabilistic ("lottery") stands are allowed, or if there is any asymmetry in the distribution of citizens' policy preferences. Plott remarks
that "it would only be an accident (and a highly improbable one) if
an equilibrium exists at all."[11]

This result is closely related to Arrow's paradox. In cases in which
public preferences are such that there exists no package of policies
which a majority prefers to all others—that is, when there is a cyclical
majority and no unique majority winner—neither does there exist, by
the same token, any set of policies which a party can advocate with
the assurance that the other party cannot find policies that will beat
them. There is no equilibrium.

Failure to find equilibrium may indicate a deficiency in these theories, or it may not. In some situations party stands may in fact be
indeterminate and quite unpredictable. For the sake of scientific inquiry, one would hope that such situations are rare.

In any event, for our present purposes it is possible to find certain
coherent predictive themes in the spatial modeling literature, particu-
larily when we contrast the two different families of spatial models
described in this and the following section.

Many—perhaps most—spatial models of electoral competition can
properly be labeled *public opinion* theories, since they propose that
candidates' or parties' stands are affected solely by the policy opinions
of an undifferentiated mass public. As we have indicated, Hotelling's
original model was of this type; so is much of the leading work by Otto
Davis and his associates in the Carnegie group.[12] Public opinion theories are closely related to the economic theory of democracy since
they postulate how, empirically, the normatively desired outcome of
centrist party stands could occur.

Two main predictions flow from public opinion theories. Most of
them predict that:

1. the midpoint of public opinion exerts an important influence
   upon the stands that parties or candidates take.

All public opinion theories imply that:

2. there are no systematic differences between the stands of opposing parties.

That is, the positions taken by opposing candidates may not be identical, due to the nonexistence of equilibrium strategies or because of
random error or other factors; but in these theories no variable is
specified that could account for the differences between them.

The first prediction is more familiar and perhaps more significant
than the second; it is critical to the economic theory of democracy.
It is less strong than is often supposed, however, because of the slippery nature of the concept of "importance." Only under certain narrow
assumptions do the theories predict that both parties converge exactly
at the midpoint of public opinion. Under more general conditions, the
best they can do is to show that a candidate standing further from the
midpoint than a certain distance could always be defeated by a midpoint strategy—and the boundary is a very loose one, at that.[13] This
prediction is quite difficult to put to empirical test, but because of its
normative importance an attempt to do so will be made in chapter 3.

The second prediction is less familiar but has stronger empirical
implications, and will be tested in chapter 4. Although seldom made
explicit, it follows quite directly from the assumptions of public opinion theories. In all such theories, regardless of varying provisions
concerning turnout, shape of opinion distributions (even bimodality),
or anything else, the influences on the candidates of opposing parties
are exactly the same. Both candidates face identical electorates. They
make identical calculations about what issue position is optimal. Nothing in these theories distinguishes between the parties in any way or
pushes them to take different stands.

This identity of influences depends on four critical assumptions
concerning actors, motivations, and the absence of transaction costs
or information costs:

   a. *Single arena and unified actors.* Candidates' stands are influenced
only by anticipation of *general* elections, in which only the two candidates (or unitary "parties") and voters take part.

   b. *Pure vote seeking* by candidates and parties, without any concern for the substance of their stands.

Assumptions *a* and *b* together ensure that Republican and Democratic candidates do not have differing policy goals of their own, and

that they need not take special account of the policy preferences of
Republican and Democratic primary voters or convention delegates.

c. Pure policy voting by citizens, with perfect perceptions and fixed
issue salience; no effects of candidates' personal images, canvassing,
media advertising, or other factors on voting decisions.

d. Turnout which is either universal or which responds only to
candidates' stands, and does so only directly; no effects of precinct
workers, registration drives, or the volume of publicity on how many
people vote.

Assumptions *c* and *d* rule out any need for money or campaign
work; hence candidates need not be concerned with differing policy
goals of Republican and Democratic money givers or activists.

These four assumptions of public opinion theories are not very
plausible as descriptions of the real world. We draw attention to them
in order to suggest why predictions based on them may go wrong, as
well as to indicate ways in which alternative theories can be developed.

Responsible Party Theories and Party Cleavage Theories

A number of American political scientists, most notably Woodrow
Wilson and E. E. Schattschneider, have put forward a type of normative theory of elections and democracy which differs markedly from
the economic theory of democracy, and which accords with Goldwater's call for "a choice not an echo." "Responsible party" theories
call for centralized, well-disciplined political parties, each taking policy
stands which are clear and are substantially different from the stands
of the opposing party. Voters are supposed to choose the party whose
stands are closer to their own policy preferences. The winning party,
whose stands please more voters, then enacts those policies.[14]

The economists offer a critique of these theories which, at first blush,
seems quite compelling. The responsible party theories appear to focus
on expressive rather than instrumental aspects of elections. They guarantee voters a "real choice," and thereby give more citizens the pleasure of voting for a party near them—a shorter walk to one of Hotelling's dime stores—than would be the case if both parties stood for
the same thing; but by the same token, the theories seem to ignore the
outcome of the electoral process. The parties are asked only to differ,

with no other restrictions on their stands. There is no guarantee that either party will stand for the policies most favored by the public. This seems an odd sort of democracy, which ensures only that the less unpopular party takes office.

A closer look shows that there is more to it than this. The responsible party theories in their more sophisticated form involve a somewhat different notion of democracy from the economists' aggregation of individuals' policy preferences, and they rest on a different model of man. The voter is not conceived of as a perfectly informed citizen with fixed policy preferences, who votes for the party or candidate that most nearly agrees with him. Instead, the citizen is one who can afford to obtain only limited and imperfect information about politics. He knows only vaguely what the government is doing, what alternative policies can be pursued, and how various policies would actually affect his interests. Thus it is the task of political parties to inform, to educate, and to persuade. This they do not only by offering a clear choice but also by explaining the consequences of the programs they advocate and the reasons voters should support such programs. The winning party is not simply the one which more nearly agrees with the policy preferences of a majority of voters; it is the one which can convince a majority of voters to agree with its policies.

There is a strongly populistic thrust to these responsible party theories, which maintain that the poor and the downtrodden are the most likely to be confused about the nature and consequences of public policy, and to be most in need of a political party to mobilize them and explain what policies would work to their benefit. In Europe, it is sometimes implied, the socialist parties play this part of uplifting and guiding working people and the poor; in the United States the Democratic Party does (or should do) the same thing. In general, it is argued, distinct party stands open the possibility of leadership, which can achieve a higher form of democracy than one in which policy preferences are perfectly aggregated but may not reflect voters' true interests.

The relationship between these normative prescriptions and empirical reality has presented a problem for responsible party theorists. They have had difficulty in accounting for how party differences would come to exist at all, and have had still more difficulty in showing how (as they generally hope) any existing party differences could be made greater. Spatial models of the public opinion sort, as well as pre-

Hotelling common sense, seem to show that parties have strong incentives to converge and *not* take different stands. Responsible party advocates have often resorted to exhortation or to reform proposals like the celebrated American Political Science Association report,[15] which lacked any promising strategy for implementation.

Within the spatial modeling literature, however, there have been a number of efforts (not all of them successful) to develop empirical theories of party differences. These theories are in the economic tradition, and therefore do not capture the full spirit of such responsible party ideas as the educational function of parties, but they do at least offer possible accounts of how differences between parties' policy stands could arise, and can therefore be associated with the responsible party theory. Spatial models which predict party differences will be called *party cleavage* theories.

The first efforts in this direction must be counted as unsuccessful. In 1937, Lerner and Singer introduced a limited form of elastic demand into Hotelling's model of store locations. They postulated that if customers had to travel too far to both stores, they might not buy at either, even if one were a little closer than the other.[16] The political analogy would be abstention due to alienation: if citizens don't like either party, they may choose not to vote at all.

Lerner and Singer argued that if transportation costs made demand highly elastic with respect to store location, two merchants would not necessarily converge at the middle of Main Street; practically any location would yield the same profits. Arthur Smithies, using a more general concept of elastic demand, concluded that under high transportation costs the merchants would locate at opposite quartiles, not at the median. Turning to the political analogy, he argued that by 1936 the Republican and Democratic parties were no longer taking similar stands; he conjectured that they did not feel free to compete for the undecided vote at the center, but had to worry about losing support at the extremes of political opinion.[17]

Anthony Downs, too, tried to allow for nonconvergence of competing parties by postulating efforts to prevent alienated supporters with extreme opinions from abstaining. Downs argued that the shape of opinion distribution, as well as the elasticity of turnout with respect to voters' issue distance from parties, would affect parties' choices of issue stands: if there were a bimodal distribution, he asserted, parties would remain "poles apart" in ideology[18] (see figure 2).

Downs's book had such a great impact on political scientists that it is still widely believed that spatial models can account for both convergence and nonconvergence of parties and candidates, by considering only the parameters of public opinion: the location of the midpoint of the distribution, the elasticity of turnout, and the shape of the distribution. But that impression is incorrect.

Downs's result depends critically on his additional (but often forgotten) assumptions restricting party mobility: that parties cannot

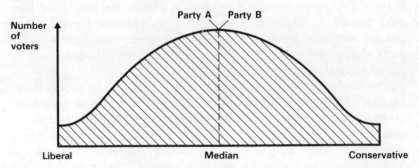

a. Unimodal distribution. Parties converge at the midpoint of public opinion.

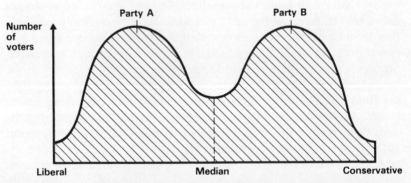

b. Bimodal distribution. According to Downs, parties diverge and stand at the modes.

Figure 2   **Downs: The Effect of the Shape of Opinion Distribution**

"move ideologically past" each other, or cross the midpoint of opinion. Subsequent work has shown that, without such a restriction, abstention due to alienation, with or without a bimodal opinion distribution, is not sufficient to produce a theoretical prediction of divergent party stands. Depending on other conditions, bimodality and alienation might bring about convergence at the midpoint, or the nonexistence of equilibrium.[19]

The models of Lerner and Singer and of Smithies, which lack mobility restrictions, should therefore be considered public opinion rather than party cleavage theories; they do not actually predict party differences.

Downs's is a party cleavage theory, albeit an unusual one, because of its dependence upon limited party mobility. Downs justified this aspect of his theory in terms of parties' need to preserve credibility by avoiding sudden shifts: a rationale which could be adequate if the credibility factor were very strong and if bimodality were extreme and persistent over time. In effect, party differences would depend upon initial historical accident plus inertia. When and whether bimodal distributions occur is a question not easily answered, since data based on equal-interval alternatives are usually lacking. There is some empirical evidence indicating that the alienation effect on turnout is not very powerful—perhaps not strong enough to pull parties' positions substantially away from the midpoint of opinion in Downs's bimodal case —and that abstention due to indifference, which could negate the prediction of divergence, is about equally prevalent.[20]

Most party cleavage theories work in a different way, for which the shape of opinion distributions is irrelevant and neither abstention due to alienation nor mobility restrictions are needed. These theories— some of them developed by the same scholars who have also set forth public opinion theories—postulate one or more specific factors which could push parties' issue stands apart in predictable directions. Such factors include the policy goals and opinions of voters in party primaries or of convention delegates; opinions of party activists and election workers; opinions of financial contributors; and the policy views of the candidates themselves.[21]

These party cleavage theories work within the same spatial modeling apparatus as public opinion theories: the unidimensional or multidimensional issue space; rational politicians, whose behavior can be explained in terms of goals and beliefs; politicians' working assumptions about voters, including single-peaked preferences and voter agreement on issue dimensionality; and complete mobility of candidates and perfect information about voters' preferences.

They also acknowledge that public opinion theories may describe an important part of what happens in a campaign. Candidates like to win elections; they know that citizens vote partly on the basis of policy preferences; and they are influenced in their choice of issue positions by calculations of what stands would best please the public.

But these party cleavage theories contradict or modify the assumptions of public opinion theories in some or all of the following ways, which introduce various transaction costs and information costs and different motivations.

a_1 *Multiple actors and arenas.* Parties act as loose coalitions, not monolithic "teams." Candidates are selected through complex nomination processes, often involving primary electorates, party activists, financial contributors, party leaders, and convention delegates. General elections involve not only candidates and the public but also party activists and financial contributors. All these actors have policy preferences which may differ systematically by party.

a_2 *Effects of nomination politics on issue stands.* The actors who influence nominations play an important part in the determination of nominees' issue positions, through two processes. First, they select the nominee from a set of pre-nomination candidates with various past issue stands, and thereby choose issue positions with the man. Second, prenomination candidates may choose their stands in anticipation of nominators' desires. In either case, prenomination stands tend to persist into the general election campaign.

b_1 *Policy motivations in nominations.* Those who influence nominations seek to win elections, but they also seek to nominate candidates who stand for policies they approve of.

b_2 *Policy motivations of candidates.* Candidates, too, want to win and to be nominated, but they also hold policy opinions of their own which they sometimes express in campaigns.

c_1 *Influence of expenditures on voting.* Citizens vote on other grounds in addition to their policy preferences, including party loyalty, their images of candidates' personal characteristics, and broad feelings about group benefits or government performance. The favorable impact of these factors can be increased by candidates' expenditure of money on television speeches and advertisements, direct mail and telephone campaigns, billboards, pamphlets, and the like.

c_2 *Policy motivations of money givers.* Private contributions are a significant source of funds. Contributors give, in part, because they agree with candidates' policy stands.

d_1 *Influence of money and workers on turnout.* Turnout is affected by a number of nonpolicy factors, including the level of campaign publicity, registration drives, and precinct work. The magnitude of these factors depends on the amount of money and the number of campaign workers a candidate can muster.

d_2 *Policy motivations of campaign workers.* Campaign activists participate, in part, because of agreement with candidates' policy stands.

According to some party cleavage theories, the factors affecting a candidate's issue positions are complex; they may not result in the optimality of a single, easily calculated strategy like standing at the midpoint of public opinion. (Indeed, as is the case with public opinion theories, if these theories allow for correlations between intensity and direction of opinion or do not impose a priori restrictions on opinion distributions, we know that in general no single optimal position exists for either candidate.)

The basic argument, however, is that if a candidate wants to get nominated, increase his turnout, and win votes, he must adjust his issue stands to please the policy-oriented activists, delegates, and money givers of his party. His stands will be influenced by their opinions and by his own, as well as by those of the general public.

Still, the economic way of thinking raises a nagging difficulty about this argument. How can party activists or others get away with insisting that candidates respond to their policy preferences? Why doesn't the logic of competition drive them to give up more and more of their own policy wishes in order to beat the other party, until both parties end up with identical vote-seeking stands? Some party cleavage theories simply ignore this problem and assume that activists do insist on having their own way, whether or not it is rational to do so. In order to keep fully within an economic framework, however, it is necessary to argue either that party differences are limited to nonequilibrium situations (that is, parties pick their favored policies from sets of cycling alternatives), or that the political market is imperfect due to voters' lack of information or collusion between the parties.[22]

Party cleavage theories predict that:

1. The midpoint of public opinion has some influence on candidates' positions.
2. Candidates' positions are also affected by the candidates' own policy opinions, and/or by the opinions of convention delegates, primary electorates, party activists, or financial contributors.
3. To the extent that party cleavages on policy are congruent across these categories of political actors, candidates of the opposing parties take systematically different positions.

Party cleavage theories, then, predict that, to some degree, candidates' policy stands echo the public and echo each other, as is called for by the economic theory of democracy and is predicted by public opinion theories. In the next chapter we will see to what extent this is actually true of presidential candidates. But party cleavage theories, unlike public opinion theories, also predict a significant degree (and a systematic direction) of choice or contrast between the stands of opposing candidates, as prescribed by responsible party theories of democracy. In chapter 4 we will explore the extent and nature of candidate differences.

3

Public Opinion and Candidates' Policy Stands

As we have seen, the economic theory of democracy calls for a candidate's policy stands to echo the policy preferences of the public, and many spatial models—especially those of the public opinion variety—predict that the midpoint of public opinion on issues has an important influence upon the stands that a candidate takes. To what degree is this prediction correct?

The evidence suggests that it tells part of the story, but only part. Candidates do tend to stand closer to the public than would happen by chance, but the correspondence is far from perfect. On many issues, candidates' stands diverge markedly from the midpoint of public opinion. Before turning to the evidence, however, we must take note of the methodological difficulties involved in finding out precisely how close together a candidate and the public are. The problem does not so much lie with determining candidates' stands; although ambiguity is widespread (see chapter 6), some comments can be found on most issues, and outright contradictions of those comments are so rare that it is usually possible to speak of—and ascertain—*the* stand which a candidate takes on any particular issue.

The primary difficulty lies instead with the manner in which public opinion has been measured. It is common practice in polls to ask people only whether they "approve" or "disapprove," whether they "favor" or "oppose" a stated policy. The pro and con responses convey little information about which policies people most prefer, or whether preferences have dimensionality, or how citizens' preferences are distributed along continua of policy alternatives. It is difficult to judge which specific policy is at the midpoint of a distribution, or to judge where, on the whole distribution of opinion, the particular policy endorsed by a candidate would fall. Only questions which ask for choices among a number of specific policy alternatives can be readily used for this purpose.

Moreover, even knowledge of a candidate's stands and of the full distribution of public opinion on a number of issues would not be sufficient to measure the overall closeness or distance between a candidate and the public. Ideally, one should aggregate the distance between candidate and public on many issues into a single overall measure of distance—not merely counting issues, or adding them up, but weighting issues by their salience or importance to citizens, and perhaps also taking account of interactions among issues. This is very hard to do, both because we generally lack good measures of the relative importance of issues to people, and because it is not usually possible to measure distances on different issues in a comparable way so that they can be aggregated.

In the face of such difficulties we have used two techniques which, although less than ideal, shed at least some light on the question of distances between candidates and the public. Given a set of issues, each technique counts how often a candidate is—according to a particular criterion—close to the public, and how often he is distant.

The first, and preferred, technique is to consider a number of issues about which multiple-alternative questions have been asked, so that on each we can estimate where the quartiles of opinion lie and we can judge whether a candidate's position is or is not in the second or third quartile: that is (by definition), whether the candidate stands as close to the median as half the public does. We can then perform a statistical test.

If there were no relationship at all between a candidate's position and the median of public opinion—if the candidate's stand on each issue were drawn randomly from the whole distribution of Americans' opinions on that issue—there would be a probability of exactly one-

half that he would stand in the second or third quartile on any given
issue. On the average, considering many issues, he would stand that
close to the median on about half the issues. If we find, using a binomial test, that a candidate stands in the second or third quartile of
public opinion significantly more than half the time, that indicates
that public opinion is influencing his issue stands.

The first technique can be used only on issues for which we can find
multiple-choice poll data. In order to investigate a broader set of issues,
we must turn to a second technique: judging how often a candidate
takes stands which are closer to alternatives preferred by a plurality of
the public, than to alternatives rejected by a plurality. The frequency
of agreement with a plurality of the public cannot easily be subjected
to statistical test since the probability of chance agreement on each
issue depends upon the size of the plurality on that issue, but it gives
at least some indication of the distance between candidate and public.

The same data limitations which make it difficult to locate midpoints
and estimate candidates' distances from them, also prevent us from
finding out whether preferences are single-peaked and whether preferred points are distributed symmetrically. Thus we cannot be sure
whether the midpoint can be identified with the optimal democratic
outcome; nor, if we accept the empirical parameter approach, can we
be sure whether the conditions are met under which spatial models
predict midpoint stands. We proceed on the assumption that the midpoint is of normative interest and that (either because the conditions
are met or because they are assumed) spatial models do predict influence by the midpoint, but the conclusions must remain tentative.

Americans' Policy Preferences

Throughout the post–New Deal historical period—in other words, for
at least as long as opinion surveys of national samples have been conducted—the policy preferences of Americans have followed certain
lines of continuity. There has remained an undercurrent of reverence
for individual rights, and mistrust of big government, rooted in Lock-
ean liberalism.[2] Since the Great Depression, however, the general public has favored (within a largely free enterprise or capitalistic economic
system) an active role for the federal government in many specific
areas: regulation of the economy; adjustment of labor-management

disputes; and assistance with jobs, education, medical care, and relief or welfare for the destitute.

This is not to say that public preferences have remained constant. Over the years the public has come to favor more extensive economic regulation and broader social welfare policies. In foreign policy, the inter-war isolationism of the 1930s gave way to internationalist desires to defeat the Axis and then to oppose the Soviet Union, followed by a tendency toward neo-isolationism after the Korean and Vietnamese wars. There was increasing support for laws promoting equal treatment of blacks and other minorities, followed by resistance to school and neighborhood integration. Enthusiasm for civil liberties rose and fell with the apparent seriousness of threats from domestic fascism or communism, or of unrest among college students, blacks, or others. Similarly, preferences for strict law enforcement increased in the 1960s and 1970s.[3]

The time span within which a presidential nominee confronts the public is a relatively brief one, however; public opinion rarely shifts dramatically during the course of a campaign. Thus, in order to provide a baseline for comparison of candidates' stands, we can examine in more detail the state of Americans' opinions at the time of a particular election.

For this purpose we gathered together the responses to a large and diverse set of questions asked by several different survey organizations in 1967 and 1968. (The topics and sources of these 122 survey items are listed in the Appendix.)[4] Our review of the responses focuses on the policies favored by pluralities of the public, and—where ascertainable—on policies at the midpoint of continua of opinions.

There are, of course, many uncertainties in reading the tea leaves of public opinion, not the least of which is the nagging concern that, given low levels of information and imperfect question wording, poll results may be meaningless. This misgiving is particularly justified in the case of obscure or unfamiliar issues: a colleague has dubbed it the "Gulf of Aquaba caveat," after one of our more doubtful items. On the other hand, it can be argued that even if the opinions of some or most individuals are unstable, such aggregate indices as marginal distributions may be stable and meaningful.

According to the polls, by 1967–68 most people had become sick of the Vietnam war. Early in 1968, just before President Johnson's decision not to run for reelection, 63% disapproved of Johnson's handling of the war and 49% thought it had been a mistake to send U.S. troops. Further, nearly half the people considered Vietnam the most important problem facing the country. Yet there was a curious unwillingness to liquidate the U.S. involvement by withdrawal; indeed, many Americans still wanted to escalate U.S. efforts. While most (66%) approved withdrawing "some" American troops if they were replaced with South Vietnamese, and a plurality had long opposed invading North Vietnam, there was no great demand for unconditional troop withdrawals. More wanted to reduce the number of American troops (35%) than wanted to increase it (17%), but the center of gravity of opinion was close to the status quo of keeping 500,000 American troops in Vietnam (32%).

Americans were even more hawkish on bombing policy. While the public overwhelmingly (65% to 27%) opposed using nuclear weapons, most people favored the bombing of North Vietnam with conventional high explosives: in June 1968 a plurality of 42% wanted to increase it, compared to 19% for stopping it and 22% for keeping it the same. A big majority opposed an unconditional halt in bombing North Vietnam, and even a halt subject to very harsh conditions won support by only a small plurality.

Most Americans also opposed making major concessions in a peace settlement. They were willing to turn the whole problem over to the United Nations (60%), or to settle for a neutral Vietnam (66%), but there was considerable resistance to the idea of a coalition government. Most people (52% to 26%) opposed negotiating even "minimum representation" in the South Vietnamese government for the Viet Cong. A plurality disapproved of a coalition government even if it were freely elected.

1968 was a year of great concern about "law and order," a phrase which seemed to lump together problems of drug abuse, student demonstrations, street crime, and riots in black ghettos. Fully 81% of Americans agreed that "law and order has broken down in this country." The predominant response was to favor stronger law enforcement —sometimes to the point of repression—but to oppose new or increased remedial programs.

Most Americans wanted to cut or keep at the same low level the "war on poverty" (68% versus only 23% for expansion) and aid to the cities (69% to 15%). They wanted federal "community action" grants to be kept at the current level or reduced. (Those favoring the present level or increases—unfortunately lumped together in the survey question—only moderately outnumbered those favoring reductions, 54% to 35%.) More people wanted to cut back (31%) than wanted to expand (14%) aid for welfare and relief payments, and—in accord with the Protestant ethic—a clear majority of 58% to 36% opposed a guaranteed income, even at the low level of $3,200 a year for a family of four.

On the other hand, Americans approved helping the poor to get jobs: a strong majority (78% to 18%) wanted the federal government to "guarantee" work, and most favored retraining programs (75%) and work projects (56%). Further, there was some support for urban renewal, low income housing, rat control, and summer camps for ghetto youth.

Most people wanted to deal severely with riots, crime, or protest of any sort. The majority (54% to 41%) thought that the best way to handle looting during race riots was to shoot looters on sight. Most (69%) felt that violations of law and order had been encouraged by the courts; 63% thought that courts did not deal harshly enough with criminals, and most favored "conservative" appointments to the Supreme Court. They overwhelmingly favored registration (71%) and licensing (73%) of guns, and a majority wanted to draft student protesters.

In foreign affairs, Americans were cautious about relations with communist nations: most (78%) wanted to negotiate our differences, but a plurality (38% to 31%) opposed permitting even nonmilitary trade. Most people favored keeping our troops in West Germany (63%) and strengthening the NATO alliance (65%). Attitudes toward China had mellowed somewhat since the depths of the Cold War, yet a substantial minority of 34% thought we "might as well" fight China before she developed a strong nuclear force, and a plurality (32% to 23%) still opposed admitting China to the United Nations.

Indeed, the predominant mood about foreign affairs seemed to be support for current policies (even in Vietnam, in the sense that there was no agreement on any other alternative), but unwillingness to undertake new actions, whether belligerent or conciliatory. Most people (51% to 13%) advocated leaving Cuba alone. Few wanted the United

States to do anything more than verbally protest the recent Soviet occupation of Czechoslovakia. There was some support for foreign aid
in general (40% pro, 28% con), but with serious reservations about
the amount of money to be spent (50% for decreases, 7% for increases.) Most Americans sympathized, on several detailed points, with
Israel's aims in the Middle East conflict but wanted to avoid any involvement in a war there and opposed sending troops (77% to 9%)
or arms (59% to 24%) to help Israel in the event of war. In case
of a future war like Vietnam, a substantial majority of 63% favored
at least sending weapons, but only a small minority (16%) favored
sending U.S. troops or even pilots. The Vietnam war had dimmed
Americans' enthusiasm for foreign adventures.

Domestically, most Americans favored such social welfare programs
as government-assisted medical care, not only for the aged (86%), but
(by 51% to 39%) for everyone. People were opposed to federal control of elementary and secondary education, but 47% favored expanding college scholarship programs, compared to 9% for cutbacks. They
felt, in general, by 40% to 30%, that the federal government was getting too powerful.

In order to combat inflation, which was then proceeding at a rate
of about 5% per year, Americans overwhelmingly (73% to 12%)
favored reducing federal spending, especially on the space program
and farm subsidies. A plurality (48% to 40%) approved of wage
and price controls, but strong majorities opposed increasing taxes or
raising interest rates.

Most people generally approved of labor unions, and thought that
public employees like teachers (59% to 34%) and nurses (58% to
34%) should be permitted to unionize. But they did not think workers should be required to join unions, and opposed (by 39% to 17%)
repealing section 14-B of the Taft-Hartley Act, which permitted state
"right to work" laws. Furthermore, the public advocated some major
restrictions on collective bargaining. Most people upheld the right of
industrial workers—like rubber, automobile, or railroad workers—to
strike; but a strong majority (69% to 22%) favored compulsory arbitration after twenty-one days. And most wanted to forbid any strikes
by public service workers—garbage men, teachers, policemen, firemen,
or nurses (66% to 29%)—or even by defense workers (55% to 34%).

Most Americans in 1968 wanted the federal government to slow down its efforts to attain racial integration: 54% thought it was pushing too fast, as against 17% too slow. They supported equal access to public accommodations, guaranteed by the Civil Rights Act of 1964, by 52% to 33%, and a narrow plurality approved open housing laws, but a plurality of 43% to 38% thought that questions of job discrimination should be left to the states and local communities. Most (44% to 38%) wanted the government in Washington to stay out of school integration. This latter sentiment foreshadowed the potent busing issue of later years.

Discontent with the selective service system had risen substantially during the Vietnam war; by 1968 nearly half the people thought there was a lot of draft dodging and considered the current system "unfair." Most favored such changes as allowing alternative nonmilitary service and ending graduate student deferments; most thought that deferment of undergraduates based on class standing was unfair. Still, there was little support for fundamental change. A majority (53% to 36%) favored the draft "as it now works," and most (54% to 31%) opposed a lottery system without deferments. While a large majority (80%) wanted to increase pay for the armed services, only a minority thought this would make the draft unnecessary. Apparently the earlier opposition to proposals for an all-volunteer army continued.

Environmental issues had not yet attracted much attention in 1968. Most people did favor expanding government programs to curb air pollution (50% expand, 9% cut) and water pollution (50% to 5%); the overwhelming majority (80%) thought it would be a good idea to require that electric and telephone lines be placed underground in urban areas. Only a minority, however, (44%) was willing to pay even $15 a year in increased taxes to control air pollution.

Finally, the public by large majorities of 60–75% favored sweeping reforms in the presidential electoral system: holding a nationwide primary election instead of party conventions; putting a limit on the total amount of money which could be spent for or by a candidate; permitting eighteen-year-olds to vote; shifting the presidential election to September and inauguration to November; and abolishing the Electoral College, deciding election of the president by total popular vote. Similarly, there was strong support for congressional reforms: requiring congressmen to disclose their financial assets and income, and forbidding campaign contributions for "personal work connected with legislation."

Candidates' Closeness to
Public Opinion

Given this climate of opinion, what was the response of the presidential candidates who came before the public in 1968? To what extent did their policy stands coincide with the voters' preferences?

The 1968 election is a favorable one with which to begin our analysis of responsiveness to public opinion. (Later in the chapter we turn to data from 1964 and 1972.) This is not because 1968 was a "typical" election—one would be rash to cite any single election as typical—but because it put spatial models of the public opinion sort on very strong ground. Neither Humphrey nor Nixon was an unusual candidate; neither appeared to take far-out stands. Their contest had all the marks of a "me-too" election, in which one would expect maximal responsiveness to the general public. If we find public opinion to have only a limited influence on candidates' stands even in 1968, it will be possible to argue a fortiori that in other elections the public was unlikely to have had more influence.

Only the presence of George Wallace in 1968, as a minor party candidate, is somewhat awkward for purposes of investigating two-party electoral competition. A true three-party election, like a three-person game, may be theoretically indeterminate; even a two-and-a-half party election like that of 1968, in which Wallace could be considered as anchored at one extreme of the issue continuum, might theoretically lead to a pushing of Nixon and Humphrey away from Wallace's issue stands, or to a pulling of the major party candidates toward him. Without dismissing such possibilities out of hand, however, it can be argued that Wallace did not seriously alter the structure of two-party competition. Not only did his vote turn out to be small, and his issue stands fixed at the conservative pole; most important, he took a visible position only on a few "law and order" and civil rights issues. Any unusual effect on Humphrey's and Nixon's stands (and none is apparent) would probably be confined to those issues.

For 1968 we have information on public opinion from the 122 survey questions discussed in the previous section. There is no way of testing whether they capture the dimensionality of preferences at that time; we must simply hope that they do so. These items do not in any precise sense constitute a random sample of issues (such a sample is scarcely conceivable), but they do cover a wide variety of policy areas, with few obvious gaps and little clustering of topics. If there is any apparent bias in the selection, it is a tendency to emphasize matters of relatively high public concern, and those within the current American political agenda.

Our collection of campaign texts and transcripts for 1968—156 of Nixon's and 120 of Humphrey's—includes nearly all the candidates' major addresses and most statements, interviews, and position papers as well as a number of remarks to local rallies made during the autumn campaign. Some important pre-autumn materials are included as well. Gaps in the coverage were filled from a clipping file of *New York Times* reports on the candidates.[5]

We repeatedly combed through these speeches, statements, position papers, and the like, summarizing the candidates' stands on each issue listed in the Appendix. On most issues it was possible to discover a single, uncontradicted stand by each candidate, which could then be compared with the public opinion data concerning that issue.

It was possible to use the closeness-to-the-median technique on 21 issues for Nixon and 23 issues for Humphrey. On those issues the prediction of public influence is supported, at least in part.

Both candidates took positions in the second or third quartiles more than half the time. Richard Nixon, in fact, was that close to the median on 19 of the 21 issues, or 90%; a proportion which (according to a one-tailed binomial test) had less than a .001 probability of occurring by chance. But Humphrey stood close to the median on only 15 of the 23 issues, or 65%; a proportion substantially lower than Nixon's and not quite significant at the $p = .10$ level by the same test (see table 2).[6]

Because of the uncertainties in measurement these findings must be interpreted with caution, but they indicate that public opinion had some effect on the candidates' positions. Further, they suggest that Nixon's rhetoric was more responsive to the public than was Humphrey's. Whether Nixon had more skill (or fewer compunctions) at saying what people wanted to hear, or whether his own beliefs were actually more in tune with public preferences in 1968, we cannot say.

Perhaps most striking, however, is the fact that a major party candidate, Humphrey, stood rather far from the median on more than one-third of the issues. Humphrey certainly did not echo the public exactly. Even Nixon's closeness to the median should not be overestimated on the basis of this rather easy test: a candidate could stand in the second or third quartile on all issues even if his position were only slightly influenced by the public on each issue.

Table 2	Closeness of Candidates' Positions to the Median of Public Opinion, 1968	
Candidate's Stand	Nixon	Humphrey
In the second or third quartile	90% (19)[a]	65% (15)[b]
In the first or fourth quartile	10% (2)[c]	35% (8)[d]
	100% (21)	100% (23)

One-tailed binomial probabilities: Nixon $p < .001$, Humphrey $.10 < p < .25$.

Entries are based on all issues for which it was possible to ascertain the median and quartiles of public opinion, and the candidate's position.

a. Appendix, items 3, 7, 10, 13, 14, 25, 39a, 40, 47, 49, 50, 52, 55, 76, 98, 99, 102, 104, 106.

b. Items 5, 6, 9, 10, 13, 25, 49, 50, 52, 53, 55, 76, 99, 104, 106.

c. Items 9, 59.

d. Items 3, 7, 14, 39a, 40, 47, 59, 103.

On most of the issues it was impossible to estimate the location of quartiles; we could only use the second technique, judging how often each candidate took positions close to a plurality of the public. The resulting proportions are not easily subjected to statistical test; they give the impression of being fairly substantial, but far from perfect. Nixon stood with a plurality of the public 79% of the time, on 65 of 82 issues; Humphrey did so on a slightly smaller 69%, or 59 of 85 issues (see table 3).

Both candidates, in other words, took popular positions more often than unpopular ones. At the same time, it is quite apparent that on a number of issues the candidates did not agree with the public.

A clearer understanding of the exact relationship between the candidates' stands and public opinion can be gained by looking closely at Nixon's and Humphrey's positions on the specific issues which went into our findings.

Table 3   Agreement of Candidates' Positions
                              with Pluralities of the Public, 1968

	Nixon	Humphrey
In agreement with the plurality opinion	79% (65)[a]	69% (59)[b]
Opposed to the plurality opinion	21% (17)[c]	31% (26)[d]
	100% (82)	100% (85)

Entries are based on all issues for which it was possible to ascertain the candidate's position.

a. Appendix, items 1, 2, 3, 7, 10, 12, 13, 13a, 14a, 16, 18, 19, 20, 21, 22, 24, 25, 26, 27, 28, 29, 30, 31, 32, 35, 36, 39, 39a, 40, 40a, 44, 46, 47, 49, 50, 51, 52, 55, 61, 62, 63, 64, 69, 70, 71, 72, 76, 77, 78, 83, 84, 85, 86, 87, 88, 91, 95, 96, 98, 99, 102, 104, 106, 109, 111.

b. Items 1, 2, 4, 5, 6, 8, 9, 10, 11, 12, 13, 13a, 14a, 18, 19, 20, 21, 22, 24, 25, 26, 27, 29, 30, 31, 35, 36, 39, 40a, 43, 44, 46, 49, 50, 51, 52, 53, 55, 56, 58, 62, 63, 64, 77, 78, 83, 87, 88, 91, 92, 94, 95, 99, 104, 105, 106, 107, 109, 111.

c. Items 9, 14, 17, 23, 38, 43, 48, 54, 56, 59, 60, 75, 79, 80, 90, 92, 105.

d. Items 3, 7, 14, 16, 17, 23, 28, 38, 39a, 40, 47, 48, 54, 59, 60, 76, 79, 80, 81, 82, 84, 85, 90, 93, 96, 103.

On many issues—45 of 72, or 65% of those on which both took a stand—Nixon and Humphrey both took positions which were close to prevailing public opinion. The Vietnam war provides a good example: both candidates embraced policies of gradual and tentative de-escalation similar to those the public wanted, though in some cases slightly more dovelike than the average American.

Nixon and Humphrey, like most of the public, opposed increasing the number of American troops in Vietnam, or using them to invade

North Vietnam. Nixon ruled out "further escalation on the military front"; he favored "small unit actions," and disclaimed any interest in "conquering" North Vietnam. Humphrey, too, explicitly opposed "military escalation" or an invasion of North Vietnam. At the same time both candidates, like the public, rejected rapid de-escalation of the war. Nixon considered it "dishonorable" simply to pull out, and opposed "precipitate withdrawal." Humphrey rejected "unilateral withdrawal" by the United States.[7]

Both candidates agreed with the public that more of the fighting should be turned over to the South Vietnamese and that gradual U.S. withdrawals should be made. Humphrey said his platform pointed toward "reduction of American combat forces as the South Vietnamese are able to carry a greater share of their own burden . . . ." Nixon repeatedly urged that the South Vietnamese should be trained and equipped: "As they are phased in, American troops can—and should be—phased out." He promised to pursue de-Americanization "far more vigorously."

Nixon said nothing about when withdrawals would begin, how rapid they would be, or whether a residual force would remain in Vietnam. In fact he declared that the U.S. military presence "should remain at its present level" for a time, and should not be cut back before there was "clear indication that the enemy is ready to negotiate." Humphrey was only a little more specific, and expressed only slightly more urgency: "I would sit down with the leaders of South Vietnam to set a specific timetable by which American forces could be systematically reduced while South Vietnamese forces took over more and more of the burden." He indicated that the pace of withdrawal would be slow. "The schedule must be a realistic one—one that would not weaken the overall allied defense posture." And, despite earlier hints that withdrawals might start in late 1968, he made no commitment to an early beginning: "If the South Vietnamese army maintains its present rate of improvement, I believe this will be possible next year . . . ."

Although Humphrey and Nixon deviated somewhat from the public on certain aspects of bombing policy and the shape of a desirable outcome in Vietnam (see below), they agreed on other points. Both opposed using nuclear weapons, and both also opposed an unconditional halt in conventional bombing. Both implied they would accept a neutral government for South Vietnam if it resulted from free elections, but rejected the idea of "forcing" a coalition government on the South Vietnamese.

In other areas of foreign policy, too—indeed, on more than two-thirds of the foreign policy issues on which both candidates took stands—both Nixon and Humphrey echoed public desires rather closely. Both candidates, like most Americans, rejected isolationism. Both, in harmony with the public, approved of foreign aid under some circumstances. Nixon had declared that "we can preserve our hard-won abundance only by bringing the have-nots within the affluent society." "[T]here can be no sanctuary for the rich in a world of the starving." He advocated modest programs of aid for agricultural development, highways, and education in Latin America; food relief for Biafra; and nuclear desalinization of seawater in the Middle East. Humphrey spoke of helping the Third World as being in our self-interest and a moral obligation as well; he advocated a more extensive aid program.

Humphrey and Nixon agreed with the public that the NATO alliance should be strengthened and U.S. troops should be kept in West Germany. Humphrey favored "strengthening and maintaining our key alliances for mutual security particularly including NATO . . . ," and opposed a "one-sided retreat" by ourselves or our allies. Nixon declared that "NATO must be strengthened, with our European Allies not only asked for a greater contribution, but also given a greater voice in the policies of the Alliance." He indicated that U.S. troops should be kept at the prescribed force level and their equipment should be improved; he also favored U.S. and allied "determination to uphold access rights to Berlin."

Reacting to the Soviet intervention in Czechoslovakia, both candidates expressed disapproval but shared the public's reluctance to take strong action. They urged that the Soviets be condemned, but did not advocate sending fresh American troops to Europe or otherwise attempting to bring about Soviet withdrawal.

Humphrey and Nixon agreed with the overwhelming public sentiment that the United States ought to sit down and talk with the leaders of the communist countries, and specifically with the Soviet Union. Nixon declared that, after an era of confrontation, "the time has come for an era of negotiation," and advocated "intensive and sustained" negotiation with the Soviet Union. He called for a series of summit meetings. Humphrey urged a shift from confrontation and containment to "reconciliation and peaceful engagement"; he proposed annual meetings between the United States and the Soviet Union "at the highest level."

Along with a majority of the public, both candidates rejected the idea of making preemptive war on Communist China. Both, in differing degrees, wanted to improve relations. But—again in harmony with the public—neither advocated seating China in the United Nations at present. Similarly, both shared the public's reluctance to do anything about overthrowing the Castro government in Cuba. Nixon said the United States should maintain and tighten its current economic blockade, but rejected any kind of military operation as too risky. Humphrey avoided mentioning Cuba, but when asked whether his proposals to trade with China applied to Cuba as well, he replied that the possibility should be examined.

Humphrey and Nixon agreed with the public, for the most part, on policy toward the Middle East. They thought that Israel should be recognized by the Arab nations; Nixon said a settlement should include "recognition of Israeli sovereignty." Humphrey declared that "[t]he existence of the state of Israel must be accepted by all its neighbors." Both concurred with the public that Israel ought to have the right to send ships through the Gulf of Aquaba and the Suez Canal. Nixon said that access for the ships "of all nations" through the reopened Suez Canal and the Straits of Tiran should be guaranteed. Humphrey declared that Israel "must have free navigational rights in all international waters, including the Suez Canal and the Gulf of Aquaba." Both unmistakably indicated that they shared the public's opposition to sending arms or troops to help the Arabs in the event of a new war. The whole thrust of their positions was sympathy for Israel. Indeed, as we shall see below, they went farther than the public wanted in favoring aid to Israel.

On a number of domestic issues, too—especially those unrelated to party cleavages—the candidates agreed closely with each other and with the public. Both advocated increasing military pay. Humphrey proposed a "thorough overhaul" of the military pay system "to assure that military compensation and benefits for all uniformed personnel are more equitable and more comparable with standards of civilian life," and favored improved living conditions—housing, schools, and medical care—for servicemen and their families. Nixon too advocated better housing and living conditions, higher pay, and increased benefits.

The unpopular draft deferments for graduate students were opposed explicitly by Humphrey, and implicitly by Nixon, who asked, "Why should your son be forced to sacrifice two of the most important years of his life, so that a neighbor's son can go right along pursuing his interests in freedom and safety?"

Both agreed that programs to combat water pollution should be expanded. Nixon wanted to "perfect and expand" regional and federal approaches, developing better pollution control devices, standards for measuring pollution, and enforcement procedures; he would have the federal government set the example by "eliminating, as soon as possible, all pollution from federal facilities . . . ." Humphrey referred approvingly to the Water Quality Act of 1965 and the Clean Water Restoration Act of 1966; he proposed a Heritage Riverways Program, which would "begin rescuing and renewing America's rivers" by providing funds to river basin commissions and states, and a similar Save Our Shores Program, which would—in addition to zoning and public purchases—provide incentives to private landowners to "conserve public values."

Nixon and Humphrey indicated that they shared some of the public's skepticism about the space program. Humphrey said of the unmanned moon landing that he did not think it necessary to repeat "that kind of exercise," though he favored continuing the space program in general. Nixon asserted that "America must be first in space," but said space was an area where "some necessary trimming needs to be done . . . ."

Both candidates reflected the public's desire to cut back on farm subsidies. Nixon often urged that farmers' dependency on government should be reduced; he criticized current farm legislation as a "patchwork" which was "unsuitable for the long term." Humphrey condemned federal "over-control" and "over-paternalism" toward farmers, and quietly endorsed a report which recommended a lower level of subsidy payments. However he later declared that he wanted the basic farm programs improved and made permanent, and "adequately" funded.

Both candidates, like the public, favored giving 18-year-olds the right to vote. Nixon: "I am for the 18-year-old vote." Humphrey: "I propose the voting age in national elections be lowered from 21 to 18."

Both agreed in substance with Americans' desire to abolish the electoral college. Nixon criticized the system which "disenfranchises" the minority in each state, and said that if the electoral college were continued, he favored apportioning each state's electoral vote to represent the actual popular vote in the state. Humphrey made a nod in the same direction, citing the Democratic Party platform, which urged "reform of the Electoral College . . . ."

Even on issues of domestic welfare, economic policy, and civil rights, where the candidates tended to disagree with each other (see chapter 4), there was some common ground on which they both voiced agreement with the public.

Nixon and Humphrey echoed the public sentiment that the federal government was getting too powerful. Nixon condemned the "vast proliferation" of federal programs since World War II, which, he said, had caused a tangled web of confusion, siphoned off top management from the states, caused local fiscal poverty, and bred an atmosphere of alienation. He claimed that modern problems demanded a diversity of approach, and local direction and coordination; most of his policy proposals did in fact involve local government or private efforts.

Humphrey went along with the idea that circumstances demanded "a far greater measure" of local initiative and responsibility and "less direct Federal control" than then existed. His heart did not seem to be in it, though; many of his specific proposals pointed in the opposite direction. As he self-consciously noted, calls for decentralization had become "almost ritualistic" for politicians in 1968.

Both candidates, like the public, favored proposals for federal revenue sharing. Nixon said that "we should begin to return tax revenue to states and the local communities in the form of bloc grants . . . ." allowing them to determine their own priorities. Humphrey urged allocation of "a limited per cent of the federal tax, $5 to $10 billion annually to go to the states, primarily by population."

Humphrey and Nixon differed greatly over questions of federal aid for employment and income maintenance, but both favored retraining programs. Both mirrored the public in rejecting the slogan (if not the substance) of a guaranteed income. Nixon: "I do not accept . . . a guaranteed annual income or a negative income tax . . . ." Humphrey: ". . . I am not one who believes in a guaranteed annual income."

Both candidates warmly approved of the popular Head Start preschool program for poor children. Nixon praised it as a "successful" part of the War on Poverty, most other parts of which he condemned; he said we should "go forward" with it, and expand it "as the need grows." Humphrey favored expansion: ". . . we ought to do more of it." Both supported federal college scholarships, though they put more emphasis on loans. Nixon said, "I will support existing programs which aid needy students, and will call for their expansion when it is indicated." Humphrey called for a "solid system" of loans, work/study opportunities, and grants, and for an increase in federal financial aid to college students.

Both candidates—Humphrey more wholeheartedly than Nixon—endorsed the popular Medicare program for the aged; both, like most Americans, favored at least some general federal programs to help people get medical care.

Both, like the public, favored some federal aid for low-income housing, particularly through guaranteeing loans by private enterprise. Nixon endorsed Senator Percy's National Home Ownership Foundation plan, and said the FHA should also take greater mortgage risks in slum areas. Humphrey advocated tax and other incentives for building "new communities," and a National Urban Development Bank, which would use federally guaranteed bond issues to raise funds to invest in housing mortgages.

Nixon and Humphrey agreed with the public feeling that farmers, and such public employees as teachers and nurses, ought to have the right to join unions. Nixon said, "I believe in the right of unions to organize . . . ," and specifically applied this statement to teachers and other government employees. Humphrey called the right of all workers to organize and bargain collectively "basic" to the free enterprise system. Humphrey explicitly favored "organized farm bargaining," and advocated including farm workers under the National Labor Relations Act. Nixon said we must explore ways to give the farmer "a stronger hand in bargaining" for prices.

Both candidates—with Humphrey again expressing more enthusiasm than Nixon—supported existing civil rights laws dealing with public accommodations and housing.

On questions related to "law and order" the two candidates generally took quite different positions, but even in that area they both sometimes followed public opinion. They agreed with the public that keeping law and order is more a local than a federal problem. Nixon

declared that the "primary responsibility" for dealing with crime "con-
tinues to rest—as it should—with the local and state government. We
want no centralized federal police force in this country." Humphrey
affirmed in similar language that "[t]he prevention of crime and the
enforcement of law against violence are essentially state and local responsibilities. We do not want in a strong national government a federal police force." (Beneath this surface agreement, however, Humphrey advocated policies which would substantially expand the federal
role.)

Nixon and Humphrey—again with specific differences between them
—both advocated registration of guns and licensing of gun owners.

Across a wide variety of issues, then, both Humphrey and Nixon
took positions which corresponded fairly closely with what the average
American favored. But this correspondence was by no means universal. On many issues one candidate, or even both, deviated markedly
from public opinion.

Candidates' Divergences from
the Public

In some cases—on 11 of 72, or 15% of the issues on which both took
positions—both Nixon and Humphrey disagreed with the public. Both,
for example, opposed the popular move of increasing the bombing of
North Vietnam. Nixon stated that bombing was at "about the right
level" and should be continued for some time. "I would not raise the
level of bombing." He opposed the use of nuclear weapons or "area
bombing" of nonmilitary targets in North Vietnam. Although he argued
against an unconditional halt to the bombing, he left open the possibility of stopping it in response to limited concessions. Nixon asserted
that bombing was "the trump card in the negotiations, and I would
not give up that trump card unless we were to get in return from the
North Vietnamese some kind of evidence, some move on their part,
that they would de-escalate their assaults on American men." "My
view is that we should stop the bombing when whoever is president
is convinced that it will result in less American lives lost . . . ."

Humphrey went even further. He dramatically promised that, "As
President, I would stop the bombing of the North as an acceptable risk
for peace . . . ." However he qualified this commitment: before taking

action he would "place key importance on evidence—direct or indirect, by deed or word—of Communist willingness to restore the demilitarized zone between North and South Vietnam. If the government of North Vietnam were to show bad faith, I would reserve the right to resume the bombing." The condition of restoring the demilitarized zone was not so very different from the "reciprocity" or "restraint and reasonable response" which Humphrey had previously required as conditions for stopping the bombing, and was not unlike Nixon's insistence on "some move" of de-escalation. This qualification meant that Humphrey did not diverge from the public much more than Nixon did, but the fact remains that both candidates—contrary to their images in some circles as "hawks"—were somewhat more pacific on this matter than the public.

Similarly, neither candidate shared the public's rejection of allowing a coalition government to be elected in South Vietnam. Nixon said that "any individual in South Vietnam who gave up the use of force and who agreed to accept the democratic processes would be allowed both to vote and to participate in government." Humphrey advocated free elections in South Vietnam, "with all people, including members of the National Liberation Front and other dissident groups, able to participate in those elections if they were willing to abide by peaceful processes." "I say: let the people speak. And accept their judgment, whatever it is."

Both candidates took the minority position that some nonmilitary trade with communist countries ought to be allowed, and even encouraged. Nixon favored a policy of "trade and building bridges" with the Soviet Union and Eastern Europe, but denying long-term credits and excluding strategic materials; he urged using trade pragmatically, as a weapon to loosen Soviet control of Eastern Europe. Humphrey strongly favored "bridge-building" through commercial, cultural, and educational means. He asked for discretionary authority for the president to remove restrictions on trade and investment in Eastern Europe, and proposed reciprocal TV and radio exchanges. Going further than Nixon, he advocated lifting restrictions on nonstrategic trade with mainland China.

Humphrey and Nixon were both more willing than the public to come to the aid of Israel. Humphrey declared that "[u]ntil permanent peace in the Middle East is achieved, and the arms race ended, continued United States military assistance to Israel, including supersonic planes such as Phantom jets, is justified." Nixon supported a policy that would "give Israel a technological military margin to more than offset her hostile neighbors' numerical superiority," including, if necessary, supplying Israel with F-4 Phantom jets.

Both candidates resisted the popular demand for a Medicare plan which would cover the whole population. Nixon declared, "I am against . . . a compulsory health insurance program for everybody." Humphrey did not "at the present time" favor extending Medicare into a nationwide health insurance program covering all citizens.

Both braved public opposition to the 10% income tax surcharge of 1968. Humphrey called the surcharge "absolutely essential," and predicted it would "break the back" of the wage-price spiral. Nixon favored the surcharge, in conjunction with a budget cut; he praised Congress for acting "courageously" in an election year. He did, however, later add that it should be repealed "as soon as possible," or "once the war is ended."

Humphrey and Nixon, unlike the public, opposed wage and price controls. Humphrey advocated "voluntary" and "cooperative" efforts including government guidelines, but said, "The United States must achieve price stability without wage and price controls." Nixon—in words he may have come to regret later when he imposed controls—flatly condemned wage and price controls as "the most harmful tool in the economist's kit." He even criticized federal price and wage guideposts, as focusing on symptoms instead of causes.

The two nominees differed over some questions of civil rights, but both endorsed existing federal legislation on equal employment, and approved the Supreme Court's school desegregation decision of 1954, in apparent conflict with the public.

Finally, both candidates disagreed with the public over the selective service system. Humphrey urged "radical reform" of the existing draft, and adoption of the "Fair and Impartial Random" lottery which was later put into effect. Nixon wanted to go much further—as he ultimately did as president—to stop the draft altogether, and move to an all-volunteer armed force, as soon as reduced manpower requirements in Vietnam would permit. He favored keeping the selective service structure on stand-by, for use only in case of "some all-out emergency."

As to why both candidates deviated from the desires of the general public in so many instances, we can only speculate. Some cases may be explicable as responses to the citizens who felt most strongly about issues, when those intense individuals happened to hold opinions substantially different from their less concerned fellows. Other possible interpretations of deviations from the public, among which we are unable to distinguish with these data, include interest group influence, collusion between the parties for their own benefit, or enlightened leadership of a confused citizenry.

In addition to the cases of deviation by both Humphrey and Nixon, there were a number of issues on which one candidate disagreed with the public, while the other conformed to public desires or took no stand at all. We will see later that many such divergences can be explained by the nature of party cleavages: one candidate or the other took a position corresponding to the unique opinions of his party identifiers or activists but conflicting with those of the general public. Such cases will be discussed in greater detail in chapter 4; they are mentioned here in order to complete the picture of candidates' relations with the opinions of the general public.

Humphrey, for example, took much more liberal stands than the public on a number of urban questions. Contrary to the tendency of public opinion, he advocated increasing federal aid to the cities and expanding the "war on poverty." Humphrey offered a new "Marshall Plan for America's cities," involving a "massive commitment," which he acknowledged "will cost money—a great deal of it." He proposed the creation of a National Urban Development Bank to help finance projects, especially in the inner cities, at the rate of billions of dollars each year. The bank would start with an appropriation of federal funds, and would then sell federally-guaranteed bonds to private investors; it would underwrite risky loans. He said it was true that "I would increase the poverty program . . ."; he urged expansion of programs like the Job Corps, Head Start, and other elements of the war on poverty.

Similarly, Humphrey proposed income maintenance programs which amounted to a significant expansion of the welfare system, against the public's wishes.

Humphrey's stand on "law and order" deviated rather significantly from popular attitudes. He contended that riots were caused by injus-

tices, and tied riot prevention to his Marshall Plan for the cities: "As
we reduce the human misery of our ghettoes; establish social justice
for all Americans; and eliminate discrimination, we will sharply reduce
the threat of riots born of discontent." He said that riots must be put
down promptly and firmly, but disagreed with the public sentiment
that looters should be shot; he advocated rapid introduction of manpower, with the emphasis on "men rather than guns" and "arrests
rather than shooting." He declared that "[l]ooters and arsonists must
be punished according to the law . . . ."

Whereas most Americans felt that certain student protesters should
be drafted, Humphrey favored the "FAIR" (Fair and Impartial Random) selective service system, which would assure that "the power to
draft is never used to stifle dissent or to punish those who may violate
other laws."

Humphrey disputed the popular notion that the courts had not been
harsh enough with criminals and had encouraged violations of law and
order. He declared that "the court decisions are not a significant factor
in the crime increase . . . . These rules are designed to protect the innocent and to assure the liberties of all Americans." He frequently condemned the "scapegoat approach" of attacking the Supreme Court.

From the opposite side, the conservative one, Nixon found himself
out of step with the public on certain questions of social welfare and
economic policy. His proposals for job assistance fell far short of the
popular federal "guarantee" of work. Nixon opposed urban renewal:
he was against "spending hundreds of millions to clear more slum
acres, to displace more families, and to build more public housing."
Nixon also deviated from public opinion in opposing compulsory arbitration. "I believe the Federal government ought not to intervene with
the give-and-take of collective bargaining unless there are compelling
reasons" of national health and safety.

In the area of foreign policy, Humphrey differed substantially from
the public on several issues. Contrary to majority opinion, he called
for a "steady increase rather than a steady decrease" in the amount of
foreign aid. He did not go as far as most Americans in opposing future
military interventions abroad: while agreeing that "the United States
cannot play the role of global gendarme," he refused to promise that
U.S. troops would not be used, and said that when violence transcends
national frontiers, "[w]e must . . . be prepared to fulfill specific and

clearly-defined mutual-defense commitments approved by the President
and the Congress of the United States."

Humphrey did not completely share the public's opposition to negotiating a coalition government for Vietnam. He said, carefully quoting
Robert Kennedy, that he was opposed to "forcing a coalition government on the government of Saigon, a coalition with the Communists
even before we begin the negotiations." But—making a rather fine
distinction—"we expect that the National Liberation Front and the
Viet Cong will play some role in the future political process of South
Vietnam, but that should be determined by the negotiators and particularly by those people of South Vietnam."

Apparently Nixon, unlike the public at that time, lacked any strong
commitment to make the United Nations a success, for he rarely mentioned the organization at all. In one of his few allusions to the UN, he
disagreed with the majority which wanted to turn the problem of Vietnam over to the United Nations. Nixon predicted that the Soviet Union
would veto any Western proposal for a UN role: "So, until you get
Soviet cooperation, the possibility of a UN force in Vietnam just isn't
there at all."

Insurgent Candidates and
Deviations from the Public

The 1968 election did not prove such an easy mark as might have
been expected for public opinion spatial models; the 1964 and 1972
elections ought to put such models to a still harder test.

Barry Goldwater in 1964 and George McGovern in 1972 can be
called insurgent candidates. They won their parties' nominations with
issue-oriented appeals and with the help of dedicated bands of activists. Both were reputed to take policy stands far out of the mainstream
of American politics, away from the center of public opinion. Goldwater's and McGovern's stands will be described in detail in chapter 5,
in the context of changes in position; here we deal only with how
close their stands actually were to public opinion.

For Goldwater, the plurality technique was applied to his stands in
relation to the public's answers to forty-four policy questions asked by
the Gallup poll during 1963 and 1964.[8] Our findings support the conventional wisdom: Goldwater offered an authentically conservative

choice, one which differed markedly from the policy preferences of the average American.

Goldwater, unlike the public, advocated a very hard line in the Cold War. He disagreed with the pluralities of Americans which favored ratification of the nuclear test ban treaty (by 63% to 17%), increasing trade with and selling surplus wheat to the Soviet Union (55% to 33% and 60% to 31% respectively), initiating direct airline service to Russia (53% to 29%), and agreeing to an arms reduction treaty with the Soviets (46% to 40%). Similarly, Goldwater was doubtful about U.S. membership in the United Nations (the public favored staying in by 79% to 8%). He opposed building up the UN Expeditionary Force (a buildup was approved, 62% to 19%) or deploying a UN army in Vietnam (the public favored such a move, 58% to 19%). Goldwater generally disapproved of foreign aid, which a 58% to 30% majority of Americans favored.

On domestic questions, Goldwater resolutely opposed most forms of federal government action. In disagreement with the public, he expressed grave doubts about the progressive income tax. Unlike most Americans, Goldwater opposed national civil rights laws, even those relating to public accomodations, which the public approved by 61% to 31%. He objected to the Supreme Court decisions on reapportionment of state legislatures, which the public supported by 47% to 30%, and favored the "court of the union" proposal for review of Supreme Court decisions by state chief justices, which the public rejected by 53% to 18%. Goldwater opposed the popular (78% to 17%) idea of federal gun controls.

To be sure, Goldwater was not wholly out of touch with public opinion. Many Americans in 1964 had reservations about federal civil rights laws for blacks: a large majority (72% to 21%), like Goldwater, opposed withholding education aid from segregated schools, and only a bare plurality (48% to 43%) rejected a "states rights" approach to integration in general. There was, in harmony with Goldwater's stands, opposition to railroad "featherbedding" (52% to 25%), and a large majority (70% to 24%) disapproved of the Supreme Court decision banning school prayers. In foreign policy, there was agreement (71% to 15%) with Goldwater's stands for keeping Communist China out of the UN, even to the extent of not wanting the United States to "go along" with any UN decision to admit China

(44% to 42%), and for dealing firmly with Panama over the Canal Zone and (at least right after the Tonkin incident) being tough in Vietnam: 48% wanted the next move to be a tough one, with only 26% for conciliation.

All in all, however, Barry Goldwater was in broad and substantial disagreement with the American public. The gulf between Goldwater's views and those of the average American was so great that he disagreed with a plurality of the public on fully 68% of the issues we examined (see table 4).

Table 4   Goldwater's Stands and Public
                     Opinion, Early 1964

Goldwater in agreement with a plurality of the public	32% (9)
In disagreement	68% (19)
Total issues	100% (28)

Entries are based on 44 policy questions asked by the AIPO between January 1963 and October 1964, as reported in Gallup, in *The Gallup Poll* (1972). Sixteen issues were omitted because Goldwater's stand could not be ascertained.

The Gallup questions cannot be considered a random sample of all issues, but their most glaring deficiency—the neglect of domestic social welfare questions—probably makes Goldwater seem closer to the public in table 4 than he actually was. Again, we have no statistical test by which to judge whether a discrepancy like that between Goldwater and the public might have appeared in this set of issues by chance. The discrepancy is so large, however (much larger than the deviations by Humphrey or Nixon in 1968 which are reported in table 3), that it strongly suggests that Goldwater's stands were not much influenced by public opinion, and did not correspond either to the economic theory of democracy or to the predictions of public opinion theories of electoral competition.

The case of McGovern is different, in rather intriguing ways which do not easily fit the usual interpretations of the 1972 election. This becomes apparent when we apply the same plurality technique to Gallup data from 1971 and 1972.[9]

On some issues, McGovern's stands differed from the preferences of most Americans. He went against large majorities in favoring lesser penalties for possession of marijuana (28% to 60%), in proposing amnesty for Vietnam draft evaders (24% to 62%), and in supporting the busing of school children for racial balance (22% to 66%). On certain aspects of Vietnam policy, too, such as opposing continued military aid after a U.S. withdrawal, McGovern's stands disagreed with a majority (39% to 51%) of Americans.

It is also likely—although the data are missing or inconclusive—that most Americans opposed McGovern's guaranteed income proposals, and that majorities were unwilling to go as far as he suggested in progressive taxation or in cutting the defense budget. There was, on the other hand, much more sentiment for reducing defense expenditures than for increasing them (42% to 9%), and Americans did oppose tax loopholes for the rich.

On most of the twenty issues we were able to consider, however—on 70% of them, in fact—McGovern was in agreement with a plurality of the public (see table 5). Rather than being an extremist, McGovern was in substantial accord with the opinions of the average American.

A solid majority of Americans (62% to 34%), like McGovern, favored withdrawing all U.S. troops from Vietnam by the end of 1972. (There was ambivalence about the bombing of North Vietnam, with small pluralities first approving and then disapproving of it.) A major-

Table 5	McGovern's Stands and Public Opinion, Early 1972
McGovern in agreement with a plurality of the public	70% (14)
In disagreement	30% (6)
Total issues	100% (20)

Entries are based on 34 policy questions asked by the AIPO between January 1971 and October 1972, as reported in *The Gallup Poll* and in the *Gallup Opinion Index*. Fourteen issues were omitted because McGovern's stand could not be ascertained.

ity (64% to 31%) approved of letting abortion be a matter between a woman and her doctor. Large majorities, along with McGovern, favored government job guarantees (80% to 10%), national health insurance (69% to 18%), spending more to control pollution (80% to 10%), and increasing opportunities for blacks (67% to 21%) and for women (64% to 20%). Majorities also agreed with McGovern in favoring gun control (62% to 26%), in opposing legalization of marijuana (81% to 15%) or reduction of penalties for selling marijuana (80% to 16%), and in favoring the 18-year-old vote for state and local as well as federal elections (60% to 35%).

We must bear in mind the imperfections of this method of analysis, especially the limited number of issues and the fact that issues could not be weighted by importance, so that the significance of McGovern's disagreement with the public on a few crucial matters may have been understated. Still, our findings indicate that the real distance between McGovern and the public was not great—much less than for Goldwater, and about the same as for Humphrey or Nixon. Perceptions of a wildly left-wing McGovern, at odds with public opinion, seem to be much exaggerated. Evidence will be offered later that such perceptions may have resulted from misleading attacks by McGovern's enemies and from non-issue-related objections to McGovern among the general public.

At any rate, the main effect of our findings about Goldwater and McGovern must be to reinforce the findings on Nixon and Humphrey: they indicate that the economic theory of democracy is not completely fulfilled, and that the influence of the midpoint of public opinion is not all-determining.

Policy Stands, the Public, and Democracy

We cannot conclude from these findings that spatial models which predict an important influence of public opinion are simply wrong. Those theories like Hotelling's which unconditionally predict convergence exactly at the midpoint of public opinion are plainly incorrect, as are certain other spatial models to the extent that they flatly predict convergence. Yet the "important influence" prediction is a slippery one, and within the terms of many spatial models (if we grant the empirical parameters approach) there are several possibilities consistent with our findings. The nonexistence of equilibrium, or the existence of an equilibrium elsewhere than at the midpoint, could follow from particular preference distributions, candidate goals, and/or turnout processes, and could lead candidates to take non-midpoint stands consistently with the theories. Alternatively, it is possible that spatial models' assumption of dimensionality (single-peakedness) of preferences was not met in our cases and that the midpoint positions as measured were not in fact majority winners. Finally, of course, it is possible that measurement errors led to overestimating candidates' deviations from the midpoint of public opinion.

For evidence bearing more conclusively on the validity of certain types of spatial models, the reader is referred to the next chapter, where the contrasting predictions of public opinion and party cleavage theories are tested. At the same time, however, the findings of this chapter suggest that more goes on in electoral competition than the unalloyed influence of public opinion that is found in many spatial models. The Goldwater case can be rationalized in populistic terms only with considerable straining. (It is no answer to say that spatial models point out how to win votes and that Goldwater paid for the sin of ignoring them; these theories are supposed to predict candidates' behavior.) The substantial deviations from public preferences on some issues by Humphrey, McGovern, and Nixon—and especially the fact that, with Humphrey and Nixon, one candidate often agreed with the public while the other disagreed—also point toward features of the electoral process not incorporated in the public opinion variety of spatial model.

By the same token, we cannot make any conclusive judgment on the economic theory of democracy. The findings do suggest some of this sort of responsiveness in the American electoral system; most candidates do appear to be somewhat influenced by public opinion. Three of the four candidates examined here agreed with the public more often than not. As we will see in the following chapter, there are indications that this process occurs more often on issues of consensus between followers of the two parties than on issues of party cleavage.

The possible workings of the economic theory of democracy can be illustrated by the Vietnam war issue in 1968. In the contests for party nominations that year, aspiring candidates took a wide variety of stands on Vietnam, with Eugene McCarthy and Robert Kennedy decidedly "doves" on the left side, and Ronald Reagan and George Wallace "hawks" on the right. Economists would presumably note with approval that the Republican and the Democratic parties both nominated centrist candidates (Nixon and Humphrey), whose Vietnam stands were closer to the midpoint of public preferences.

The centrality of Humphrey's and Nixon's positions is displayed graphically in figure 3, which shows the median public perceptions of the various candidates' stands in relation to median self-ratings by the public at several points in the election year. As we have stressed, one should not uncritically accept perpetual data as indicators of candidates' true stands. In this instance, however, (with the exception perhaps of the low-visibility candidate, Reagan) the median perceptions correspond fairly closely with our analysis of candidates' Vietnam stands as taken in their speeches and statements.[10]

In the Vietnam case the nomination process appeared to act as a filter, screening out candidates with unpopular stands. On other issues, and in other elections, the process might work in other ways, for example by forcing all leading contenders for nomination to anticipate the will of the voters and take popular policy stands, or by discouraging those with outlying stands from ever trying. (The dispersion and intensity of Vietnam preferences, not reflected in party cleavages, may have encouraged an unusual diversity of stands by prenomination candidates in 1968.)

Before concluding that the economic theory of democracy describes an important aspect of American politics, however, we would have to grapple with the question whether this echoing of public preferences gets translated into policy, or whether it represents no more than empty campaign rhetoric which is later ignored. The theory might assert that campaign promises are kept, or that office holders are under

Figure 3   **Candidates' Vietnam Stands, 1968.**
Entries are median perceptions and self-ratings by the public from four ORC surveys. Standard errors of the means range from .03 to .07. Standard deviations of the self-ratings range from 2.07 (November) to 2.21 (February).

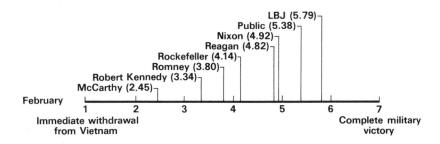

February

1   2   3   4   5   6   7

Immediate withdrawal   Complete military
from Vietnam   victory

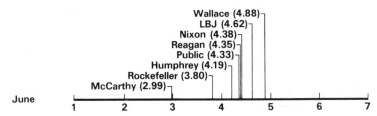

June

1   2   3   4   5   6   7

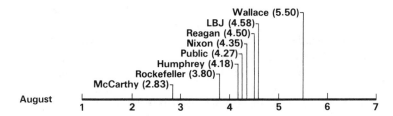

August

1   2   3   4   5   6   7

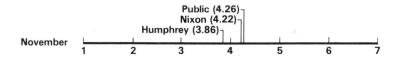

November

1   2   3   4   5   6   7

the same competitive pressure as campaigners and must, in order to retain power, respond in the same way to the citizenry's policy preferences; but it is also possible that competitive pressure and public scrutiny relax between elections, and that policy is less democratic than is rhetoric. This is an empirical question which cannot be answered with data on elections alone, and upon which little scholarly evidence has been offered.

We would also have to face the question of causal inference: whether a correspondence between politicians' stands and public preferences means that the public is influencing politicians or that the politicians are influencing the public. A related question is whether expressed preferences are "authentic," and coincide with citizens' true interests, or whether they are manipulated by elites or molded by an oppressive system.

Again the Vietnam issue of 1968 offers an illustration. We cannot tell whether the nomination of two candidates favoring a slow ("honorable") end to the war, and the election of one of them, represented a triumph of democracy or a perversion of it. Certainly Nixon's stand was close—uncannily close—to the stated preferences of most Americans. But we cannot be sure whether he passively reflected the will of the people; or whether his eloquence engineered that expressed will; or whether years of talk by the Kennedy and Johnson administrations concerning Vietnam had created public acquiescence. Perhaps the vision of "dominoes" toppling in Southeast Asia and exhortations about the need to defend the self-determination of the freedom-loving South Vietnamese against invasion from the North—together with decades of emphasis on the evils of communism—blinded Americans to the realities of the war, alienated them from sympathy with the Vietnamese people, and created inauthentic preferences based on false information.

It is our view that individual presidential candidates rarely succeed in affecting what policies the people prefer, if indeed they try to do so. But possibilities of manipulation of opinion over long periods by incumbent presidents and by parties and interest groups (to say nothing of the economic, social, and nation-state systems themselves) cannot be dismissed so easily. Such matters are crucial to the workings or nonworkings of democracy, and we will encounter them more than once in the following pages.

In any event, our findings suggest that the economic theory of democracy—if it works at all—does not work to perfection. Even setting aside the questions of causal inference and manipulation of preferences, the simple correspondence between candidates' policy stands and the preferences of the public is imperfect. One important reason for this, the role of party cleavages in the electorate, has already been mentioned and will be discussed in detail in the next chapter. Among other possible reasons—including collusion between parties or influence by special interest groups—we cannot distinguish. Nor, indeed, can we be sure to what extent a well-defined popular will (an optimal social choice, a majority winner among policy alternatives) exists but is not realized through the electoral process; or to what extent democracy is technically impossible because there are cyclical majorities, no majority winner, no equilibrium.

We can be confident, however, that elections do not always cast up candidates who invariably stand for policies which the public prefers to all others. There is no perfect, frictionless working of the economic theory of democracy.

4

Party Cleavages on Policy

While the economic theory of democracy advocates similarities in candidates' stands, responsible party theories call for clear differences between the policy stands of opposing parties. Spatial models of the party cleavage variety—but not of the public opinion type—predict that some systematic differences do occur. But are there, in fact, any significant differences between Republican and Democratic presidential candidates? If so, what issues do they concern, how great are they, and what causes them?

If we look at recent presidential elections, we find that there have indeed been party differences on a persistent set of issues. The differences are significant, but by no means immense; they tend to be greatest when an insurgent candidate captures the nomination of one party. They generally reflect (and are caused by) party cleavages—differences between the policy preferences of Democratic and Republican party activists, money givers, and identifiers.

The Nature of Party Cleavages

American political parties can be viewed as enduring coalitions of more or less like-minded individuals who engage in various sorts of party activity: giving substantial sums of money, running party organizations, canvassing precincts, or just declaring loyalty to a party and voting for its candidates. Since the New Deal, Republican and Democratic partisans have differed in certain regular ways, regardless of the nature or level of their activity.

On issues of domestic social welfare, Democrats have tended to favor an active federal government, helping citizens with jobs, education, medical care, and the like; Republicans have wanted less government spending and lower taxes. On labor-management relations and regulation of the economy, Democrats have allied themselves with labor and Republicans with business. There have also been (with some shifts over time) party differences on civil rights, civil liberties, and occasionally foreign policy.

Money being a prime factor in any political equation, a party's monetary benefactors constitute an important element in the coalition. In the past, the major contributors to the two parties have differed substantially. To be sure, both parties have drawn upon the well-off, and both can, without gross injustice, be called factions of "the money party." But, since the New Deal, businessmen in general—and particularly the executives of the largest manufacturing corporations, banks, and investment houses—have tended overwhelmingly to give money to the Republican rather than to the Democratic party. Corporations themselves, despite the Federal Corrupt Practices Act, have given huge sums to Republican campaigns, through contributions in kind (billboards, furniture, office space, mailing lists, postage, airplanes, automobiles); through money conveyed by attorneys, executives, and trade associations; and through the loan of employees' time and efforts.

Democrats, on the other hand, have regularly received contributions in kind or money from labor unions, from professionals and public officials, and from certain sectors of business: merchandising, construction and building materials, hard and soft drinks, publishing, advertising, and entertainment. Starting in 1936, organized labor in particular has played a profound part in providing money and workers for the Democratic party.[1]

Survey evidence on the policy preferences of money givers is sparse, but much can be inferred from their public statements and actions and from their economic self-interest. Most Republican-contributing businessmen have favored lower federal taxes, and opposed domestic welfare programs in fields like education, employment, and medical care which would require substantial spending. They have also opposed public ownership or regulation of business, and favored regulation of labor unions and restrictions on the rights to unionize and to strike.

Contributors to the Democratic party have tended to hold quite different policy views. Organized labor has actively worked for social welfare policies which would benefit their rank and file (if not always the nonunionized poor) in the areas of health, jobs, and education. Labor has favored the broadest possible rights to organize and to strike, and has advocated government regulation of business. Those segments of the business world which have regularly supported the Democrats have favored at least certain important aspects of the traditional Democratic program: those in the construction and building materials industries, for example, have hoped for spending on public works and highways.

Active workers in the two parties have diverged along similar lines of cleavage. On this point survey data are available and show quite large differences: McClosky and his associates found in the 1950s that many more Democratic than Republican delegates to the national conventions wanted to increase federal aid to education and wanted to increase social security and public housing. The Democratic delegates were less inclined than Republicans to want more regulation of trade unions, and much less eager to decrease regulation of business; they were considerably more willing to increase public ownership of natural resources and to increase regulation of public utilities. Beyond these central economic concerns, Democratic delegates were also more likely to want increased enforcement of racial integration, and increased reliance on the United Nations, American participation in military alliances, and foreign aid.[2]

Much the same differences in opinion have been found between Republican and Democratic delegates to other national conventions, and also between workers in the regular party organizations and between Republican and Democratic "occasional activists"—those who help in campaigns, belong to political clubs, attend rallies, persuade others how to vote, and the like. In most cases the differences have been quite substantial, especially on issues of domestic social welfare and economic regulation.[3]

Between the ordinary identifiers of the two parties—those who generally consider themselves Republicans or Democrats—the differences

in policy preferences have not been nearly so great as those between
the activists. But the fact is that some noticeable differences have per-
sisted, and they almost invariably run along the same lines as the
cleavages between the activists of the two parties. Survey research from
the 1930s through the 1970s regularly revealed that citizens who called
themselves Democrats were more favorable than Republicans toward
government programs dealing with social welfare: unemployment, education, housing, social security, medical care, the minimum wage, urban
renewal, fighting poverty. Democrats were more eager than Republicans to regulate business and public utilities, to subsidize farmers, and
to tax high incomes, but less eager to regulate trade unions. These
party differences were generally greater in the 1930s and 1940s, and
in the 1960s and 1970s, than in the politically quiescent 1950s.[4]

On civil rights, Republican and Democratic identifiers differed very
little in the 1950s, but by 1964 Democrats were more favorable toward integration than Republicans and blacks had become a firm and
important part of the Democratic coalition. Certain issues of life style,
and some related to "law and order," also began to divide Republicans
and Democrats in the 1960s. Cleavages on foreign policy were shallow
and shifting, with Democrats somewhat more internationalist than
Republicans until the 1950s, when (perhaps as a result of Eisenhower's leadership) the Republicans caught up with and in some respects surpassed the Democrats in internationalism.

Party differences on domestic social welfare issues and on the regulation of business and labor (and, in its special way, on civil rights)
were rooted in the social and economic composition of the parties as
established in the New Deal realignment. During the 1924–36 realigning era, class and ethnic issues came to the fore and were given partisan meaning by Al Smith's candidacy, the Great Depression, and the
New Deal. Many working-class people, especially union members and
such minorities as Catholics, Jews, and blacks, joined the Democratic
party, while upper-income Americans remained mostly Republican.
Most of these new Democrats were not converts from Republicanism
but were new entrants to the two-party electorate, either young people
coming of age or older citizens who had remained disaffiliated from
political parties or had backed the Progressives.[5]

These new party affiliations tended to remain stable over time, presumably because of continued policy agreement with the parties, if

also as a result of inertia and social reinforcement. Parents passed their party affiliations along to their children, together with similar life circumstances and a tendency to hold similar policy views. Party cleavages on policy, in other words, were founded upon real social and economic differences between the followers of the two parties— differences that endured for a long time and were congruent with differences between the activist cores of the two parties.

In order to explore the nature of party cleavages in more detail, and to lay the foundation for discussion of their influence on candidates' policy stands, we can again use 1968 as a case in point. For the 1967– 68 period, breakdowns of opinion were obtained by party identification on 63 of the 122 survey questions. They were divided into party cleavage and noncleavage issues (labeled "PC" or "NC" in the Appendix) on the basis of a statistically significant difference between the preferences of Republican and Democratic party identifiers.[6]

In 1967–68, as in most of the post–New Deal period, Republican and Democratic party identifiers did not differ very sharply on most policy questions. On about half of the 63 issues there were no appreciable differences at all between party groups; disagreement fell short of statistical significance. Thirty-two party cleavage issues were found —that is, issues upon which party differences were statistically significant. But even those differences were moderate in size: nearly half of them were less than 11 percentage points, and only one-fifth were greater than 20 percentage points.

Issues of foreign policy, in particular, and relatively low-salience domestic issues such as election reform and school prayers, involved little or no party cleavage. Fifty-nine percent of foreign policy issues, compared with 42% of domestic, showed no significant party differences; only 11% of the foreign policy issues, compared with a substantial 45% of domestic issues, involved differences of 11 or more percentage points (see table 6).

On some domestic issues, however, particularly those concerning social welfare policies, Republicans and Democrats did disagree markedly. Thirty-six percent more Democrats than Republicans, for example, favored federal medical assistance; 29% more Democrats supported aid to education; 21% more favored government job assistance. Democrats were considerably less prone than Republicans—by a difference of 29%—to think that the government had gotten too powerful. More Democrats were favorable toward programs for guaranteed income (by 16%) and guaranteed work (by 6%).

Democrats also tended to give more support than Republicans to the rights to unionize and to strike. Nineteen percent more Democrats than Republicans said that teachers should be permitted to join unions; 18% more thought that nurses ought to be permitted to join a union and that farmers ought to establish one. Twenty-one percent more Democrats thought that teachers should be allowed to strike, and 18% more advocated the same right for garbage men.

Table 6   Magnitude of Party Cleavages by Issue Area, 1967–68

Amount of Difference Between Opinions of Republicans and Democrats	Issue Area		
	Foreign	Domestic	Total
None (0–5%)	59%	42%	49%
	(16)	(15)	(31)
Low (6–10%)	30%	14%	21%
	(8)	(5)	(13)
Medium (11–20%)	11%	28%	21%
	(3)	(10)	(13)
High (21%–)	0%	17%	10%
	(0)	(6)	(6)
	100%	100%	100%
	(27)	(36)	(63)

Entries are based on the issues given in the Appendix.

Difference between means is significant at $p < .05$ by one-tailed t test. Difference in the dichotomized table is significant at $p < .025$ by chi-square test. (Yule's Q = gamma = 0.73.)

Democrats in 1967–68 were somewhat more favorable than Republicans to civil rights for blacks: 17% more Democrats than Republicans favored equal employment legislation, and 16% more favored federally enforced integrated schooling. There were smaller but still significant differences on integrated public accommodations and on open housing.

In other issue areas, party differences were not so deep. Issues of "law and order" were largely new to the 1960s; on some of these matters Democrats took a less hard line than Republicans. Fewer Democrats (by 8%) thought the courts had been too soft on criminals, and many more (by 26%) wanted liberals appointed to the Supreme Court. But more Democrats (by 11%) favored forbidding the use of guns by young people.

On some questions of foreign policy there were significant party cleavages in 1968, but these were not large and did not follow any very clear pattern. Democrats tended to be more favorable to foreign aid for Asian development (by 9%), and to maintaining or increasing the amount of foreign aid in general (by 12%) but—perhaps because of their Catholic members—less favorable (by 6%) to aid for birth control. Democrats, more than Republicans, strongly supported the United Nations (7%), favored negotiating with communist countries (6%), and were reconciled to the admission of China to the United Nations (12%). Democrats were also less enthusiastic (by 13%) about bombing Vietnam and less inclined (by 6%) to give military aid to Israel. In these respects Democrats seemed to be dovish internationalists, favoring more peaceful activity—but less military action —than Republicans did. On the other hand, Democrats were somewhat more willing to keep U.S. *troops* in Vietnam (8%), and were more inclined to react belligerently to the Soviet invasion of Czechoslovakia (7%) and to contemplate war with China (10%).

For the most part, the differences between party identifiers reflected enduring aspects of the party coalitions and corresponded closely with the cleavages dividing the activists and money givers of the two parties. Differences between party identifiers can therefore be used as indicators of party cleavages in general. If we then analyze candidates' behavior in the light of these differences, we can gain some insight into how, and indeed whether, presidential candidates respond to party cleavages in their policy stands.

Candidate Differences on Party Cleavage Issues

A preliminary answer to this question emerges when we review, in a summary way, the rhetoric of presidential campaigns from 1932 onward. For a more conclusive answer we will later return to our 1968 data.

In every election from 1932 through 1976 there were detectable differences between the policy stands of the Republican and Democratic candidates. Those differences generally followed the same lines as the party cleavages in the electorate and among activists.

In 1932, the policy differences between Roosevelt and Hoover were surprisingly mild: Roosevelt steered clear of specifics, and the policy stands he did take did not contrast sharply with Hoover's. Both candidates, for example, favored a balanced federal budget and assigned primary responsibility for dealing with the depression to the states. Both candidates favored inflationary policies (combined with a balanced budget and reduced operating expenses!), and both wanted to rehabilitate silver, though neither suggested abandoning the gold standard. But New Deal party conflicts were foreshadowed by a few specific differences.[7]

On job relief, Roosevelt was more favorable than Hoover toward unemployment insurance and public works employment, especially in reforestation, although the magnitude of public works projects to come was scarcely hinted at. Roosevelt gave the impression of favoring more RFC (Reconstruction Finance Corporation) loans, and more distribution of them to small rather than big businesses. Roosevelt went further than Hoover in advocating regulation of Wall Street securities markets and holding companies; he favored more disclosure by and regulation of public utilities, but gave little indication of favoring public ownership. On banking, too, Roosevelt more strongly advocated regulation and the protection of depositors.

On the older party cleavage issues of the tariff and prohibition there were also some differences between the candidates. Roosevelt flatly favored repeal of prohibition and immediate amendment of the Volstead Act to permit the sale of beer; Hoover, acknowledging that prohibition had failed, still emphasized the need to protect the rights of dry states. Roosevelt favored a "competitive tariff for revenue" and urged reciprocal negotiations; Hoover more definitely supported the protective aspect of tariffs, and opposed negotiations which would reduce U.S. tariff autonomy.

The Roosevelt-Landon election of 1936, and the contests between Roosevelt and Wilkie in 1940 and Roosevelt and Dewey in 1944, were characterized by candidate differences similar to those of 1932, still moderate in degree but sharpened somewhat by disputes over New Deal programs.

The 1948 election between Truman and Dewey displayed clearer candidate differences, along well-developed lines of New Deal party cleavages which still persist thirty years later. For an incumbent president, Truman was unusually active and specific in the campaign, perhaps in hopes of counteracting his low standing in the opinion polls. He adopted a comparatively leftist campaign strategy (largely worked out by Clark Clifford) late in 1947, and began to carry it out as early as his State of the Union message in January 1948; he continued to follow it in messages to the Republican congress, at the Democratic convention, in the postconvention legislative session, and in the campaign itself.[8]

Truman proposed a 50 percent rise in social security payments and an extension of coverage; a national health insurance program; slum clearance and low rent housing projects (as well as housing construction subsidies and strengthening of rent controls); federal aid to education; and increases in the minimum wage (from 40 to 75 cents an hour) and in unemployment compensation. Dewey took vague me-too positions, favoring increases in the minimum wage and social security, and federal aid for housing, but without mentioning magnitudes; he deplored "socialized medicine" and said little about education.

On civil rights, Truman in February issued recommendations which were remarkably comprehensive for the time. He proposed a fair employment practices commission, an antilynching law, protection of voting rights, District of Columbia home rule, and a permanent commission on civil rights, as well as issuing executive orders against discrimination in federal employment and completing desegregation of the armed forces. Truman privately resisted the ADA's and young Hubert Humphrey's successful struggle to put some of these proposals in the Democratic platform, but Truman subsequently claimed credit for the platform. Dewey favored civil rights only in general terms, and was ambiguous about the FEPC.

One of the most important Truman-Dewey differences concerned labor relations. Truman had vetoed the Taft-Hartley Act, with its restrictions on unions and on strikes; when it was repassed over his veto, he condemned it and urged repeal. Dewey called the Taft-Hartley veto message "the wrongest, most incompetent, most inaccurate document" put out of the White House in 160 years; he defended the Taft-Hartley Act (carefully referring to it as the "Labor-Management Relations Act of 1947"), while promising unspecified changes where necessary. Yet even on Taft-Hartley the candidates' differences were somewhat unclear and seldom repeated. As a result, some voters misperceived their stands.[9] This should alert us to the fact that even on party cleavage issues candidates are often ambiguous (see chapter 6), and that candidate differences are not always visible in detail to all members of the general public.

Truman was more favorable than Dewey to reclamation and to integrated public power projects like TVA, and to the immigration of displaced persons from Europe. Both candidates favored farm price supports, and agreed on most foreign policy issues, including the Marshall Plan for Europe and aid to the Chinese Nationalists. Truman was, however, more inclined toward imposition of a peacetime draft and universal military training.

In 1952, Eisenhower and Stevenson differed somewhat along the lines of party cleavages. Stevenson proposed uniform wages and hours legislation; expanding the coverage and increasing the benefits of social security; repealing the Taft-Hartley Act and starting over with (rather similar) labor legislation; and a federal equal employment commission and curtailment of the Senate filibuster, which had been used by Southerners to block civil rights legislation.[10]

Candidate differences in 1952 were blurred, however, both by Stevenson's centrism and by Eisenhower's vagueness and his endorsement —in general terms—of traditionally Democratic programs. Eisenhower said that the New Deal accomplishments in housing, workmen's compensation, unemployment insurance and social security had become "rights" not to be tampered with; he favored "expanding" social security. (At the same time he spoke of cutting "billions" from federal spending in order to balance the budget and halt inflation.) Stevenson's espousal of price supports for farmers at 90% of parity was upstaged by Eisenhower's endorsement of support legislation then on the books (which provided that amount) and his declaration that a fair share for farmers was not merely 90% of parity but "full parity."

Both candidates agreed in opposing "socialism" of any sort, and in wanting to get communists or "security risks" out of government, with a nod to protection of civil liberties. Perhaps the clearest differences between the candidates were on two peripheral party cleavage issues: Stevenson's advocacy of federal (and Eisenhower's of state) control of offshore "tidelands" oil, which had just been awarded to the federal government by the Supreme Court; and Stevenson's greater enthusiasm for public power and reclamation projects.

Foreign policy differences in 1952 were slight, with Eisenhower somewhat more eager for the "liberation" from Soviet influence of the "captive peoples" of Eastern Europe, and Stevenson more favorable to the United Nations and world law, and to foreign aid for countries like India. On Korea (much like Vietnam in 1968), both candidates rejected escalation against China but also rejected quick withdrawal; both favored gradual disengagement, with Eisenhower emphasizing the replacement of American troops by Koreans, and Stevenson placing hope in firmness and negotiations.

In 1956 the differences between the same two candidates were still more muted. Eisenhower remained vague and aloof from the campaign, and continued his verbal acceptance of traditional Democratic policies like federal aid to education; Stevenson and the Democrats tended to voice agreement with Eisenhower's program and to blame congressional Republicans for obstructing it. Even on social welfare issues the differences between Eisenhower and Stevenson were slight. Stevenson did advocate federal grants and loans to subsidize a national health insurance system, which Eisenhower opposed, and Stevenson favored raising the minimum wage while Eisenhower preferred broadening its coverage, but on employment, housing, and education, scarcely any differences were discernible.[11]

On civil rights the candidates could hardly be told apart: the Republican platform was somewhat more approving than the Democratic of the *Brown* school desegregation decision, but Stevenson endorsed the decision explicitly and urged that the president should create a climate of acceptance, while Eisenhower (saying he was sworn to uphold the *whole* Constitution) declined to endorse the *Brown* decision. Stevenson's advocacy of public help to private enterprise in developing atomic power closely resembled Eisenhower's "partnership" concept. Of all domestic issues, only farm policy (then a matter of significant party cleavage) clearly divided the candidates, with Stevenson advocating high price supports and Eisenhower opposing them, in favor of his "soil bank" program and the hope of parity prices through the marketplace.

It was in certain aspects of defense and foreign affairs, not party cleavage issues at the time, that Eisenhower and Stevenson had the most visible differences—modest ones at that. Stevenson proposed that the United States should suspend H-bomb testing if other countries would do likewise; he said he would go anywhere at any time to confer about halting the tests. Eisenhower wanted strong safeguards against cheating on any test ban, and said he was doing everything possible for peace consistent with the national safety; he declared that the subject was inappropriate for public discussion. Stevenson also expressed the hope that the draft could "in the foreseeable future" or "ultimately" be abolished and replaced with a professional army; Eisenhower said the draft was needed.

The 1960 Kennedy-Nixon election involved somewhat greater candidate differences, rather like those of 1948.

Kennedy and Nixon disagreed, for example, on medical care for the aged, federal aid to education, the minimum wage, and depressed areas legislation—in each case lining up in accordance with party cleavages. Kennedy urged adoption of the Anderson-Kennedy bill providing federal medical insurance to all the aged (without a means test) for hospital and nursing costs, financed through the social security system. Nixon favored the already enacted Kerr-Mills bill, which provided federal subsidies to state-operated programs for medical assistance to the indigent; he also proposed unspecified aid for voluntary state-operated insurance programs, but opposed the compulsory, federal, and social-security-financed aspects of what was later called Medicare.[12]

Kennedy advocated low-interest federal loans for college construction, and federally insured loans to college students, as well as federal aid for school construction and teachers' salaries, preserving "complete local control" of school systems. Nixon favored loans, scholarships, and expanded NDEA (National Defense Education Act) fellowships for students, as well as tax deductions for students' parents. He also backed assistance for school construction through matching grants, but disagreed with Kennedy by opposing aid for teachers' salaries, on the grounds that it would "lead toward dictation from Washington as to what is taught in our schools . . ."; Nixon cast a tie-breaking vote in the Senate against an education bill which included teachers' salaries.

Kennedy supported the Fair Labor Standards amendments of 1960, which would have raised the minimum wage from $1.10 to $1.25 per hour and extended its coverage to some five million additional employees. Nixon favored extending coverage to only three million and raising the minimum wage to only $1.15; he argued that greater increases would lead to unemployment.

Kennedy sought to repass and sign the $251 million depressed areas bill (twice vetoed by Eisenhower), which would provide long-term development loans and technical assistance for industry, and loans and grants for public facilities, vocational training and retraining, slum clearance and urban planning. Nixon favored a much smaller ($80 million) Republican redevelopment bill. During the campaign he endorsed the bill proposed by Republican Senator Scott, for a $200 million program consisting of half federal funds.

The extent of these differences should not be overemphasized. Nixon in the campaign stood somewhat closer to public opinion and to Kennedy than he had as a member of the Eisenhower administration. The positions of both candidates were shrouded in ambiguity and confusion; they did not make very clear the budgetary differences between their programs. Nixon, for example, referred to the Scott depressed areas bill as a $200 million program, making it sound like the Democratic bill even though only half the amount was to come from the federal government; he emphasized several specific localities in Scott's Pennsylvania where he claimed the Republican bill would have provided more aid than the Democratic. Indeed in most post–New Deal elections the Republican candidates, finding themselves on the unpopular side of social welfare party cleavage issues, have tended to be especially vague on those issues.

On issues of little or no party cleavage, the differences between Kennedy and Nixon were mostly slight. About civil rights—not then a party cleavage matter—they said little and differed little, except that Kennedy favored home rule for the District of Columbia—a proposal with partisan as well as racial implications. Even on labor relations the candidates' differences were minuscule, except that Kennedy favored and Nixon opposed authority for government seizure of industry in national emergency strikes. (Nixon charged that Kennedy also favored compulsory arbitration, but Kennedy denied it.)

In foreign affairs, Kennedy expressed somewhat more enthusiasm for foreign aid, especially to Africa. The candidates both urged toughness against communist countries, and each seized upon minor policy differences to imply the other was "soft"—with Nixon opposing Kennedy's suggestions that the president should apologize to Khrushchev over the U-2 incident and that the United States should not commit itself to defend the Quemoy and Matsu islands off China, while Kennedy proposed and Nixon opposed encouraging an exile invasion of Castro's Cuba. (Whether Kennedy knew that an invasion plan was already underway, and why Nixon, knowing of the plan, claimed that it would be an unthinkable violation of U.S. treaties and international law, is still a matter of dispute.) Kennedy advocated somewhat more military spending and a greater diversity of forces than Nixon did.

The 1968 election, which we will later examine in depth, brought differences between Nixon and Humphrey, along party cleavage lines, quite similar to those of 1948 and 1960. The unusual elections of 1964 and 1972, with their insurgent candidacies of Goldwater and McGovern (to be discussed below and in chapter 5), entailed even clearer differences along traditional party lines at the same time that some new kinds of differences were introduced.

In 1976, too, Carter and Ford disagreed along the usual party lines, although Carter (more like Stevenson than like Kennedy or Humphrey) did not go all-out for the policies of liberal Democrats.[13]

Carter was more favorable than Ford to public service employment of the sort provided in the Humphrey-Hawkins bill, though Carter expressed some reservations about it. Carter, but not Ford, advocated a national health insurance system. Carter advocated tax reform—the closing of "loopholes," and more progressive taxation—of a sort opposed by Ford.

On civil rights, Carter conveyed an impression of being more pro-black than Ford, but the specific differences on policy were hard to discern: both opposed mandatory busing for school integration, while promising to enforce any court decisions on the point; both favored open housing laws banning discrimination, but opposed active federal efforts to integrate housing.

Carter adopted somewhat more pro-labor positions than Ford, agreeing to sign, but not to work for, repeal of the Taft-Hartley "right to work" section 14-B. On the newer party cleavage issues, Carter was more favorable than Ford to "pardoning" (but not giving amnesty to) Vietnam draft resisters, and to permitting abortions. He made clear that he personally disapproved of abortions, but opposed a constitutional amendment banning them.

So far we have compared candidate differences with party cleavages in rather general terms. For a more precise analysis we must return to the election of 1968. In the previous section we reviewed in detail party differences in public opinion for that year. By comparing this information with the candidates' stands in 1968, we can perform a test of party cleavage as against public opinion theories of electoral competition.

On each of our thirty-two party cleavage issues from 1967 and 1968, we examined Nixon's and Humphrey's stands to see whether differences between the candidates (if any) ran in the same direction as differences between the opinions of Republican and Democratic party identifiers, or in the opposite direction from them. For example, if Democrats were more favorable toward federal aid to education than Republicans were, did Humphrey favor it more than Nixon? Taking all issues, if the prediction of public opinion theories were correct and there were no systematic differences between the stands of opposing candidates, we would expect that by chance the differences between candidates and those between identifiers would run in the same direction only about half the time. If, on the contrary, candidates' and identifiers' differences ran in the same direction significantly more than half the time, public opinion theories would be refuted and party cleavage theories would be supported. There would be definite evidence of systematic candidate differences on policy.

Our results, shown in table 7, are unmistakable. Humphrey's and Nixon's stands differed in a systematic fashion that is compatible with party cleavage theories but quite inconsistent with public opinion theories.

There were measurable differences between the two candidates' stands on 30 of the 32 party cleavage issues, and in the vast majority of cases—26 of the 30, or 87%—the candidate difference paralleled differences between party identifiers. When Democrats favored more federal help with medical care, or more aid to education, than Republicans did, Humphrey advocated more medical care and more aid to education than Nixon did—and so on over the 26 issues. There is less than one chance in 1000 that this proportion could have arisen accidentally (see table 7).[14]

Table 7	Party Cleavages and the Direction of Candidate Differences, 1968
Candidate differences parallel to those of their party identifiers	87%* (26)[a]
Candidate differences opposite to those of their party identifiers	13% (4)[b]
	100% (30)

*Significantly greater than 50%, at $p < .001$, by a one-tailed binomial test.

Entries refer to all the cleavage issues given in the appendix upon which there was a measurable difference between the candidates' stands.

a. Items 3, 9, 14, 21, 25, 39, 42, 43, 46, 48, 51, 62, 63, 64, 69, 70, 74, 76, 77, 78, 79, 80, 85, 86, 89, 109.

b. Items 4, 13, 24, 27.

A fuller picture of how much Nixon and Humphrey differed, and in exactly what ways, can be gained by looking in detail at their positions on party cleavage issues.

Just as rank-and-file Democrats were more favorable than Republicans toward programs of job assistance, Humphrey advocated such programs more strongly than Nixon. Nixon proposed to expand job opportunities through private action, at little government expense, by increasing Small Business Administration loans, by setting up a Domestic Development Bank, and by giving tax incentives to corporations which hired and trained the unskilled. He favored a national job census, a national skill census, and a computerized job bank to help with job placement. Nixon supported retraining programs through tax incentives to private industry—a Human Investment Act and a New Enterprise program to train blacks in management. But none of this amounted to a federal "guarantee" of jobs, and in fact Nixon opposed

direct federal action to train the unemployed or to put them to work
on public projects. He maintained that "we ought to get rid of the
Job Corps . . . ," which he called a "costly failure."[15]

Humphrey, too, called for the federal government to help private
enterprise provide jobs, through retraining, voluntary efforts, and job
placement. But he went much further. He approved retraining programs like the Manpower Development and Training Act and the Job
Corps, and called for "an expanded effort" along those lines. He proposed a comprehensive federal training program under which all adult
family heads younger than sixty-five would be entitled to training or
retraining for jobs; they could keep 50% of their earnings under the
program. Further, he declared that "[t]he idea of guaranteeing decent
jobs to anyone who will work at them makes sense." He advocated
"public service employment," at first insisting that the federal government should *not* become the employer of last resort, but later accepting the idea: for those unsuited or unable to find jobs, even after
training, "the federal government should provide employment by financing the major part of the cost of unskilled jobs with state or local
agencies or with nonprofit institutions like hospitals."

The question of income maintenance, too, divided the nominees in
the same way it divided Republican from Democratic party identifiers.
To be sure, Nixon supported the social security and railroad re-
tirement programs, and even proposed some liberalization of them:
automatic cost-of-living increases, higher limits on allowable earnings,
increased widows' benefits, and extension of universal coverage down-
ward from age seventy-two to sixty-five. He advocated direct distribution of food in every county where food programs didn't exist, and
favored simpler distribution of food stamps. He acknowledged that
welfare should meet the immediate needs of those who couldn't help
themselves—the disabled, the aged, and the sick. But he opposed
Humphrey's proposal of a 50% increase in social security benefits as
"dangerous and cruel" and too expensive. He recited many objections
to the idea of guaranteed income, and said he did not accept it. The
main thrust of his proposals, in fact, was to *cut* the amount of money
spent on income maintenance. He spoke repeatedly of the need not for
"more millions on welfare rolls—but more millions on payrolls . . . ."
He opposed "permanent welfarism." He asserted that second- and
third-generation families were living on welfare as semipermanent

wards of the state, and that "something is drastically wrong with the program. Both the goals and the means of aiding the chronically impoverished must be restudied."

Humphrey, on the other hand, called for substantial increases in a variety of income maintenance programs. He was wary of the "guaranteed income" symbol. Saying he did not believe in it, he went on, like Nixon, to emphasize the importance of providing jobs. He too said that the welfare system must be "totally revamped"; he wanted to make changes to avoid disrupting family life, to liberalize incentives to work (deducting from payments only 50% of earnings), and to establish eligibility by personal statements. But the main thrust of Humphrey's proposals was to increase income support. He favored food stamp and commodity distribution programs in every county where severe problems of hunger existed, and school lunches year-round for every needy child. Humphrey called for a 50% across-the-board increase in social security benefits, with automatic future rises to reflect price increases (unlike Nixon, he was willing to finance these increases partly out of general revenues); he favored raising minimum and maximum payments, with proportionally more going to widows and single workers. He advocated a great expansion in coverage and an increase in benefits of unemployment compensation; and an increase in the size and duration of the benefits, as well as the coverage, of workmen's compensation.

For poor people beyond the reach of job or social security programs, Humphrey said the federal government should set nationwide "standards of need"—at least as high as the official poverty level—and underwrite 100% of the financial burden of assistance up to that level. For those not fitting existing federally-aided assistance categories, he said a new program should be introduced to provide allowances directly from the federal government.

Nixon warmly endorsed the goal of improved education. He specifically exempted educational programs from his general plan to cut the budget, and urged a "massive upgrading" of such efforts as Head Start and Follow Through, compensatory and remedial programs, and vocational education. He supported federal help for bilingual education, and aid for private school pupils. However, he strongly emphasized state and local control of education programs, and called for "bloc grants" of federal funds, with states setting standards for their use. As in other policy areas, Nixon advocated programs which would require little or no direct federal spending but would involve informational or organizational activities, work by volunteers, and participation (with tax incentives) by private enterprise. Thus he called for a Defense Department information program to show Vietnam veterans the "opportunities and rewards of teaching," and for a National Student Teacher Corps of volunteers to work in the ghettos. Nixon promised to study improved administration and coordination of educational programs. He approved of tax advantages for donations to colleges, called for tax incentives for private businesses to cooperate with schools in job training, and advocated a National Institute for the Educational Future, a "clearing house" for ideas about elementary and secondary education.

Humphrey, like rank-and-file Democrats, more strongly favored direct federal aid to education. He proclaimed a "civil right" to education, which would guarantee everyone educational opportunity from age four through college and adult education. Like Nixon, he paid homage to local control: ". . . education is basically a state and local responsibility, and should remain so." But at the same time he proposed sweeping federal assistance, for preschooling (available to all poor children from age three, and eventually to all children); for the handicapped; school construction and operating costs; year-round teacher training (expanding it "substantially"); vocational education (tripling the number of students involved); and higher education (a "massive increase" in aid). Humphrey acknowledged that these programs would be expensive, but argued that we must be prepared to pay the price. He urged setting up a federal trust fund for education, with the revenue from federally owned oil shale deposits.

Just as Democrats tended much more than Republicans to support federally assisted medical care, the candidates differed in the same way. Humphrey proposed loans and scholarships to medical students, and support for building new medical institutions. He advocated expanding urban and rural health centers, intensifying health research, and establishing a Health Service Corps. He expressed great enthusiasm for the Medicare program for the aged, and proposed several extensions: putting doctors' bills on the same insurance basis as hospital bills; providing protection against drug costs; and extending coverage to disabled Social Security beneficiaries. He wanted to enlarge preventive and rehabilitative services for the mentally retarded and for the deaf, blind, and emotionally disturbed. Humphrey stopped short of advocating the expansion of Medicare to cover all citizens (see chapter 3), but he moved in that direction, favoring comprehensive prenatal care to all low income women; medical care for all poor children during their first year of life (to be extended to age six, and, in the case of crippling disabilities, to age twenty-one); and a commission on health care insurance to recommend ways of assuring that everyone could afford treatment for catastrophic illnesses.

Nixon seemed to be embarrassed by Humphrey's attacks on his opposition to Medicare in the early 1960s; late in the campaign Nixon asserted that he favored the program and in fact wanted to "improve and extend" it. His only concrete suggestions, however, were to improve administrative efficiency and to allow the elderly full income tax deductions for their drug and medical expenses. Nixon urged an increase in the supply of doctors and nurses, but proposed no programs to bring it about. He opposed cutting federal spending on medical care, but said virtually nothing about increased spending except to favor additional funds for hospital construction under the Hill-Burton Act. Nixon strongly opposed a compulsory health insurance program, saying it would be foolish to "destroy" the system of medical care and research by making federal medical programs available to everyone.

On questions of union-management relations, Democrats tended to be more favorable to unionization and strikes than Republicans. The presidential candidates reflected this cleavage too, though only in muted form. Both upheld unionization in general. Nixon said, "I believe in the right of unions to organize . . . ," and specifically applied this sentiment to government employees. Humphrey expressed more enthusiasm for unions, calling the right of all workers to organize and bargain collectively "basic" to the free enterprise system. He more explicitly favored "organized farm bargaining," and advocated including farm workers under the National Labor Relations Act, while Nixon betrayed ignorance of the fact that the NLRA did not already apply.

Nixon made clear his opposition to strikes by public employees: "So whether it's strikes by teachers or strikes by sanitation workers or strikes by policemen or firemen, I am unequivocally against such strikes and believe that both federal and state law should stand firmly against them." Humphrey said little about strikes, perhaps in order to avoid offending either the general public or his union constituency. But he did imply support of the farm workers' boycott of California grapes, which Nixon deplored as "illegal."

On questions of civil rights, differences between the candidates were again small, but paralleled those between partisans. Democrats favored more federal efforts to achieve integration than Republicans did, in general, and in the specific areas of public accommodations, housing, employment opportunities, and schools. Humphrey warmly endorsed existing law in these areas. He said he stood "squarely behind" the 1954 desegregation decision and the Civil Rights Act of 1964; he referred to the 1957 and 1960 Civil Rights Acts, the comprehensive 1964 Civil Rights Act, the Voting Rights Act of 1965, and the Civil Rights Act of 1968 as "historic progress," and part of "one of mankind's great stories." Humphrey proposed no new legislation, but supported "all efforts" to implement title VI of the 1964 act in order to desegregate the schools, and favored "[v]igorous enforcement" of the 1968 fair housing law.

Nixon expressed some ambivalence about civil rights legislation already on the books. He declared that the legal revolution concerning housing, jobs, education, voting, and public accommodations had been a "needed revolution," but complained that it had not brought "peace, or satisfaction, or the fullness of freedom." He gave no indication of wanting to repeal any civil rights laws, but did not propose to extend them either; and his posture toward enforcement was slightly less firm than Humphrey's. He promised to use title VI of the 1964 act to cut off federal funds from school districts which practiced deliberate segregation, but not for "creating racial balance" by busing. (This was the only manifestation of Nixon's allegedly antiblack "Southern strategy" that could be found among his specific policy proposals; see chapter 5.)

The new issues of "law and order" aroused some partisan disagreement over whether the courts should treat criminals more harshly, and whether liberals or conservatives should be appointed to the Supreme Court. Nixon, in accord with the tendency of Republican identifiers, frequently asserted that "some of our courts have gone too far in weakening the peace forces in this country as against the criminal forces—and Congress should act to restore the balance." Specifically, he criticized the *Miranda* and *Escobedo* decisions concerning coerced

confessions, and the *Wade, Gilbert,* and *Beasley* decisions on the identification of assailants by victims. He favored legislation to overrule
Miranda and *Escobedo* (by constitutional amendment if necessary),
and to permit prosecution appeals of rulings on the admissibility of
evidence. Nixon also advocated appointment to the Supreme Court of
"strict constructionists" sharing his views on criminal justice.

Humphrey, on the other hand, maintained that court decisions were
not a significant factor in the crime increase, and generally endorsed
the Warren court's rulings on rights of the accused, saying that they
were designed to protect the innocent and assure the liberties of all
Americans. He condemned the "scapegoat approach" of attacking the
Supreme Court. Humphrey indicated that he favored appointing liberals to the Court by endorsing President Johnson's nomination of the
liberal Abe Fortas to be chief justice.

Democrats tended to favor somewhat stricter gun controls than Republicans did, and Humphrey and Nixon differed in the same way.
Humphrey declared that if the states did not "promptly" pass registration and licensing laws, the next Congress must do so. Such federal
legislation would require registration of all long guns and hand guns
under simple and speedy procedures; licensing of all importers, manu-
facturers, and dealers in guns and ammunition; and licensing of all
owners and users of guns, under standards insuring "responsible usage
in the public interest." Nixon, on the other hand, wanted to handle
licensing and registration at the local level, and would consider federal action at some unstated time only if the states did not "adequately
handle the problem." He was skeptical about what gun control could
accomplish, and emphasized a different approach more congenial to
gun owners: anyone convicted of using a gun in a major crime should
receive a mandatory prison sentence.

Although both candidates favored allowing eighteen-year-olds to
vote (see chapter 3), they divided in the same direction as their party
followers in enthusiasm for it. Nixon wanted the states to decide such
matters, and merely asked them to "carefully consider" giving the
eighteen-year-olds the right to vote. Humphrey called for federal action through a constitutional amendment.

In the area of foreign policy, where party cleavages were much
weaker, the pattern of correspondence was broken. The candidates
did not always divide in the same way as party cleavages. In fact, there

was no significant tendency in that direction: 5 instances of correspondence, 4 of reversal, and 2 in which the matter could not be
ascertained.

Taking the instances of correspondence first, just as Democrats
favored a somewhat higher level of foreign aid than Republicans did,
so did Humphrey call for a "steady increase" in the amount of aid.
Meanwhile, Nixon rejected "permanent welfarism" abroad, and advocated cuts in foreign aid. In particular he criticized "showcase projects" like steel mills. Humphrey advocated aid for food production,
commodity agreements to stabilize prices, guarantees to encourage
private capital investment, multilateralism, regionalism, modernization
of the monetary system, and trade preferences for the exports of underdeveloped countries. He criticized Congress's action in cutting Alliance for Progress funds as "irresponsible and short-sighted," and
called for higher appropriations for aid to Latin America.

Democrats were less favorable than Republicans toward the bombing of North Vietnam; similarly Humphrey, as we have seen (chapter
3), expressed somewhat greater willingness to stop the bombing than
Nixon did.

Support for the United Nations was more vigorous among Democrats than Republicans. Nixon scarcely mentioned the UN, thereby
indicating that his commitment to the organization was less than enthusiastic. Humphrey, in contrast, spoke repeatedly of the need to
strengthen the United Nations. He made the UN central to his foreign
policy, promising to try to place international peacekeeping soldiers
rather than American soldiers in troubled areas including Vietnam. He
urged UN members to earmark units of their armed forces for peacekeeping, and proposed to use American military assistance funds to
help them do so; he called for a United Nations peacekeeping fund,
beginning with twenty million dollars; he promised to call a new San
Francisco conference on peacekeeping, and urged establishment of a
permanent panel of fact finders and mediators. Humphrey also supported creation of a UN Staff College and a UN Training Center for
Peacekeeping.

Democrats were more eager than Republicans to negotiate with the
communist countries. Accordingly, Humphrey made arms control negotiations a major theme of his campaign. He favored a U.S.-USSR
agreement, first to freeze and reduce offensive and defensive strategic

arms, and then mutually to reduce all armaments. Humphrey called for mutual thinning-out of troops in Europe, and sought agreements to end nuclear testing; to control chemical, radiological, and biological weapons; and to halt regional arms races in the Middle East and elsewhere. He repeatedly urged prompt ratification of the Nuclear Non-Proliferation Treaty.

Nixon, while urging an "era of negotiation" and calling for a series of summit meetings with the Soviet Union, emphasized that he wanted to negotiate from a position of strength, and set rather modest negotiating goals. His specific negotiating proposals were innocuous: improved communications, "Open Skies" exchanges of information on the location of forces (echoing Eisenhower), and the like. He expressed only "hope" that the United States and her opponents could "one day" limit their armaments, without pledging any effort to do so. Nixon endorsed the nonproliferation treaty, but expressed "concern" over some of its provisions, and (because of the Soviet invasion of Czechoslovakia) wanted to postpone ratification.

Just as Democrats tended to take a softer line than Republicans toward admission of the People's Republic of China to the United Nations, Humphrey took a somewhat softer line than Nixon. Humphrey wanted to "actively build bridges of cultural exchange and of commerce and trade to one of the great land masses of this earth, Communist China . . . ." He advocated the interchange of scholars, journalists, and artists, and an end to restrictions on nonstrategic trade. Without specifically mentioning United Nations membership, he said that, should China decide to become a "responsible, participating member of the community of nations, we will welcome it. And we should, now, encourage it." Nixon opposed a UN seat for China at the present time, though he did not rule it out for the future, provided that China indicated by deeds that she wanted "to be a part of the civilized family of nations and not an outlaw nation." He rather mildly anticipated "eventual conversations" with the leaders of China, and declared that we could not afford to leave China forever outside the family of nations; but in the short run he opposed recognition or trade. Nixon barely hinted at the major changes to come in relations with China and the Soviet Union.

On four foreign policy issues, the pattern of correspondence between candidate differences and party cleavages was reversed. Though

Democrats expressed more belligerence concerning preemptive war
with China than Republicans did, Humphrey was more friendly than
Nixon toward China, and therefore presumably more strongly opposed
to war with that country. Humphrey also showed signs of favoring
troop withdrawals from Vietnam slightly more than Nixon did (chapter 3), even though Republican identifiers favored them more than
Democrats.

Republicans supported foreign aid for birth control more than Democrats, but Humphrey was the one who favored "[l]eadership toward
family planning in the developing nations on a scale many times larger
than now being considered," whereas Nixon cast doubt on what population control could accomplish, and made no proposal for U.S.
action.

Finally, Democrats tended to support a more forceful reaction to
the Soviet invasion of Czechoslovakia, but it was Nixon who called it
"an outrage against the conscience of the world," and urged that ratification of the nonproliferation treaty be delayed in retaliation. Humphrey merely said the world should condemn the "tragic action" of
the Soviets; he did not propose any action at all, and specifically rejected the idea of delaying the nonproliferation treaty. In general,
Humphrey was more consistently a pacific internationalist than were
rank-and-file Democrats.

On foreign policy issues taken as a whole, then, the candidates
showed no significant tendency at all to respond to party cleavages.
It was on every domestic issue examined that the difference between
Nixon's and Humphrey's position corresponded to the difference between Republican and Democratic party identifiers. This perfect congruence on domestic policy, together with the preponderance of domestic issues among significant party cleavages, accounts for the fact
that on the total set of issues the candidates responded to the direction of party cleavages nearly 90% of the time.

Looking beyond the question of direction of differences, we also
have some evidence, though it is less conclusive, that the *amount* of
difference between the candidates on a given issue depended upon
the amount of party cleavage on that issue.

On this point we could use all sixty-three issue items, cleavage and
noncleavage, for which party identification breakdowns were available.
On the fifty-four issues upon which both candidates took stands, the

amount of difference between candidates was coded as relatively "high" or "low," and the amount of party cleavage was categorized as high or low also, taking an 11% difference between Republican and Democratic identifiers as the threshhold of "high" party cleavage. As can be seen in table 8, there was a positive relationship between the two variables: on issues of little or no party cleavage, Nixon and Humphrey tended to take similar positions, and on issues of high cleavage, they tended to take substantially different positions. This relationship is significant at better than the $p = .025$ level.[16]

This was only a tendency, of course; on some issues of low cleavage—for example, negotiating and trading with the communists, court treatment of criminals, wage and price controls, and military pay—Nixon and Humphrey differed markedly. On some issues of high cleav-

Table 8   Party Cleavages and the Magnitude
of Candidate Differences, 1968

	Extent of Party Cleavage	
Amount of Candidate Difference	Low (0–10%)	High (11%–)
High	34% (12)[a]	68% (13)[b]
Low	66% (23)[c]	32% (6)[d]
	100% (35)	100% (19)

Yule's Q = gamma = 0.61.

Difference significant at $p < .025$ by chi-square test.

The table is based upon all issues for which party identification breakdowns were available and both candidates' stands could be ascertained.

a. Appendix items 2, 9, 21, 23, 26, 43, 60, 78, 82, 85, 88, 91.

b. Items 3, 14, 39, 42, 46, 48, 51, 69, 70, 74, 76, 80, 86.

c. Items 1, 4, 5, 6, 7, 8, 11, 12, 13, 13a, 14a, 20, 24, 27, 35, 36, 37, 38, 40a, 59, 77, 109, 111.

d. Items 25, 62, 63, 64, 79, 89.

age, such as unionization of teachers, nurses, and farmers, differences between candidates were minor. The bulk of the relationship resulted from substantial candidate differences on social welfare matters, and small differences (in whichever direction) on most foreign policy issues.

The limited survey evidence available indicates that voters fairly accurately perceived this contrast between candidate differences on foreign and domestic issues. The average American saw Nixon and Humphrey as standing very close together on the Vietnam issue, with Humphrey only slightly more dovish and both standing very close to the average American's own opinion. On the urban crisis, however— compounded of the party cleavage issues of law and order, race, and social welfare—the average American saw Humphrey as considerably more liberal than Nixon, and as more liberal than the average voter. According to these public perceptions, Humphrey and Nixon stood apart by only .17 standard deviations of public opinion on Vietnam, but by .77 standard deviations on the urban crisis (see figure 4).[17] As we will see, these perceptions and the reality behind them had important implications for issue voting.

The evidence indicates, then, that both the amount and the direction of differences between candidates are determined in part by the nature and extent of cleavages between their parties. A contrary interpretation is possible, of course: that, through selective recruitment or opinion change, party cleavages respond to candidates' positions rather than vice versa. This possibility cannot be wholly dismissed, as we will note in our discussion of policy realignments. In the case of 1968 and most other elections, however, it is not likely to have been the dominant process. The principal lines of party cleavage had been much the same since the New Deal and thus long antedated the campaign of 1968. Moreover, the bulk of our opinion data (including responses on eighteen of the thirty-two party cleavage issues) was gathered before the autumn campaign and could not have been affected by it. Lastly, the typical campaign speech is an unlikely vehicle for political persuasion, as will become apparent from our discussion of ambiguity in chapter 6. Realignments do occur, and candidates' stands may sometimes play a part in them. Ordinarily, however, candidates merely echo (and perhaps reinforce) existing cleavages; they act less often as leaders than as the led.

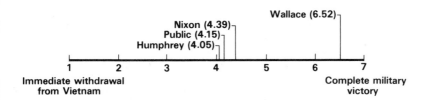

Nixon (4.39)
Public (4.15)
Humphrey (4.05)
Wallace (6.52)

1   2   3   4   5   6   7
Immediate withdrawal   Complete military
from Vietnam   victory

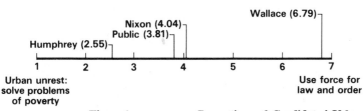

Nixon (4.04)
Public (3.81)
Humphrey (2.55)
Wallace (6.79)

1   2   3   4   5   6   7
Urban unrest: Use force for
solve problems   law and order
of poverty

Figure 4   **Perceptions of Candidates' Urban and
                                 Vietnam Stands, Autumn 1968.** En-
                                 tries are median perceptions and self-
                                 ratings from the SRC election study,
                                 provided through the ICPR. Standard
                                 errors of the means range from .04
                                 to .06. Standard deviations of self-
                                 ratings are 1.97 on Vietnam and 1.93
                                 on urban unrest.

At the same time, we cannot be nearly so confident about which
elements of the party coalitions affect candidates' stands and how
much they affect them. The findings are consistent with several different party cleavage theories, including Downs's theory with its restrictions on party mobility; the Davis and Hinich model of primary elections; Wittman's theory of unitary policy-oriented parties; or indeed
any theory that takes account of party activists, money givers, candidates' own opinions, or other elements of party cleavage (see the discussion in chapter 2). Our data do not permit us to distinguish among
them, and the prospects of doing so in the near future are not bright,
because of difficulties in data collection and in distinguishing the separate effects of collinear variables.

By the same token, however, since the various strata of the parties
have tended to stand together on party cleavage issues, it is not such

an urgent matter to assess their separate influences on candidates'
stands. The central point is that on such issues the distinctive opinions of the party coalitions, *taken as a whole*, strongly affect the issue
positions of their candidates.

One would expect this regularity to endure even as the particular
content of party cleavages changes; and even as particular electoral
institutions (such as the use of direct primaries, or public financing)
vary. In any electoral system which allows for special influence by
identifiers or activists, so long as identifiers or activists have policy
goals that differ by party, parties and candidates presumably have
incentives to respond to party cleavages.

Insurgent Candidates, Distinct
Choices, and Policy Realignments

In some elections, candidates' policy differences appear to be greater
than usual and to encompass new issues, which may then enter into
party cleavages for the first time.

It is difficult to speak with any precision about whether the candidates in one election offered a clearer choice—stood further apart on
the issues—than the candidates in another election. In principle it
should be possible to do so in terms of the dispersion of public opinion; we ought to be able to judge, for example, whether Goldwater
and Johnson in 1964 stood far apart, near the quartiles of public opinion (or perhaps separated by two standard deviations) on various
issues, while Eisenhower and Stevenson in 1956 stood rather close
together, say within half a standard deviation of each other. In practice, however, we can seldom make such statements, because the measurement of public policy preferences has not been precise enough
to reveal distributions of opinion and to let us judge where on those
distributions a given candidate stands. (This is the same problem we
faced in chapter 3 in measuring closeness to the midpoint of opinion.)
Often the best we can do is to enumerate the specific differences between candidates and make judgments of relative distances, as was
done at the beginning of this chapter. For some recent elections we
can use public perceptions of candidates' stands on issue scales and
make direct comparisons with opinion distributions on the same scales,

so long as we remember that perceptions are only rough indicators of candidates' objective positions.

With these qualifications in mind, we can generally confirm the impression that differences between candidates are sharper than usual when one of them is an insurgent, nominated by ideological forces outside the main body of his party, like McGovern in 1972 or Goldwater in 1964. This apparently obvious point needs some modification, however. The policy statements of Johnson and Goldwater in the autumn of 1964, and of Nixon and McGovern in the autumn of 1972, were not nearly so different from each other as one might expect.

Certainly voters *perceived* a distinct choice in the 1972 election, as we can see in figure 5 and table 9. Nixon and McGovern were seen by the average voter as standing substantially further apart than one standard deviation of public opinion, on four issues (overall liberalism, Vietnam, busing and jobs) out of the fourteen surveyed by the Center for Political Studies (CPS). On another five issues they were viewed as approximately one standard deviation apart. Only on three issues were they seen as not very different from each other. By contrast, as figure 4 indicated, in 1968 Nixon and Humphrey had been seen as less than one standard deviation apart on both the major issues for which perceptual data are available.

On the same party cleavage issues which had divided Nixon and Humphrey in 1968, McGovern and Nixon were perceived as quite different from each other. McGovern was seen as much more liberal than Nixon on the urban unrest question, which combined law and order, civil rights, and social welfare; and as more liberal on government assistance with jobs and standard of living, on medical insurance, and on school integration through busing.

In addition, McGovern and Nixon were seen as distinctly different on some new issues which had not entered into earlier party cleavages: McGovern was thought much more eager to get U.S. forces out of Vietnam (contrast the 1968 similarity of Nixon and Humphrey in chapter 3 and figure 4); more tolerant of marijuana use; more sympathetic to campus protesters; and more in favor of progressive taxation.

Voters also saw moderately large differences between Nixon and McGovern on aid to minorities and rights of the accused. Overall, McGovern was seen as more "liberal" (a concept which by 1972 had

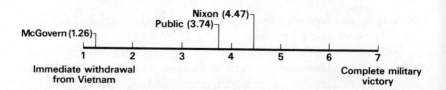

McGovern (1.26)
Public (3.74)
Nixon (4.47)

1 2 3 4 5 6 7

Immediate withdrawal
from Vietnam

Complete military
victory

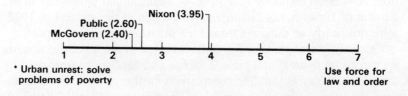

Public (2.60)
McGovern (2.40)
Nixon (3.95)

1 2 3 4 5 6 7

* Urban unrest: solve
problems of poverty

Use force for
law and order

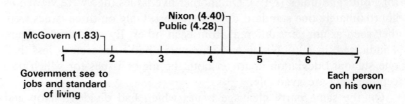

McGovern (1.83)
Nixon (4.40)
Public (4.28)

1 2 3 4 5 6 7

Government see to
jobs and standard
of living

Each person
on his own

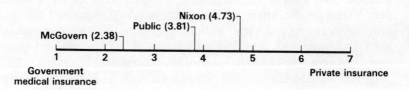

McGovern (2.38)
Public (3.81)
Nixon (4.73)

1 2 3 4 5 6 7

Government
medical insurance

Private insurance

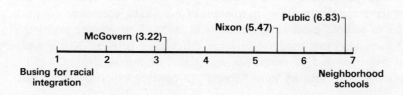

McGovern (3.22)
Nixon (5.47)
Public (6.83)

1 2 3 4 5 6 7

Busing for racial
integration

Neighborhood
schools

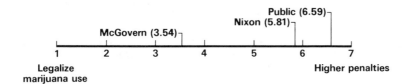

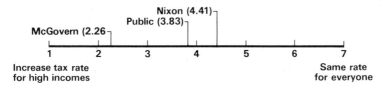

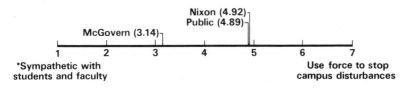

Figure 5

Perceptions of Candidates' Stands, 1972. Entries are median perceptions and self-ratings from the CPS (formerly SRC) Michigan election study, provided through the ICPR. Standard errors of the means range from .03 to .07. Standard deviations of self-ratings range from 1.66 (busing) to 2.43 (health insurance), with most close to 2.00.

*Postelection data; other items are preelection.

	Table 9		Perceived Candidate Differences, 1972	
Issue	Nixon's Position	McGovern's Position	Absolute Difference	Standardized Difference
Liberalism*	5.02	2.16	2.86	2.23
Vietnam	4.47	1.26	3.21	1.62
Vietnam*	4.57	1.28	3.29	1.73
Busing	5.47	3.22	2.25	1.36
Jobs	4.40	1.83	2.57	1.25
Jobs*	4.49	2.28	2.21	1.12
Marijuana	5.81	3.54	2.27	1.05
Health insurance	4.73	2.38	2.35	.97
Campus disturbances*	4.92	3.14	1.78	.96
Tax rates	4.41	2.26	2.15	.91
Tax rates*	4.20	2.75	1.45	.63
Minority aid*	4.09	2.36	1.73	.88
Urban unrest*	3.95	2.40	1.55	.74
Accused rights*	4.29	2.96	1.33	.63
Pollution	2.79	2.19	.60	.31
Women's rights	3.56	2.90	.66	.29
Inflation	3.09	3.25	.16	.10
Inflation*	3.27	3.06	.21	.14

Entries are median public perceptions of the candidates' positions on seven-point scales; the absolute value of differences between those positions; and the differences divided by the standard deviation of public self-ratings on each issue.

*Postelection data; all other data are preelection.

come to apply to nearly all these issues) by more than two standard deviations. Only on inflation, pollution, and (oddly) equality for women did voters perceive little difference between Nixon and McGovern.

The unusually great magnitude of perceived differences between the candidates in 1972 can be emphasized if we contrast them with perceptions in 1976. In that year, Ford and Carter were seen as standing more than one standard deviation apart on only one issue out of ten (generalized liberalism), and as standing approximately one standard deviation apart on only two additional issues (jobs and health insurance.) On every one of the ten issues which were surveyed in both years (liberalism, busing, jobs, marijuana, health, tax rates, minority aid, urban unrest, rights of the accused, and women's rights), Ford and Carter were seen as standing closer together than Nixon and Mc-Govern had. In some cases—busing and marijuana, for example—they were perceived as much closer (see figure 6 and table 10).

The divergent 1972 perceptions are partly consistent with our analysis of the candidates' speeches and statements. (McGovern's stands are described in the next chapter.) But it is not the case that the average perceptions corresponded exactly to the candidates' objective positions as taken in their policy pronouncements. Study of the candidates' speeches indicates, for example, that McGovern and Nixon differed more on women's rights, taxes, and pollution—and less on marijuana and busing—than the public was aware.

The contrast between perceptions and reality is even more apparent in the way McGovern was seen as standing far from the public's median preferences—far to the left—on practically all the issues: farther from the public than Nixon on all but two of the fourteen CPS issues. This image of a McGovern out in left field was the main ingredient of perceptions of a distinct choice in 1972. Yet we saw in chapter 3 that a comparison of McGovern's explicit policy statements with public preferences did not support this image. McGovern stood about as close to the public in 1972 as Nixon or Humphrey had in 1968.

In order to understand the erroneous perceptions of McGovern's positions it is not sufficient to speculate that voters remembered earlier, more leftist stands; the changes between winter and autumn were small, and in fact our finding (see table 5) of McGovern's closeness to public opinion was based on the early stands. More likely there was reliance on such cues about policy stands as the radical nature of some of McGovern's most fervent supporters. Beyond that, caricatures of Mc-Govern's stands by his opponents probably played a part, and the public was especially susceptible to misperceptions of his stands because of misgivings about McGovern's personal qualities.

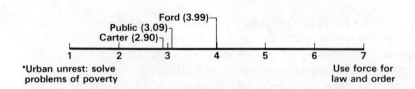

*Urban unrest: solve   Use force for
problems of poverty   law and order

Ford (3.99)
Public (3.09)
Carter (2.90)
1   2   3   4   5   6   7

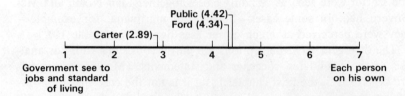

Government see to   Each person
jobs and standard   on his own
of living

Public (4.42)
Ford (4.34)
Carter (2.89)
1   2   3   4   5   6   7

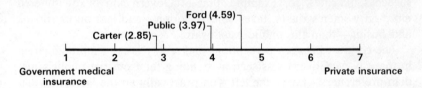

Government medical   Private insurance
insurance

Ford (4.59)
Public (3.97)
Carter (2.85)
1   2   3   4   5   6   7

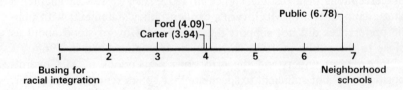

Busing for   Neighborhood
racial integration   schools

Public (6.78)
Ford (4.09)
Carter (3.94)
1   2   3   4   5   6   7

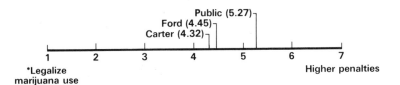

*Legalize
marijuana use   Higher penalties

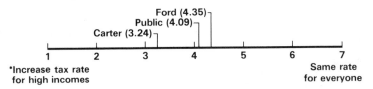

*Increase tax rate
for high incomes   Same rate
for everyone

Figure 6   **Perceptions of Candidates' Stands, 1976.** Entries are median perceptions and self-ratings from the CPS election study. Standard errors of the means range from .036 to .050. Standard deviations of self-ratings range from 1.71 (busing) to 2.38 (health insurance), with most around 2.00.
*Post election data; other items are preelection.

Turning to the Johnson-Goldwater election of 1964 we can confirm that the degree of choice between candidates was unusually distinct, even more so than in 1972. But again this point must be qualified: it was considerably less true of Goldwater's moderate autumn stands and Johnson's vague campaign utterances than of Goldwater's early stands and Johnson's record in office.

Johnson had championed and signed the 1964 Civil Rights Act, while Goldwater voted against it. Goldwater wanted to cut back on the social welfare programs and "War on Poverty" which Johnson was expanding. Goldwater wanted to tighten restrictions on labor unions which Johnson favored loosening. Johnson—at that time— urged avoiding heavy U.S. involvement in a Vietnam war which Goldwater was eager to win. Goldwater urged confrontation and "victory"

Issue	Ford's Position	Carter's Position	Absolute Difference	Standardized Difference
Liberalism	5.11	3.10	2.01	1.50
Busing	4.09	3.94	.15	.09
Jobs	4.34	2.89	1.45	.72
Jobs*	4.70	3.03	1.67	.98
Marijuana*	4.45	4.32	.13	.06
Health insurance	4.59	2.85	1.74	.73
Tax rates*	4.35	3.24	1.11	.49
Minority aid	3.89	3.06	.83	.41
Urban unrest*	3.99	2.90	1.09	.57
Accused rights	3.83	3.65	.18	.08
Women's rights*	3.47	3.18	.29	.14

Table 10   Perceived Candidate Differences, 1976

Entries are median public perceptions of the candidates' positions on the Center for Political Studies seven-point scales; the absolute value of differences between those positions; and the differences divided by the standard deviation of public self ratings on each issue.

*Postelection data; all other data are preelection.

against the Soviet Union, while Johnson had worked for peaceful coexistence and a nuclear test ban treaty. (Goldwater's stands are treated in detail in the next chapter.)

Thus Goldwater succeeded to some extent in giving life to his campaign slogan, "a choice not an echo," although the pressures of campaigning worked against it. Many of the 1964 candidate differences, like those of 1972, followed the established lines of party cleavage, while others involved new issues (especially civil rights and foreign policy) which had not previously divided the parties. It is characteristic of insurgent candidates that new issue differences are introduced.

We can extend the analysis of clear electoral choices if for a moment we abandon the two-party perspective and consider third-party candidates. It is plain that their positions are often quite distinct from those of the major party nominees. Almost by definition, the differ-

ences do not involve established major-party cleavages; indeed the
appearance of third party candidates, taking "extreme" stands on issues not previously dividing the major parties, often seems to herald
the breakdown or realignment of the party system.

Thus the Progressives of the 1920s foreshadowed the New Deal
social class realignment; the Populists of the early 1890s anticipated
the Bryan capture of the Democrats and the East-West realignment of
1896; the emergence of the Free Soilers and then of the Republicans
in the mid-1850s signaled the breakup of the Democrats over slavery
and the coming of Civil War and a North-South realignment. Similarly
George Wallace in 1968 (and, indeed, Strom Thurmond and Henry
Wallace back in 1948) perhaps represented forces that would later
alter the two major parties.[18]

Figure 4 indicated that George Wallace was seen as offering a clear
choice, in 1968, on the urban unrest and Vietnam issues. The Alabama governor's policy stands were not in fact terribly specific; he
indulged mainly in the sort of condemnations of past performance
that we will discuss in chapter 7. But he left no doubt that he represented Southern resistance to racial integration (especially opposing
the "guidelines" issued by HEW's "pointy-headed bureaucrats" in
Washington), and that he favored "law and order" in the sense of
tough measures against street crime and the use of force against black
urban rioters. Wallace was wary of any pronouncements about Vietnam. The public perception of him as a hawk was probably based—
and perhaps reasonably so—on his violent rhetoric about war protesters and on his choice of General Curtis ("Bomb 'em back to the
Stone Age") LeMay as his vice-presidential running mate.

What significance can we attribute to clear third-party choices? Certainly they do not fully satisfy the responsible party ideal; since a third-
party candidate rarely has a serious chance of winning, voters can
express their support only by throwing their votes away. Yet such
candidacies may perform some of the educational work advocated in
responsible party theories, alerting citizens to new issues. And they
do "send a message" to the major parties, sometimes revealing new
divisions of opinion which must be taken into account if the major
parties are to survive.

We noted that policy cleavages between the major parties often shift
with the passage of time. Even between 1932 and 1976, the differ-

ences in opinions of Republican and Democratic party identifiers—
and activists as well—became stronger on some issues and weaker on
others. Sometimes entirely new issues took on a partisan coloration
and old party issues faded away.

For example, the basic New Deal issues of social welfare measures,
labor relations, and government regulation of business were somewhat
dampened during the tranquil Eisenhower years; Democrats and Republicans differed only to a moderate extent. In the middle and late
1960s, however, the gap widened. On civil rights, there was scarcely
any divergence along party lines in the 1950s, but Republican and
Democratic identifiers came to differ markedly from the mid-1960s
onward. "Law and order" issues too began to divide Republicans and
Democrats in the 1960s. Marijuana and other lifestyle questions took
on a partisan meaning in the 1970s. Some foreign policy differences,
like those over Vietnam, appeared and disappeared from time to time.

We can refer to these shifts as *policy realignments* of the parties.
In some cases they are signs of the sort of durable change in the social makeup of the parties—sometimes entailing a swing in relative
party strength—that we associate with critical elections or realigning
eras. In other instances, shifts in party cleavages on policy may be
more temporary or modest, but they too tell us that the meaning of
the parties has changed. New wine is found in old bottles; to be a
"Republican" or a "Democrat" has come to signify membership in
a different sort of policy coalition.

There is still much to learn about how and why policy realignments
occur. In many cases we can point to plausible explanations: Eisenhower internationalizing the Republican party, for example, and de-
fusing the class-related New Deal issues in the 1950s; the Kennedy
legislative program and then Goldwater's candidacy heating up New
Deal issues in the early 1960s; Goldwater and the 1964 Civil Rights
Act making civil rights more a party matter than they had been when
Eisenhower was enforcing the *Brown* decision at Little Rock; Goldwater and then Nixon adding distinctive "law and order" stands to
the party line-up; Vietnam, and marijuana and other lifestyle questions becoming matters of Republican-Democratic disagreement with
McGovern's candidacy.

We can be less sure of the processes of change among individual
voters: whether party identifiers, following their leaders, changed their
own policy opinions; whether new voters with differing opinions joined

the parties; or whether people changed their party loyalties on issue grounds. All of these things may happen, in various mixtures, but the best evidence indicates that the first two are more common than the third.

The names of presidential candidates—especially third-party contenders and insurgents like McGovern and Goldwater (or Al Smith or William Jennings Bryan before them)—are prominent in these possible explanations of policy realignments. What part do candidates actually play?

Here again our knowledge is incomplete. It would be too much to claim that presidential candidates are the prime movers in realignments; if so, we would next have to ask why "extreme" candidates are nominated in the first place. Surely it can be no accident that three sets of unusually clear choices (counting George Wallace) were offered in the three consecutive elections of 1964, 1968, and 1972.

A more fundamental explanation would have to involve the rise of new issues among the electorate, with increased polarization of opinion on matters cutting across the old party cleavages. In giving political expression to new issues, the role of political activists is probably a crucial one; hardworking activists with intense policy preferences, for example, were responsible for winning presidential nominations for Goldwater and McGovern.

Yet we should push back further still and ask why new issues emerge, why polarization outside the old cleavages occurs. On this level, an answer can be offered in general outline. A party alignment is a response to a particular set of problems, with the parties offering alternative solutions—the Democrats trying to help debtors (and miners) with free coinage of silver, and to retreat from industrialism to agrarianism, in 1896; the same party trying to bring immigrants and blacks into the economic and political systems, and to regulate business and mildly redistribute wealth in 1928 and 1932. As time passes, technological and social change and the external environment bring forth new problems. These problems are outside the main political agenda; neither party has solutions for them; and in the failure of politics-as-usual, activists emerge and voters rally around their third-party or insurgent major party candidates.

Once the realignment process starts, it can move in any of several directions. The old parties can absorb new cleavages, differentiating themselves from each other on new issues, as in 1896 and in 1928–36.

Or a new party system (with parties new in name as well as content) can emerge, as in 1828 and 1860. Or the old parties can muddle along, not fully responding to the new issues, while party loyalties decline and alienation grows. A combination of absorbing new issues and muddling along was characteristic of the Republican and Democratic parties in the 1960s and 1970s.[19]

Insurgent candidates certainly play a part in realignments, if only as outward and visible manifestations of realigning forces. Without doubt they help to crystallize new party cleavages. As one sign of what a party stands for, a candidate with new issue stands can attract new voters who share his views into the party; and perhaps he can also convert the opinions of some old members. But the role of the insurgent campaign is a peculiar one. To judge by McGovern and Goldwater, in the autumn campaign itself the insurgent's message is somewhat blurred; his issue stands are not so unorthodox. It is through recollection of the candidate's past stands, and identification of the candidate with a movement of activists with known policy preferences, that the really "clear choice" is perceived and party lines are redrawn.

Issue Voting, Party Identification, and Responsible Parties

Issue voting—that is, voting on the basis of policy preferences—has always been of special interest to those concerned with the rationality of the citizenry or with responsible party theories of electoral democracy. Considerable scholarly debate has been devoted to the question of how much issue voting occurs, when and why, and what this implies about individual rationality or the workings of democracy.

It is probably fair to say that efforts to estimate the extent of issue voting have so far been inconclusive, because of methodological difficulties. It is no easy matter to sort out what affects what, among policy preferences, perceptions of candidates' stands, and evaluations of candidates. Nor can one easily control for spurious correlations between policy preferences and votes, which may arise from preferences on other issues, assessments of past performance, or party loyalties. The best evidence indicates, however, that the amount of issue voting—while it probably increased in the 1960s and 1970s over the levels of earlier years—has remained limited; it cannot account for most voting behavior.[20]

Our findings concerning candidates' stands help to explain why this is so. The logic of issue voting requires that there be real choices between candidates before voters can decide on the basis of policy alternatives. There has been little issue voting on noncleavage issues, therefore, because candidates' stands have been quite similar (and, in general, quite vague) on such issues. The Vietnam war in 1968 provides a good example. Even though feelings about the war were intense, and polls showed that it was considered the "most important problem" facing the country, Nixon's and Humphrey's stands were so similar and so ambiguous that there was little tendency for citizens to vote their Vietnam policy preferences in making a choice between the major party candidates.[21]

By the same token, we would expect to find more issue voting on party cleavage issues, where candidates' stands differ more from each other—exactly the sort of issue voting called for by responsible party theories. Confirmation of this fact is clouded, however, by the presence of party identification, or long-term attachments to parties. On party cleavage issues, where the opinions of Republican identifiers tend to differ from those of Democrats, and the stands of Republican candidates tend to differ from Democrats' in the same way, issue voting naturally involves Republicans voting for Republican candidates, and Democrats for Democrats. Thus precisely on the issues where issue voting is likely to be most common, we can easily mistake it for habitual voting on the basis of party loyalty. Many studies may have underrated issue voting (and overrated party voting) on party cleavage issues, and it may well be the case that voters have to a substantial extent upheld their part of a responsible party process, making choices on issue grounds when such choices were possible.

Much survey research has indicated that issue voting was more widespread in the elections of 1964 and 1972, with the insurgent candidates Goldwater and McGovern, than in previous or subsequent elections.[22] This is easily explained in terms of our analysis. Insurgent candidates offer relatively distinct choices on the issues, so that more people vote on policy grounds even if their capacity to do so remains constant. Moreover, since the contrasts between opposing candidates in those elections often touch on new issues cutting across the old party cleavages, issue voting competes with party loyalties rather than merely complementing (and being obscured by) them; even those who "control" for party identification therefore discover substantial issue voting.

Up to this point we have been concerned with issue voting in the strict sense of choice between candidates based on knowledge of their policy stands. To take the matter one step further, however, the use of party identification itself to choose between candidates—without knowing the details of policy differences between them—is not necessarily "irrational" or shameful. It can serve as an effective and sensible substitute for issue voting. If a voter considers himself a Democrat because he holds typically Democratic policy opinions (if, for example, he is liberal on questions of social welfare and labor relations), it may be perfectly rational for him to vote for Democratic candidates without knowing exactly what policies they advocate, since he can be reasonably confident that (as our campaign data confirm) Democratic candidates usually stand closer to his opinions than Republican candidates do.

Such use of party identification as a voting cue can save the average citizen a lot of time and energy; he has better things to do than to pore over the *New York Times* or *Congressional Quarterly* to see what the candidates are saying and doing. That is, the use of party identification can economize on information costs which it would not be worthwhile for the average voter to incur.[23] Even if the voter isn't sure whether Harry Truman is for or against the Taft-Hartley Act (or even if, for that matter, the voter isn't sure what the Taft-Hartley Act *is*) he can be fairly certain that Truman, the Democratic candidate, is more pro-labor than the Republican Dewey.

Of course reliance on party labels can lead to errors, if a candidate deviates from the party line or if the party and voter drift apart from their original policy congruence. It is probably most effective as a surrogate for issue voting early in alignment sequences, when opposing opinions on the most important issues are most clearly expressed in party cleavages and in corresponding candidate differences. Indeed, it is early in alignments that party identification is apparently relied upon most heavily.

In trying to assess the autonomous impact of party loyalties upon voting, scholars have encountered methodological problems much like those hampering the study of issue voting: it is hard, for example, to distinguish the effects of party identification on the vote, from the effects of intended vote (or policy preferences) upon declared party loyalty. The available evidence (perhaps overinterpreted in early survey research) indicates that party affiliations have had major effects on voting decisions, and that that influence—while declining somewhat in the late 1960s and the 1970s—remained substantial.[24]

The use of party identification, then, provides a way—albeit an imperfect one—by which voters can contribute to a responsible party process. Electoral outcomes can be strongly affected by the shifting balance of policy-related party loyalties in the electorate, together with policy-related defections from party affiliations; outcomes may thus reflect the balance of preferences on issues of party cleavage.

Our attention in this section has centered on the behavior of voters and how it is shaped by candidates' stands. But candidates' behavior also has, in itself, direct bearing on the workings of electoral democracy.

Our findings on the effects of party cleavages reinforce the conclusion of chapter 3, that the economic theory of democracy, in which candidates converge at the midpoint of public opinion and the winner neatly embodies the ideal democratic outcome, do not work to perfection. Such a process may operate to some degree on all issues, and perhaps to a high degree on noncleavage issues, but on issues of party cleavage the candidates differ, and there is no assurance that either one will represent a perfect social choice.

By the same token, there is some vitality to the responsible party theories of Wilson and Schattschneider and others, with respect to the policy stands taken by parties. There *are* some significant differences between the American parties, in terms of the issue stands of presidential candidates on party cleavage issues. Other evidence indicates that these differences are not confined to campaign rhetoric but appear also in presidential action and in congressional voting and legislation, as well as party platforms. The alternation of parties in power makes a difference in policy.[25]

As we have seen, it is difficult to make precise statements about how great or small party differences are. The examples we have given show that the differences have not been enormous: they concern matters of degree, within the broad center of American politics, and how

important they are is a matter for individual judgment. Obviously
neither major party has yet challenged the capitalist economic system. Nor has either recently questioned the U.S. role as a world military power. Even on issues which are central to party cleavages, positions are not usually spelled out in detail or emphasized for the public;
candidates taking the less popular stand (Eisenhower or Nixon on
jobs, education, and medical care; Humphrey on income maintenance,
and law and order) tend to camouflage their positions and sound
rather like their opponents.

Any assessment of whether, in our more-or-less responsible party
system, the parties are "too" similar or "too" different, falters on this
uncertainty about the facts, and also depends upon one's reaction to
the normative arguments discussed in chapter 2. Those arguments
began with the point that party differences increase the expressive
satisfaction of voting, by providing real choices, but that they interfere
with the economic theory of democracy.

From one long-term perspective, it can be argued that the very existence of party differences—let alone their magnitude or the particular
content of party alignments and cleavages—does not matter much at
all. Party differences may merely interfere with the economic theory
of democracy in the short run, producing a zigzag pattern of policy
making, in which the ship of state veers first to the left and then to
the right as the voters reject the excesses of each party in turn; but in
which the net effect, over a period of years, is much the same as if
government had followed a straight course of always enacting the most
favored policies.

The best answer to such an argument, and the strongest defense of
responsible parties from a democratic theory perspective, is that which
emphasizes the educational role of parties and which claims that party
differences do not merely produce an erratic summation of the public's
policy preferences but that they affect those preferences: in particular,
that the poorest and least informed citizens are helped to see what
policies serve their interests. We cannot be certain to what extent such
a process actually occurs, however. The confusion associated with
nonpartisan elections, and the traditional rally-to-the-Democrats by
low-income citizens in autumn presidential campaigns, suggest that
parties have at least some reminder value to citizens; but the party as
cue is by no means the same thing as the party as educator. The quality

of the campaign rhetoric we have examined does not seem sufficient, either in clarity of stands or in abundance of explanatory fact and logic, to exert much persuasive influence on citizens' policy preferences. Those who want parties to persuade and inform are justified in their discontent with the American party system.

Granting that party differences do (or at least potentially could) exert a long-term effect on policy making by affecting policy preferences, we would still have some reservations about whether this is desirable in a normative theory of democracy. The responsible party theory relies on party elites for leadership in changing preferences, and there is a thin line, if any, between leadership and oligarchy. What is to guarantee that parties will educate their followers to the followers' true interests? There is nothing in the theory to prevent the Democrats from leading poor people astray by getting their support for legislation favoring organized labor, or from misleading working people by asking only for "more" within the confines of the capitalist system; nor would anything prevent the Republicans from deceiving small businessmen and professionals into benefiting giant corporations.

The dilemma is that processes which can or do bring about party differences involve getting elites unequal influence over what those differences are, and therefore give unequal influence over the directions in which citizens can be persuaded. In the United States there is a semblance of a responsible party system because the active, the organized, and the wealthy—especially business and organized labor—exert a special influence over the stands that parties take. Faith that these or other elites will always act for the benefit of the people generally, or for the benefit of the disadvantaged, may be a weak foundation upon which to rest electoral democracy.

5 Constancy and Change in Policy Stands

The logic of electoral competition suggests a good many reasons why we might expect candidates to take shifting or inconsistent positions on public policy. If, for example, citizens' policy preferences changed in the course of an election year, we would expect vote-seeking candidates to alter their positions in response.

More broadly, the ideal strategy for an unscrupulous candidate would seem to consist of telling each individual voter exactly what he wanted to hear, when he wanted to hear it. How better could a politician maximize votes than by having a different set of policy stands designed precisely to please each individual voter? Barring that as impractical, a candidate could presumably gain votes by shaping his stands to suit each particular audience he spoke to—talking tight budgets to bankers but free spending to the poor. At the very least, we might expect candidates to profit by adapting their positions to fit the distinctive sentiments of whatever city or region of the country they happen to be speaking in.

Even if, for some reason, candidates could not vary their positions systematically to please different audiences, we might still expect that they would vary their stands randomly (within a certain range and with a certain central tendency) so as to take a "lottery" stand that would maximize votes among risk acceptant citizens. This is one plausible reading of Shepsle's theory of political ambiguity,[1] to be discussed in both this and the following chapter.

Most spatial models have been concerned with static equilibrium and have postulated that each candidate takes a single fixed policy stand in a given election. But the use of the term "convergence," and Downs's reference to the "dynamics" of party ideologies,[2] suggest further possible motivations for changes in policy stands. Since the electoral process occurs over time, candidates might begin in ignorance of the exact distribution of policy preferences; they might try out different stands, receive feedback, and shift in the direction of increasing support, finally reaching the optimal position.[3] Or, if no equilibrium existed, they might cycle from one stand to another, seeking to dominate each new move by their opponents.

Still a different sort of change is implied by some party cleavage theories: candidates might follow a two-stage strategy, aiming their appeals first at the activists and primary electorates of their parties, in order to win nomination, and then redirecting their appeals to the public at large.[4]

Finally, one can imagine complex ways in which candidates might vary their stands in order to activate different groups at the times they are most needed—perhaps raising money early, then appealing to the general public, and then at the last moment trying to mobilize campaign workers to get out the vote on election day. Such considerations could lead to a dynamic model of issue stands.[5]

The Rule of Constancy

It is something of a surprise to find, despite all the possible expectations of inconsistency or change, that constancy of policy stands is the rule. Most candidates take a single stand on each issue they deal with, and stick to it—or at least do not contradict it—throughout the remainder of the campaign.

To be sure, we must distinguish carefully among different theories of change. We will see that several of them have some validity. For example, in the rare cases when policy preferences shift markedly during a campaign, candidates' stands do tend to move in response. Furthermore, by using hints and nuances and forum selection, candidates do try to convince different audiences that they stand for different policies. Incremental convergence also occurs, at least in the sense that candidates usually begin an election year with highly vague and general stands, and only later—in major addresses and task force "position papers"—zero in on the more specific stands they finally decide to take. And the major exceptions to the rule of constancy are efforts by insurgent candidates to move closer to the center of public opinion.

Instances of outright variation or discrepancy in policy stands are rare, however. Candidates ordinarily remain constant to their early stands on issues. Insofar as theories imply massive change or frequent inconsistency, they are misleading.

The 1968 policy stands discussed in chapters 3 and 4, for example, were not merely central tendencies or final preelection stands; for the most part they represented *the* policy stands of the candidates, uncontradicted by other statements. Nixon and Humphrey did not (with a few exceptions, to be discussed) generally shift their stands over time, they did not generally say conflicting things to different audiences.

In order to understand this high degree of uniformity, it is helpful to know something of the mechanics of campaign rhetoric. The typical campaign speech, delivered to a partisan crowd in a shopping center or meeting hall, has virtually nothing to say about the specifics of policy. For many candidates it is the same speech (with minor variations) five to ten times a day, day in and day out. "The Speech" is a distillation of punch lines with proven audience appeal, which the candidate has sharpened and polished since his first primary campaign, and which he can deliver by heart, without the artificiality of reading or the strain of continually facing fresh texts.

The Speech sometimes includes a reference or two to problems of special local interest; its punch lines allude vaguely to policy matters; but, as we will see in chapter 6, the bulk of it deals with exceedingly broad questions of goals and performance: "Peace, Progress, and Prosperity." Only rarely do ordinary campaign remarks describe specific policies which the candidate undertakes to pursue.

Policy stands are mostly taken elsewhere, often in the course of focused discussions of particular policy areas. Some such discussions come in set speeches delivered to the national audience (like Humphrey's Salt Lake City address on Vietnam) or to specialized audiences (Nixon on agriculture in Des Moines). In 1968 Nixon used the na-

tional radio networks for at least twenty set speeches on "The All
Volunteer Armed Force," problems of the elderly, "The Security
Gap," NATO, and the like.

Some policy stands are taken in "statements" or position papers:
Humphrey on veterans, education, "Order and Justice"; Nixon on
"The Illegal Grape Boycott," the merchant marine, foreign investment
restrictions, the poultry industry. These can be prepared by research
staffs and can be released directly to the press without requiring the
time or effort of delivery by the candidate.

In addition, some policy stands are taken in "candidate forum" responses to written questions posed by magazines ("How Nixon Views
the Medical Scene," "Three Candidates Speak Out on Education"),
and in newspaper, radio, and television interviews.

The anatomy of campaign rhetoric can be illustrated more precisely
by the example of 1960. For that election (unfortunately for that
election only) we have a complete collection of texts and transcripts,
so that we can tabulate the exact frequency of different modes of
presentation (see table 11).[6]

The most common format for both Kennedy and Nixon, comprising
about half of their appearances, was informal "remarks." These were
made to campaign crowds and rallies, usually without a prepared text
and without detailed policy content. Often they merely repeated The
Speech, with a few local references thrown in.

Each candidate made about forty or fifty major prepared speeches,
constituting about 10% of his rhetoric. Some of these included specific policy discussions. Each candidate—Kennedy more often than
Nixon—issued a number of "statements." About half of these dealt
with policy; the other half announced campaign committees, celebrated
ethnic holidays, and the like. For both candidates some of the most
specific policy stands came in the fifty-one joint appearances in magazine or newspaper forums, which sometimes simply repeated stands
verbatim from speeches or statements but at other times covered new
ground. Appearances in which the candidates could neither control the
subject matter nor use prepared texts—that is, interviews, question
and answer sessions, and press conferences (as well as the four "Great
Debates")—were infrequent, altogether constituting only 6% of the
total texts and transcripts.

Most policy stands are carefully thought out, and are drafted by
research staffs, "task forces" or "study groups," and speech writers in

Table 11   Types of Campaign Rhetoric, 1960

Format	Kennedy	Nixon
Remarks	54% (317)	50% (169)
Speeches	10% (59)	13% (44)
Statements	20% (120)	14% (48)
Study papers	0%	2% (6)
Letters	1% (5)	0%
Magazine and newspaper forums	9% (51)	15% (51)
Question and answer sessions	2% (11)	0%
Interviews	1% (7)	1% (5)
Debates	1% (4)	1% (4)
Press Conferences	2% (11)	4% (12)
	100% (586)	100% (339)

Entries are based on the texts and transcripts listed in the three-volume government compendium of 1960 campaign rhetoric, *Freedom of Communications* (1961).

consultation with the candidate. They are not lightly abandoned. Sometimes a single speech or statement contains the only specific comments made about a particular policy area during the whole campaign, thus precluding the possibility of variation. When a candidate does mention a policy matter on a second or third occasion he usually does so briefly, citing the earlier discussion as representing his full position, or quoting from it. Nixon in 1968 often used set formulas to refer to his stands. He repeated identical terms for a Middle East settlement on two different occasions; he backed enough funding of the space program to ensure "steady and efficient," or "efficient and steady" progress; he incessantly repeated that some court decisions had "gone too far in weakening the peace forces in the country against the criminal forces" and that Congress should restore the balance.

Infrequent references to policy, control over formats, and a modicum of memory (now supplemented by computer indexing of past statements) make it easy for a candidate to be consistent if he wishes.

Only in face-to-face interviews, when candidates are pressed on specifics and have no prepared texts, is there much danger of accidental inconsistency.

Our best measure of candidate inconsistency is for 1968, a year for which we combed through our collection of speeches, comparing each separate mention of each issue and searching for inconsistency or change. We found that Nixon and Humphrey took inconsistent stands on only 7% of the issues. On 93% of 122 issues, each candidate's stand (if any) went uncontradicted (see table 12).[7]

While we lack data of this quality for other elections, in most of them the degree of constancy appears to have been much the same. The various theories of inconsistency and change—involving differential audience appeals, "lottery" stands, moving with public opinion, incremental convergence, and two-stage strategies—are either incorrect or largely inapplicable.

Table 12	Constancy in Candidates' Policy Stands, 1968	
	Nixon	Humphrey
Issues on which candidate took or implied contradictory stands	7% (8)[a]	7% (8)[b]
Issues with no contradiction in candidate's stand	93% (114)	93% (114)
	100% (122)	100% (122)

Entries are based on the collection of speeches described in chap. 3 and the issues listed in the Appendix.

a. Appendix items 13, 58, 59, 70, 78, 87, 99, 104.

b. Items 12, 13, 14, 16, 39, 43, 83, 106.

Moving with Public Opinion

There are indications that when public opinion on a policy changes markedly, candidates do tend to shift their own positions in order to conform. But such shifts seldom occur, because marked changes in public sentiment are rare in the course of a single election year and almost never occur during an autumn campaign. One of the infrequent examples of change in public opinion and in candidates' stands is that following the Vietnam Tet offensive of early 1968.

Prior to February 1968 both Nixon and Humphrey had advocated strong military action in Vietnam. Humphrey, as vice-president in the Johnson administration, explained and defended administration policy, bringing his abundant rhetorical energy to bear, as when he warned against "militant, aggressive Asian communism, with its headquarters in Peking, China." Nixon, while supporting the war, had kept his distance from administration policy, and from time to time indicated that stronger action should be taken.

The Tet offensive of January-February 1968, in which several population centers and even the American embassy in Saigon were temporarily occupied by the Viet Cong, seemed to show that even half a million American troops and intensive bombing were not enough to guarantee a South Vietnamese victory. The shock of Tet, after years of official optimism about "light at the end of the tunnel," transformed the public mood. According to Gallup, the proportion of Americans who labeled themselves "hawks" dropped sharply from 60% to 41% between February and March. Our own data show that by June the large (33%) support for increasing the number of American troops in Vietnam had shrunk to 17%, with 35% favoring reduction or total withdrawal.[8]

Once this public disillusionment became apparent, presidential candidates and incumbent politicians reacted to it. Following requests from the military for more U.S. troops, President Johnson convened a council of advisers and, on March 30, ordered geographical restrictions in the bombing of North Vietnam and declared he would not run for reelection. In early March, Nixon pledged that "new leadership" would end the war, though he opposed withdrawal and advocated keeping up military pressure while using leverage to get the USSR "on the side of peace." He then canceled a new statement on Vietnam scheduled for the same time as Johnson's March 30 speech and declared a series of moratoriums on the discussion of Vietnam policy, saying he didn't want to interfere with the peace talks. Finally, in August, he emphasized that "the war must be ended," and advocated a phaseout of U.S. troops and a negotiated settlement. He accepted a Republican platform plank which favored de-Americanization of the war and pledged to "sincerely and vigorously pursue peace negotiations as long as they offer any reasonable prospect for a just peace."

After the convention, Nixon's rhetoric tended to emphasize peace, Eisenhower's ending of the Korean war, and the importance of new leadership. Occasionally he espoused a hard line on specifics, opposing a bomb halt without reciprocity, urging suspension of aid and credits to suppliers of North Vietnam, and opposing reduction of U.S. combat troops until there was "a change in the enemy's attitude."

In October, however, Nixon spoke further about de-Americanizing the war, and training and equipping the South Vietnamese. He advocated stopping the bombing when that would stop the war; later he suggested stopping the bombing if it would not endanger lives and would help bring an honorable peace, and if in the long term that would save American lives. He favored a "generous peace," not imposing a coalition government but permitting the NLF to participate if it would renounce force and accept elections. By the end of the campaign, therefore, Nixon was advocating gradual disengagement and a negotiated settlement to the war.

After Tet, Humphrey too lapsed into silence about Vietnam, not declaring an explicit moratorium but simply not mentioning the war, even in major foreign policy speeches. (Since Humphrey was slow to declare his formal candidacy for president, these were billed as vice-presidential addresses.) When pressed, he argued that the war should not be made an issue so as not to upset peace negotiations. He did begin to edge toward advocating de-escalation, however, urging that the "painful and costly war" be ended, without humiliation or defeat, and suggesting the United States should meet for peace talks in any "reasonable" place. In May he said (in what was, when it angered President Johnson, called a slip of the tongue) that it would be no problem to have the NLF represented in Paris. He suggested that negotiations should continue as long as necessary in order to attain a peace with which both sides could live.

In June, Humphrey proposed an immediate ceasefire, while opposing either unilateral withdrawal or the invasion of North Vietnam. In July he spoke against imposition of a coalition government, but approved of it if acceptable to South Vietnam. He endorsed Clark Kerr's proposals, which included an "immediate standstill ceasefire" by all sides; international peacekeeping machinery; free elections in South Vietnam, with participation by all political groups including the communists; arrangements for the withdrawal of all outside military forces from

South Vietnam; economic and social reconstruction, including land reform; and protection of minorities from reprisals.

Humphrey's crucial reservation to the Kerr proposals was that instead of beginning the ceasefire by halting the bombing of North Vietnam, bombing should be terminated "as reciprocity is obtained from North Vietnam." Later, acknowledging that "reciprocity" had been interpreted as a "harsh or rigid" word, he replaced it with "restraint and reasonable response."

In the autumn, Humphrey began to contemplate unilateral withdrawals of U.S. troops: he endorsed the Democratic platform proposal for cutting back U.S. military involvement "as the South Vietnamese forces are able to take over their larger responsibilities." He suggested —and repeated, after a few days of confusion—that some U.S. troops could and should be brought home in late 1968 or early 1969.

Finally, after Arthur Goldberg and George Ball had joined his campaign staff, Humphrey made his dramatic September 30 Salt Lake City address. He advocated setting a "specific timetable" by which American forces could be systematically reduced while South Vietnamese forces took over more and more of the burden. Moreover, he declared that he would stop the bombing of North Vietnam.

As we saw in chapter 3, Humphrey's commitment to a bombing halt was conditioned upon evidence of communist willingness to restore the demilitarized zone. He was still, in effect, requiring "restraint and reasonable response." Similarly, his advocacy of troop withdrawals was contingent on South Vietnamese performance, and was indefinite as to rate and starting time. Nonetheless, Humphrey had gradually shifted from upholding a heavy war effort to favoring tentative and gradual de-escalation.

Both Nixon's and Humphrey's (and indeed also Johnson's) shifts in position can be seen, in part, as slow and careful responses to the post-Tet dovish change in public opinion. The average American perceived these changes fairly accurately: a substantial doveward shift by Humphrey and Johnson (and, less so, by Nixon) between February and June, which put both Nixon and Humphrey rather closely in harmony with the new opinions of the public (see table 13).

What is less easily explained is Humphrey's continued change of position in the summer and autumn, when public opinion was static. This change, too, along with Johnson's somewhat lesser shift to a complete bombing halt, is reflected in the perceptions of table 13, although the average American somewhat exaggerated the extent of Humphrey's change and mistakenly saw it as occurring entirely in the autumn rather than spread through the summer and fall, perhaps because of the spectacular nature of the Salt Lake City speech.

Table 13	Perceptions of Changes in Candidates' Vietnam Positions, 1968			
	February	June	August	November[b]
Humphrey's perceived position on Vietnam	5.79[a]	*4.19*	4.18	*3.86*
Johnson's perceived position on Vietnam	5.79	*4.62*	4.58	4.26
Nixon's perceived position on Vietnam	4.92	*4.38*	4.35	4.22
Public's self-rating on Vietnam	5.38	*4.33*	4.27	4.26

Entries are median perceptions and opinions, on a seven-point scale ranging from (1) advocacy of immediate withdrawal from Vietnam, to (7) advocacy of complete military victory.

Standard deviations range approximately from 1.50 to 2.00. Standard errors of the corresponding means are approximately .04–.06.

a. Rating of Johnson; Humphrey not included in survey.

b. ORC data (see Appendix). SRC data differ slightly and are not comparable with the earlier ORC surveys.

The puzzle is why Humphrey shifted when there was no evidence of a continued change in public opinion. As we can see from table 13, and as we discussed in detail in chapter 3, Humphrey ended the campaign with a more dovish stand than the public's. Contrary to an incremental theory of convergence, or a two-stage theory, or to the notion of moving with public opinion changes, Humphrey actually moved *away* from the public; he widened the gap between his own position and Nixon's.

Humphrey's summer and autumn change in Vietnam position is probably best understood in terms of factors other than public opinion on Vietnam policy. It may have had something to do with the need for campaign workers and money, both of which became more available to Humphrey after the Salt Lake City speech. But perhaps equally important was an effort, even at the cost of taking a less popular policy stand, to create a symbolic break with the Johnson administration, thus dissociating Humphrey from unpopular past performance and demonstrating his independence and strength. After the speech, journalists reported an immediate stop of the anti-war heckling which had plagued Humphrey in early September.

It would appear reasonable to expect, then, that whenever public opinion undergoes the sort of marked shift that occurred after Tet, candidates will tend to move with the public. But such changes in opinion have not been at all common; and even our one clear example involves some anomalies in candidates' reactions.

The Insurgent Exception:
Barry Goldwater Moves Leftward

It is only in the exceptional case of insurgent candidates that we find substantial changes in a number of issue stands. These changes follow the lines predicted by two-stage theories.

As was suggested in chapter 4, insurgent candidacies are characteristic of periods of electoral upheaval or realignment like the 1960s and 1970s, when new concerns about civil rights for blacks, law and order, the Vietnam war, and lifestyles cut across the Republican-Democratic party cleavages dating from the New Deal period. At such times it has been possible for candidates to win presidential nominations by taking relatively "extreme" stands that appeal to and mobilize a core of intense activists—whether Southern whites or anti-war protesters. These activists can round up delegates by packing local party caucuses and conventions, and by mounting powerful campaigns in selected primaries, canvassing door-to-door, getting out friendly voters, and dominating the turnout on election day. The insurgent strategy is particularly likely to succeed within the "out" party when the incumbent of the opposite party is relatively sure of reelection, and mainstream politicians are less eager to block insurgents from an unpromising nomination.

Rather quickly, however, the successful insurgent candidate faces a problem. The very issue stands which brought forth his core of activists are likely to alienate much of the general public. The candidate comes under intense pressure from opponents, party regulars, and money givers to "move toward the center" and adopt more orthodox stands, which are expected to win more votes in the general election. As a result, insurgent candidates tend, even before they are nominated, to shift somewhat toward the center of public opinion.

In trying to move toward the center, however, insurgents risk alienating their original supporters; they have difficulty persuading the public that they have "really" changed; and they are bombarded with charges of instability, weakness, and dishonesty, which damage their personal images. Recent insurgent candidates have not been notably successful in presidential elections.

In the early 1960s a movement of conservative political activists emerged in the South and Southwest and joined the Republican party. Many were motivated by strong opposition to social welfare spending and civil rights action by the federal government. They were joined by traditional anti–New Deal Republicans who had never quite reconciled themselves to Eisenhower's "new Republicanism," and by seekers after "law and order." Following intensive organizing efforts by F. Clifton White, the movement coalesced in early 1963 as the National Draft Goldwater Committee.[9]

Barry Goldwater had long been a leading conservative voice in the U.S. Senate. In *The Conscience of a Conservative* (1960) he set forth a number of uncompromising stands that made him a major national figure and a highly popular conservative speaker. He argued that politics should achieve maximum freedom for individuals consistent with social order, and that the growth in federal government power violated the Constitution, created dependency, and threatened despotism.

Specifically, in his 1960 book, Goldwater maintained that federal grant-in-aid programs were, in effect, a "mixture of blackmail and bribery," violating states' rights and the Tenth Amendment. The federal government should "withdraw promptly and totally from every jurisdiction which the Constitution reserved to the states." On civil rights, the 1954 *Brown* desegregation decision should be reversed by constitutional amendment; the Constitution did not require integrated schools, and in fact did not permit any interference whatsoever by the federal government in the field of education.

Goldwater also urged "prompt and final termination" of the then
large farm subsidy program, and restoration of a free market in agriculture. He strongly favored enactment of state right-to-work laws
which would forbid the widespread union shop contracts that made
union membership a condition of employment; he favored new legislation to forbid political activity by unions, and advocated the use of
antitrust laws to prevent industrywide bargaining by unions. He opposed progressive or graduated taxes, and urged that the government
"begin to withdraw"—cutting spending by perhaps 10% a year—from
social welfare programs, education, public power, agriculture, public
housing, and urban renewal.

In *The Conscience of a Conservative* Goldwater declared that the
"Soviet menace" was determined to conquer the world; the appropriate
American response was to seek not accommodation but *victory*. Every
policy should be judged by the standard, "Is it helpful in defeating
Communism?" Accordingly, Goldwater advocated military superiority
and opposed cuts in the defense budget. He opposed foreign aid, except for military or technical assistance to "friendly, anti-Communist
nations that are willing to join us in the struggle for freedom." He
criticized negotiations with the communists and cultural exchanges—
which, he said, made us tolerant of communism; he advocated withdrawing diplomatic recognition from all communist governments including the Soviet Union. Goldwater opposed any permanent ban on
nuclear testing, in order to further the development of tactical nuclear
weapons. He urged reexamination of the U.S. commitment to the
United Nations—though calling withdrawal "unfeasible."

Goldwater also urged help to the "captive peoples" of the communist world, encouraging revolt through close liaison with underground
leaders and by provision of printing presses, radios, weapons, and in-
structors—"the paraphernalia of a full-fledged Resistance." The United
States should encourage friendly peoples to undertake offensive operations for the recovery of their homelands: "For example, should a
revolt occur inside Red China, we should encourage and support
guerilla operations on the mainland by the Free Chinese. Should the
situation develop favorably, we should encourage the South Koreans
and the South Vietnamese to join Free Chinese forces in a combined
effort to liberate the enslaved peoples of Asia" (p. 124).

Goldwater added that we must ourselves be prepared to undertake
military operations against vulnerable communist regimes. Assuming

that we have nuclear weapons that can be used in land warfare, and that there is a major uprising in Eastern Europe, like that of Hungary in 1956, "we ought to present the Kremlin with an ultimatum forbidding Soviet intervention, and be prepared, if the ultimatum is rejected, to move a highly mobile task force equipped with appropriate nuclear weapons to the scene of the revolt. Our objective would be to confront the Soviet Union with superior force . . . and to compel a Soviet withdrawl" (p. 125).

Throughout the early 1960s—in *Why Not Victory?* (1962) and in newspaper columns, speeches, and interviews—Goldwater reaffirmed most of these stands, making some of them stronger and more specific. He repeated his list of programs from which the federal government should withdraw. He asserted that the time had come to "dissolve" the Rural Electrification Administration, and said that the Tennessee Valley Authority should be "sold," or "turned over," to free enterprise even if it only brought one dollar. He opposed the federal minimum wage law. He said that social security should be made "flexible" in amount and "voluntary" in coverage. He opposed the power of unions to be chosen as exclusive bargaining agents by majority vote, and (abandoning the idea of a mandatory federal right-to-work law) proposed an amendment to the Taft-Hartley Act that would outlaw the union shop except where states legislated to the contrary.

On foreign affairs, Goldwater repeated his call for encouragement of Eastern European revolts. He opposed the Nuclear Test Ban Treaty of 1963 and continued to oppose negotiations with the Soviet Union and to favor breaking off diplomatic relations. After the Katanga secession in the Congo and the UN involvement there, he said the United States should get out of the United Nations.

Goldwater criticized the outcome of the 1963 Cuban missile crisis, and urged strong action against Castro. He stopped short of advocating a U.S. invasion of Cuba, but declared that Republicans had not "shrunk because of fear" from the possibility; even the possible use of atomic bombs against Cuba "should be left up to the generals." He said that a low-yield atomic bomb might well have been used to defoliate the rain forests in Laos, and advocated interdicting North Vietnamese supply lines to South Vietnam, perhaps by dropping a low-yield atomic bomb or by naval shelling.

He also (in November 1963) indicated approval of decentralized control of atomic weapons: "If we could give the NATO command the right to decide when to use nuclear weapons, we could bring a third to half our troops home."[10] (In October 1963 Goldwater had been quoted in Hartford as favoring control by *local* commanders, but he subsequently claimed that he had been misquoted and had referred only to the supreme NATO commander.)

During this period, with the conspicuous exception of supporting the Central Arizona Water Project, Goldwater's Senate votes were generally consistent with his stated views. He voted against establishing the Arms Control and Disarmament Agency, against trade expansion, cultural exchanges, foreign aid, the Inter-American Development Bank, and a loan to the UN; he also voted against the National Defense Education Act, aid for medical schools, expanded vocational education, assistance for higher education, Kerr-Mills medical care for the aged, and research on housing for the aged. In each of these cases the legislation passed, with the support of a plurality of Senate Republicans.

By late 1963 the "Draft Goldwater" movement was in full swing. Although Goldwater himself expressed reluctance to run, he may have had thoughts of the presidency in mind. He modified his stands a bit on several controversial issues, moving somewhat toward the predominant views of the public. He concluded that we couldn't repeal the graduated income tax totally, and instead proposed a "complete study" of the whole tax problem. In mid-1963 he noted that he had once felt that we should get out of the United Nations: "I still probably do"; but in the autumn he said that he was "not clamoring" to get out, and that "at best I'm lukewarm about the UN now." By January 1964 Goldwater had softened his proposal to break off diplomatic relations with the Soviet Union, advocating use of such a threat as a "bargaining tool"; if his bluff were called, he would merely "suggest" to the Senate that recognition be withdrawn. (Goldwater later acknowledged that Senate approval was not required, but said he would "ask the advice" of the Senate or "consult" the Foreign Relations Committee anyhow.)

For the most part, however, Goldwater went into the New Hampshire primary campaign in January 1964 with his conservative flags flying. He declared that as president he would renounce the Nuclear Test Ban Treaty "if it appeared to be to our advantage to test in the atmosphere." He said that we should use "any method at our disposal," including U-2 flights, to gain information on our enemies. He again declared that Social Security should be made voluntary, and said he would have backed a veto of the public works bill.

If anything, some of Goldwater's foreign policy statements in early 1964 were even more militant than they had been previously. In January he recommended invoking a "blockade" against Cuba, telling the Cubans they had to get rid of Soviet arms and equipment. (Again in April he advocated an "economic-military blockade," and he reaffirmed this stand in July.) In February he said that the United States should tell Castro to turn the water back on at the U.S. Guantanamo base or we would send in the marines.

In April, Goldwater again recommended that the supreme commander of NATO ("probably always" an American) should have direct command over a NATO nuclear force, which would meet local invasions on the spot, with local tactical nuclear weapons. In May he said that the use of atomic weapons should be left "up to the commanders." In June he urged that the NATO supreme commander "should be given great leeway" in the decision to use or not use tactical nuclear weapons. Again in July, at the Republican convention, he said that "small" nuclear weapons (but not ICBMs or IRBMs) should "come under closer supervision" by the head of NATO.

In an interview in May, Goldwater declared, concerning Vietnam: "I would strongly advise that we interdict supply routes wherever they be, either by sea, or most importantly through North Vietnam, Laos or Cambodia, and I believe this could be done in a way that would not endanger life. . . . There have been several suggestions made. I don't think we would use any of them. But defoliation of the forests by low yield atomic weapons could well be done. When you remove the foliage, you remove the cover."[11] In the same interview, he indicated that "we might have to" take action within Red China. Shortly thereafter he said that "[i]f I had my choice I would go at the Red River Valley approaches in South China," but indicated that "[i]t's not a suggestion now," because interdiction of the supply lines in North Vietnam should be the "first step." He declared that he would not use atomic weapons in Vietnam when conventional weapons would do the job, but he would "leave it up to the commanders." In June, Goldwater said about Southeast Asia that, as president, "I would turn to my Joint Chiefs of Staff and say, 'Fellows, we made the decision to win, now it's your problem.' "

His conservative stands brought Goldwater into unusually broad disagreement with the policy preferences of the American public. As we
saw in chapter 3 and table 4, a comparison of Goldwater's early 1964
stands with Gallup opinion data showed that he disagreed with a
plurality of the public fully two-thirds of the time.

If ever a vote-seeking candidate were vulnerable to pressure from
public opinion, then, Barry Goldwater was. It is precisely under such
circumstances, when a candidate initially takes unpopular positions,
that we would expect dynamic or two-stage theories of issue stands to
have some predictive power; and in 1964 they did.

In the early phase of the campaign, Goldwater's opponents needed
to do little to attack him. Goldwater's own statements, reported (and
sometimes distorted) by the mass media, brought about self-destruc-
tion. His early New Hampshire comment on making Social Security
voluntary, for example, inspired the alarming headline: "Goldwater
Sets Goals: End Social Security . . . ." Nelson Rockefeller's staff distributed thousands of reprints of the newspaper article to all Social
Security recipients in the state. The Rockefeller staff also picked up
on Goldwater's quote (or misquote) on control of nuclear weapons
by NATO "commander*s*," and publicized it, inspiring fears of accidental nuclear war.

After Henry Cabot Lodge won in New Hampshire, however, Rockefeller went on to the Oregon primary and began to attack Goldwater
with vigor, if not desperation. He declared that *he* would not "wreck"
social security; he was *for* aid to schools; the United States needed a
responsible man for president, who would not set off war unwittingly.
The Republican party must move with the "mainstream" of American
life.

By the time of the decisive primary in California, Rockefeller and
others were making devastating attacks—some of them unfair and misleading—which put almost irresistible pressure on Goldwater's stands.
In May, Republican senator Thomas Kuchel (of California) sounded
the alarm that "odious totalitarian techniques of subversion" were
being used by a minority to capture control of the California Republican party. Rockefeller declared that a Goldwater victory would subject the party to danger of control by a "narrow extremism" which
would lead it to wither away like the Whigs. He said that voluntary
Social Security, by allowing the withdrawal of millions of participants,

would "bankrupt" the system. He called the "proposal" to use nuclear weapons in clearing the jungles of Vietnam "reckless belligerence," and characterized Goldwater's Republicanism as "narrow, doctrinaire extremism."

Goldwater's victory in California virtually assured him of nomination, but centrist Republican leaders—in a confused effort which Theodore White has called "the dance of the elephants"—tried desperately to stop him. Governor William Scranton of Pennsylvania eventually took the lead, saying in June that he would offer a choice in place of "the echo of fear and of reaction . . . ," while Governor George Romney of Michigan predicted "suicidal destruction" of the Republican party. Scranton said that we needed an American foreign policy "that thinks from the head, not one that shoots from the hip"; this was not the hour to join "extreme reactionaries," "radicals of the right who would launch a system of dime-store feudalism . . . ." He said Goldwater would take the party down "the low road into the dusty limbo of minority politics." In July, Ambassador Lodge warned the Republican platform committee against "a trigger-happy foreign policy, which would . . . destroy . . . life itself." Scranton's staff, in a later disavowed but highly damaging "letter to Goldwater" at the Republican Convention, declared: "You have too often casually prescribed nuclear war as a solution to a troubled world. . . . Goldwaterism has come to stand for refusing to stand for law and order in maintaining a racial peace. . . . In short, Goldwaterism has come to stand for a whole crazy-quilt collection of absurd and dangerous positions that would be soundly repudiated by the American people in November."[12]

These attacks from fellow Republicans, which were later to haunt Goldwater in Democratic ads in November, were supplemented during the spring and summer by barbs from other commentators. Joseph Alsop, without any evidence, voiced fears of a "shrill" and "nasty" Goldwater campaign appealing to racial prejudice; he took up the theme of Whig and Federalist oblivion. Walter Lippmann pontificated that Goldwater would "dissolve the Federal union into a mere confederation of the states . . ." and would nullify the Civil War amendments, leaving blacks unprotected by the national union; he expected the Goldwater candidacy to be the rallying point of the white resistance. He said Goldwater was "ready to confront the Soviet Union and China with a choice between capitulation and war." *Christian*

Century commented that, if Goldwater were elected, he "could very well be the *last* President of the United States."

CBS News saw Goldwater's plan to take a vacation in Germany as a signal of links between the United States and the Bavarian right wing. (The German trip was cancelled.) Roy Wilkins of the NAACP likened the Republican convention to the emergence of Hitler from the beer halls of Munich. Walter Reuther of the United Auto Workers said that Goldwater's election would be a "catastrophe," and that the whole free-world alliance would disintegrate for lack of confidence. Norman Thomas, the socialist, called the Republican platform plus Goldwater "a prescription for World War III."

After Goldwater's nomination in San Francisco, Republican governor Romney said he would support the national Goldwater campaign only if it progressed in a "responsible manner, free of hate-peddling and fear-spreading." The chorus of criticism continued through July and August, with Democrats now taking the lead. Governor Pat Brown of California perceived the "stench of fascism" in Goldwater's acceptance speech. Governor Breathitt of Kentucky said that "the extremists at San Francisco carried out—as cooly as a butcher would carve a roast—the most extensive political purge since the Moscow trials and the Nazi purge of 1934." Black baseball star Jackie Robinson declared that Goldwater was, at best, "a hopeless captive of the lunatic, calculating right-wing extremists." United Steelworkers president David MacDonald declared that Goldwater posed a "menace" to the future of "free American trade unionism," and undersecretary of labor John Henning foresaw the possibility of "forced labor camps" under Goldwater. *Commonweal* reached heights of passion, declaring that "Goldwaterism in foreign affairs has a militarist, xenophobic and virulently anti-communist flavor which closely parallels the views of fascist and crypto-fascist movements everywhere."

Let us pause for a moment and consider these attacks, not only as sources of pressure on Goldwater, but as political rhetoric in their own right. It is not necessary to admire Goldwater or his stands in order to see that many of the attacks were, at best, misleading—or, at worst, vicious distortions. Few of Goldwater's opponents bothered to grapple seriously with the substantive policy questions that he raised.

It was by no means obvious, for example, that to make Social Security voluntary would "wreck," "destroy," or "bankrupt" the system;

experts were not all agreed, and the consequences would have depended partly upon what sort of voluntariness was provided—whether the option of no pension coverage at all was allowed, or merely a choice between public and private plans. NATO commanders' control over nuclear weapons, too, involved complex technical questions concerning different types of weapons and different contingencies; it was not certain that Goldwater's proposals carried substantial danger, or indeed that they went beyond current arrangements. The "extremism" charge, based partly on Goldwater's refusal to disavow support from the John Birch Society, and on two unfortunate phrases in his acceptance speech ("Extremism in the defense of liberty is no vice. Moderation in the pursuit of justice is no virtue."), ignored the fact that he had vigorously purged his organization of "kooks," and that the booing and heckling of Rockefeller in San Francisco came from the uncontrollable galleries, not from Goldwater delegates. Perhaps most unfairly of all, the charge of racism ignored Goldwater's good civil rights record on the state and local level, and ignored the complete absence of racist appeals in his campaigning—which extended to a self-denying agreement with Johnson for a moratorium on race issues in the autumn campaign.[13]

The rhetoric of 1964 was unusually violent, leading the director of the Fair Campaign Practices Committee to comment that it was the most vicious and bitter campaign he had seen or heard of. But oversimplified and distorted charges neither originated nor ended in that year, as we will see with the attacks on John Kennedy in 1960 and McGovern in 1972. Usually such charges are made by private citizens, campaign staffs, and middle-level politicians; they sometimes come from presidential candidates and even presidents.

Why do otherwise honest and reasonable men resort to excess in the heat of political campaigns? Perhaps it is because they care so much about the electoral outcome; or they believe their attacks to give an essentially correct impression; or perhaps they doubt people's ability to understand the issues in all their complex detail. The essential point is that there is nothing to stop them. Distortion is particularly easy when candidates or their stands are somewhat unpopular to begin with.

In any event, Goldwater responded to this pressure by modifying some of his stands still more in the direction of public opinion. In

1963 he had already said he was "not clamoring" to get out of the
UN; in January 1964 he said "I can't recall" ever advocating getting
out, though he didn't think we could live in the UN if Red China were
allowed in. In June he declared, "I've never advocated withdrawing
from the United Nations; in fact I've given more support to the United
Nations than have some of my critics." As we have seen, in January
Goldwater spoke of breaking relations with the USSR as only a "bargaining tool," and said he would consult the Senate. In June he qualified his support of helping uprisings in Eastern Europe, saying he still
advocated it "[i]f that became necessary, if that were the only way
. . . ." He insisted that his discussion of using nuclear weapons in
Vietnam had only been an example of policy options, not something
he advocated.

As to the graduated income tax, Goldwater had already said in 1963
that it would not be totally repealed, and that a "complete study" was
needed. In September 1964 he announced that he would propose to
Congress "a regular program of automatic cuts in income taxes." He
later specified that this would mean "an across-the-board reduction
of 5% per year in all income taxes—both individual and corporate"
in each of the next five years. This amounted of course to a 25%
total cut, not abolition.

By late 1963 Goldwater had modified his advocacy of "prompt and
final termination" of farm subsidies, by saying it might take three to
five years to accomplish. Through most of 1964—despite intense pressure from Republican farm-state senators Mundt, Young, and Curtis
—he remained committed to termination, and even chose the National
Plowing Contest at Fargo, North Dakota, in September, as a place to
criticize "arbitrary handouts" from the government. In early October,
however, while repeating that Republicans were "pledged to return
farmers to a free market," he said it would be done "without working
any hardships" on farmers now dependent on support payments. Supports would not be "suddenly ended." Finally in mid-October, in Sioux
Falls, South Dakota, he moved one step further: ". . . I will never
propose a change in the price support program until something better
has been developed that can be gradually substituted for it." And,
apparently reversing his proposal to "dissolve" the REA, he declared
". . . I believe in a strong and healthy rural electrification program."

A shift can also be seen in Goldwater's civil rights stands. In May,

acknowledging that "at one time" he had felt it was improper for the
federal government to intervene in local school systems to promote
integration, he said, "I believe now that this is possible . . . ." In June,
he cast an unpopular vote against the Civil Rights Act of 1964, object-
ing to the public accommodations and fair employment provisions as
unconstitutional. Subsequently, however, he promised to enforce it,
and endorsed the Republican platform's call for "full implementation
and faithful execution" of the act. In his major civil rights speech of
mid-October (delivered in Chicago and later repeated on national
television), Goldwater recounted his support of the 1957 and 1960
voting rights bills, and declared that "government should not discriminate" and that the president should exert moral leadership. At the
same time he opposed busing of schoolchildren or racial quotas, and
emphasized freedom of association.

Nuclear weapons issues had become the most damaging to Goldwater; his January comment on delegation of nuclear authority to the
NATO commander—together with the May discussion of defoliation
in Vietnam, and his periodic remarks that U.S. missiles were "not dependable"—inspired the charges that Goldwater was "trigger-happy."
His spokesmen immediately asserted that Goldwater had not *advocated*
using nuclear weapons in Vietnam, but had merely pointed out that
the matter had been studied. At the end of June, in an interview with
Der Spiegel, Goldwater said that there would have to be "some measure of control" over NATO nuclear weapons, although he still felt
that the supreme commander ought to have "great leeway" in situations where expeditiousness was required. And in July at the GOP
platform hearings, he retreated even further, saying, "we can never
remove the President from the act . . ."; he would hope only that tactical nuclear weapons could come under "a little closer control" by the
NATO commander. At the time of the August Tonkin Gulf incident
he argued that President Johnson had delegated nuclear authority in
that case, but in the face of Pentagon rebuttals he backed off.

In late August, speaking to the Veterans of Foreign Wars, Goldwater reversed field and dug the pit deeper for himself, by referring
to NATO control of tactical or "conventional" nuclear weapons; he
discarded this phraseology when it was pointed out that many tactical
nuclear weapons were more powerful than the bombs dropped on
Hiroshima and Nagasaki.

In the autumn campaign Goldwater did not actually abandon his nuclear stands. He largely observed silence about nuclear issues, and encouraged statements by Eisenhower (in the televised "Conversation at Gettysburg") that warmonger or pushbutton charges were "tommyrot," and assertions by Nixon that nuclear discretion had already been given to NATO commanders by President Eisenhower. Testimony before the Joint Committee on Atomic Energy did indeed seem to indicate that such discretion, in emergency situations, had been given at least as early as 1957.

Social Security had been the other issue of most intense attacks. Here, Goldwater more distinctly changed his stand; in June he said flatly that he did not advocate making the system voluntary, and anyone who claimed he was against social security, "lies." The campaign book, *Where I Stand*, was purged of any reference to voluntariness. Repeatedly through the summer and autumn (especially in October) he emphasized that he believed in the Social Security system and wanted to make it stronger; he had voted for the Social Security legislation of 1954, 1955, 1956, 1958 and 1961. He had voted for an increase in benefits in 1964, which President Johnson had killed in conference because Medicare was omitted. He favored extension of coverage and periodic cost-of-living increases in benefits, as well as a revision of the earnings test to allow more work without losing benefits. At the end of the campaign he issued a statement summarizing these stands, concluding plaintively, "I am the true friend of social security, and I have lost patience with those who would so blatantly deceive you."

The attacks against Goldwater continued and even intensified in the autumn, however, sometimes centering on old positions which he had disavowed. The president of the New York AFL-CIO charged that Goldwater was "trying to repeal the 20th Century"; "neo-Fascists" and "union busters" had taken over the Republican party. Roy Wilkins said a Goldwater victory would bring about a "police state." Senator William Fulbright spoke of equivalence to "Russian Stalinism." Martin Luther King foresaw a "dark night of social disruption." The *Saturday Evening Post* saw Goldwater as a "grotesque burlesque" of a conservative, a "wild man." George Meany of the AFL-CIO compared Goldwater to Hitler.

Hubert Humphrey said Goldwater's freedom is the freedom "to be uneducated, to be sick, to be hungry, to be unemployed." The AFL-

CIO *American Federationist* said Goldwater's economics would lead to "mass unemployment." Secretary of agriculture Freeman said (after Goldwater's conciliatory Sioux Falls speech) that if Goldwater abolished farm subsidies, "25 percent of family farmers would go bankrupt." The chairman of the Federal Maritime Commission declared that Goldwater as president would mean that the American merchant marine "probably would be sunk," or "would be wiped off the trade lanes." President Johnson himself intoned, "We are told that we must abandon education, we must make Social Security voluntary; we should sell the TVA and get rid of public power, we should forget our farm programs."

The most damaging attacks were those that conjured up fears of nuclear warfare. Hubert Humphrey asked whose hand the voters wanted on the nuclear trigger, when with "one rash or reckless act 100 million of us would be ashes by nuclear attack." In this election "life itself, the future of the planet, the salvation of the species" were at stake. Later he warned that Goldwater's election would make the United States "a garrison state in a nightmare world, isolated from everything except a nuclear reign of terror." Goldwater's solutions were a sure path ultimately to "a terrible holocaust." Humphrey claimed that in his "hot pursuit of the mirage of total victory," Goldwater wanted to "back the Soviet Union into a corner where its only alternatives would be surrender or nuclear war." Johnson noted that "[b]y a thumb on a button, you can wipe out 300 million lives in a matter of moments. And this is no time and no hour and no day to be rattling your rockets around or clicking your heels like a storm trooper."

Perhaps most destructive of all to Goldwater was the Democrats' "daisy girl" television commercial which showed a little girl in a sunny field picking daisies. As she plucked petals and counted, a male voice counted backwards, louder and louder. When she reached ten, the man's countdown, in tones of doom, reached zero. The screen was filled with an atomic explosion. "These are the stakes," said the voice of Lyndon Johnson, "to make a world in which all of God's children can live, or go into the dark." Viewers protested and this ad was withdrawn, but only after it had done its work.

If the election returns are any indication, Goldwater's shift toward the center was not very successful. His opponents largely ignored changes and kept attacking his old stands. Many voters probably remained unaware of the changes, or refused to believe them. And we will argue in chapter 8 that, to the extent Goldwater's changes were perceived, they had a negative effect on his personal image of honesty and integrity.

When a candidate changes his stands, there is a real problem in determining his "true" position. In Goldwater's case, the earlier stands had been repeated in many columns and speeches, and printed in books; even his "slips of the tongue" seemed consistent with his general philosophy. Why should revisions, made to attract votes, be taken more seriously? And to the extent that a man's real stands are revealed by the nature of his supporters, Goldwater was somewhat tainted by foreign policy belligerency and by racism.

It is hard to deny that Goldwater tried to move toward the center during 1963 and 1964. Yet we would certainly not argue that he tried to take up a position exactly at the midpoint of public opinion. Some of his changes were substantial: the virtual dropping of opposition to the graduated income tax, to membership in the UN, and to recognition of the USSR; abandonment of encouraging uprisings in Eastern Europe; eventual acceptance of farm price supports and the REA; and rejection of his voluntariness proposal for Social Security. But other changes were minor: he always had spoken of nuclear weapons in Vietnam as an option or an idea, not a "proposal"; commitment to enforce the 1964 Civil Rights Act was not really inconsistent with opposition to its passage; and his language concerning NATO control of tactical nuclear weapons did not change very appreciably. On a good many issues he did not try to change at all. Goldwater remained, in November 1964, quite conservative and rather distant from the policy preferences of most Americans.

George McGovern Shifts Rightward

McGovern in 1972, like Goldwater in 1964, was an insurgent candidate, in the sense that he sought the nomination by taking relatively noncentrist stands and appealing to an ideologically oriented group of activists. Although his original positions were much less distant than Goldwater's from the views of the public, McGovern too came under pressure to move away from the stands that had mobilized his core of activists, and to appeal more to the general electorate. McGovern too tried to change some of his positions—albeit to a somewhat lesser extent than Goldwater did. McGovern too was not wholly successful.[14]

In the late 1960s the Vietnam war threw American society into turmoil. A large and active peace movement, centered on college campuses, agitated to get out of the war. In 1968 this movement energized the presidential campaigns of Eugene McCarthy and Robert Kennedy, who played a part in driving Lyndon Johnson from office but could not capture the Democratic nomination. At the last moment before Humphrey's nomination in that year, George McGovern declared a token presidential candidacy, in order to hold together some former supporters of the assassinated Robert Kennedy.

McGovern had been an orthodox Democratic liberal, director of the Food for Peace program under John Kennedy and then a senator with a voting record much like Hubert Humphrey's. But he became an early and strong opponent of the Vietnam war. In a Senate speech in 1963 he declared that the U.S. nuclear arsenal, the costly new "special forces," and the $3 billion and many American lives spent to date had proved powerless against the Viet Cong guerrillas. Moreover, the South Vietnamese government was tyrannizing its own citizens. "This is scarcely a policy of 'victory'; it is not even a policy of 'stalemate.' It is a policy of moral debacle and political defeat. . . . (T)he failure of our Vietnam policy should be a signal for every Member of the Senate to reexamine the roots of that policy" (24 September 1963).

Despite certain lapses like his vote for the Tonkin Resolution in August 1964 (perhaps an understandable error, given the crisis atmosphere and the deceptive information provided to Congress) McGovern generally stuck to his opposition to the war through the 1960s. Shortly after the 1968 debacle and Nixon's election, McGovern decided to make a serious run for the presidency, building upon former supporters of Kennedy and McCarthy and appealing primarily to the anti-war movement.

During much of 1970 McGovern toured the country, speaking for Democratic congressional candidates and urging quick withdrawal from Vietnam. He gathered together a young but highly skilled staff headed by Gary Hart. In January 1971 he formally announced his candidacy for president. During 1971 he continued the tour of colleges and other liberal audiences, emphasizing Vietnam. He received little national publicity, but collected a larger and larger band of enthusiastic activists, who started to plan for primary elections and state conventions.

In his talks to college students, McGovern began to go beyond the Vietnam issue to embrace a variety of positions of special interest to students: favoring, for example, less severe penalties (but not legalization) for smoking marijuana, and—especially after his September 1971 trip to Hanoi—complete amnesty for war resisters (but not deserters). In dealing with women he implied support for liberalized abortion laws. He expressed sympathy for "gay liberation," the end of legal and social discrimination against homosexuals. On some occasions he may have been carried away by the enthusiasm of his audience and hinted, or allowed listeners to believe, that he took more liberal stands on these issues than his specific commitments warranted.

In 1971 McGovern also branched out into stands on economic issues, about which he felt less knowledgeable and less comfortable than he did on foreign policy. His staff assembled a group of noted liberal economists, who in June briefed McGovern on a variety of tax reform proposals, from loophole closing to a high minimum tax on the rich. They later formed a regular advisory group, led by Edwin Kuh of MIT. By autumn the economists had worked out a comprehensive plan for income redistribution, or tax and welfare reform.

The plan had four main components: 1. The imposition of a minimum tax of three-quarters of the statutory rate on all income above $50,000 per year, regardless of source. That is, capital gains, revenue from municipal bonds, and other sheltered income would be taxed at rates going as high as three-quarters of the then top statutory rate of 77%—in other words, at 58%, as opposed to the 30-35% then actually paid on the highest incomes. 2. Raising corporation income taxes to the point where effective rates would be as high as they had been in 1960, by repealing accelerated depreciation and the investment tax credit. 3. Imposing an inheritance (as versus estate) tax on the cumulative transfers which any individual received in his lifetime, on a progressive scale perhaps reaching 100% on any transfers over $500,000. 4. Giving "demogrants" of unspecified size (but with some possible examples cited) to all members of the population, subject to income taxation so that only the poor would keep the whole grant; working people would keep some, the rich none. This would be financed by new revenue from the tax reforms, and by eliminating personal exemptions and welfare payments.

McGovern was intrigued with the plan, and gave a sneak preview of it in a *Washington Post* interview on December 22; the full plan was unveiled in a speech at Iowa State University in January 1972.

Without question the income redistribution plan was a far-reaching one, which would have profoundly transformed the U.S. tax and welfare systems. Whether or not it was "radical" depends on one's use of the term, but it was certainly not a crazy or inherently unworkable scheme. Its component parts had substantial histories of discussion, as well as support from a number of leading economists.

McGovern also began to pay increasing attention to questions of national security and the defense budget. His legislative assistant, John Holum, worked out a comprehensive and rather carefully constructed Alternative Defense Posture, which proposed to cut defense spending to $54.8 billion (from the current figure of more than $80 billion) by fiscal 1975. It rested on "zero-baseline" reasoning, beginning with estimates of foreign threats and calculating defense needs, rather than beginning with current programs and adding or subtracting increments. It proposed substantial reductions in the 4,600 existing (10,000 planned) deliverable nuclear warheads, arguing that second-strike delivery of 200 warheads each to the Soviet Union and China would be enough to devastate those countries, and that more emphasis should be put on submarine-launched missiles rather than the relatively vulnerable bombers and land-based ICBMs. It called for roughly halving the number of U.S. troops in Europe (keeping two divisions instead of four and one-third) and Asia (withdrawing completely from South Korea), and cutting aircraft carriers from fifteen to six. The Alternative Defense Posture was issued in January 1972.

By the beginning of 1972, then, McGovern had evolved from an orthodox Democrat to a purely anti-war candidate and then to one offering sweeping proposals on a whole array of issues from lifestyle to income redistribution and defense. His positions appealed to practically every faction of the fragmented American Left: peace groups, women's liberation, blacks, populists, and gay liberation. These groups —mobilized by the issue stands rather than loyalty to the man—provided the energy and manpower which, aided by new rules ensuring openness in delegate selection, eventually won McGovern the Democratic nomination.

As we saw in chapter 3, McGovern's early stands were not nearly so far out of tune with the public as Goldwater's had been. According to our Gallup data, in fact, he disagreed with a plurality of the public only 30% of the time, about the same as Humphrey's 31% and not much more than Nixon's 21%. Still, on certain salient issues —marijuana, amnesty, school busing, and probably also guaranteed income, taxation, and the defense budget—McGovern stood substantially to the left of the average voter. He came under strong pressure to modify his positions, both from the general public and from the most well-to-do and articulate elements of society.

The suggestion of a 100% tax on inheritances over $500,000, in particular, aroused strong opposition—much of it coming from the wealthy, but some of it from unexpected sources like the working men McGovern met during the New Hampshire primary campaign. Even if they made only $8,000 a year, they did not want confiscatory taxation of the rich. McGovern altered the proposal in April, to make the top tax on inheritances 77% rather than 100% and to exempt family-owned businesses.

After McGovern's strong showing in New Hampshire (gathering 37% of the vote against the 46% for Muskie from neighboring Maine) and his victory in Wisconsin, people began to take him more seriously and pay attention to his proposals. Cries of alarm went up. The *Wall Street Journal* (April 27) ran a column headed "McGovern's Program: Strong Stuff," rather accurately summarizing the tax and welfare and defense proposals, and characterizing them as "radical." That column apparently served as a call to arms for the business world. Stories began to appear (e.g., in the *New York Times*, May 10) reporting that businessmen were worried about McGovern. In June the *Wall Street Journal* summarized a lengthy series of interviews with prominent businessmen, who spoke ominously about destruction of the country and of the free enterprise system. One compared McGovern to Hitler, and another suggested he might commit suicide if McGovern were elected.

Also in April a considerably less responsible attack was launched by columnists Evans and Novak, who reported that "a liberal Senator" (possibly a creation of their imagination) was worried because

McGovern stood for "amnesty, abortion, and legalization of pot," and once middle America found out, he would lose as badly as Goldwater. This characterization of McGovern's stands was at best a half truth, since he then took no position on abortion (calling it a matter for the states to decide), and he favored reducing marijuana penalties to misdemeanors, not legalizing use. But the charge was effective. James Reston repeated it; Senator Henry Jackson took it up in Ohio, and Hubert Humphrey in the Nebraska primary; and Republican Senator Hugh Scott made what was then a damaging quip, that McGovern was the "triple-A" candidate, for amnesty, abortion, and acid (LSD).

The attacks took highly visible form in late May, when Hubert Humphrey tried everything he could to stop McGovern in the California primary. In a televised debate, Humphrey charged that McGovern's income redistribution plan would cost $72 billion (thus either mistakenly or deliberately confusing McGovern's plan with that of the National Welfare Rights Organization) and would involve "a $210 billion treasury transaction" (a fanciful figure based on the example of $1,000 demogrants and ignoring the provision that most would be taxed back and never actually paid out). He opposed "confiscatory" taxation. He attacked the McGovern defense proposal on grounds that it would "cut into the very muscle of our defense, the very security of our country" and would make America into "a second-class power" (although Humphrey had himself proposed a cut of similar size in 1971). Humphrey also argued that defense cuts would deprive California workers of jobs, and that McGovern was not fully committed to the defense of Israel.

In June, after McGovern narrowly won the California primary, Democratic politicians continued to criticize his positions. Muskie, who was expected to throw his support to McGovern, instead publicly refused to do so, and urged McGovern to "re-examine and refine" his positions on taxes and welfare and defense, for the sake of party unity. Organized labor (that is, George Meany, acting through Alexander Barkan) floated rumors that it would not work for McGovern in the general election unless he modified his stands. Humphrey predicted "disaster" in November unless McGovern shifted on welfare and military spending.

Some Republicans joined the attacks. Secretary of Defense Melvin Laird joked that the United States would have to spend $1 billion on white flags if the McGovern defense budget were adopted. Herbert

Stein, chairman of the president's Council of Economic Advisers, ridiculed the income redistribution plan and claimed (quietly hypothesizing, contrary to McGovern, that there would be no reform of the tax laws) that the plan would require a new tax of 46% on net income, in addition to current income taxes.

McGovern's response to these pressures was to retreat into vagueness on some issues, to change his position on a few of them, and—at least for a time—to deny vehemently that he had changed.

On taxation and welfare, by April he had modified only the inheritance tax provision. But he created trouble for himself by seizing upon one example of a demogrant program—based on $1,000 per person—and giving the impression that every American would actually receive a check for that amount, rather than a credit, much of which would be taxed away from all but the poor. In the face of attack he tried to make clear that $1,000 was "merely an example," and thereby seemed to retreat. But he never fully articulated the complex tax-back feature of the plan, possibly because his own understanding of it was not firm.

When pressure increased from the business world and from his finance chairman, Henry Kimelman, McGovern published a full-page "open letter" in the *Wall Street Journal*, which was technically consistent with his previous proposals but sought to reassure businessmen by implying that his plans would never be passed anyhow, because they were only "suggestions" to Congress. The letter also pointed out that McGovern had *not* flatly proposed ending various tax preferences, such as the low rate on capital gains; rather, he relied on a minimum tax on all income regardless of source, and he favored phasing out percentage depletion allowances and certain other corporate-tax-minimizing devices.

After Humphrey's sharp attacks in the California debate, and the humiliating moment when McGovern admitted he could not estimate the precise cost of his welfare plan, he announced that the entire program was being reworked and restudied. In the meantime he endorsed a face-saving plan by Wilbur Mills which would pro forma repeal all tax preferences and require Congress to review each one. Appearing before the Joint Economic Committee, McGovern was questioned about several specific deductions and exemptions, and denied that he would abolish them. For the Democratic platform his people wrote a plank which mildly advocated that "all unfair corporate and individual tax preferences should be removed," without making clear exactly which preferences were unfair; it also endorsed the Mills proposal.[15]

Over the summer a team of economists studied in detail how alternative plans might work, with McGovern involving himself closely in their deliberations. The experts abandoned the minimum tax idea, but worked out a program of loophole closing which amounted to major tax reform. It included completely phasing out the tax preference for capital gains, while enacting averaging provisions; taxing unrealized capital gains at death; repealing excessive depletion allowances; phasing out loopholes for real estate development; subsidizing municipal bonds directly and repealing their tax exemption; repealing accelerated depreciation and revising the investment tax credit; and replacing estate and gift taxes with a progressive "accessions tax." The new tax program was presented in late August before a meeting of the New York Society of Security Analysts.

The welfare side of the revised program, which McGovern unveiled at the same time, was more substantially changed. Demogrants and negative income taxes dropped from sight. Instead, McGovern offered a rather New Dealish mixture of public service jobs, increased Social Security, and (for welfare mothers and children) cash and food stamps. "Income redistribution" was not explicitly mentioned, although McGovern said he had asked leading economists to continue working on a system of tax credits and tax reductions for low- and moderate-income persons.

On defense policy, the attacks against McGovern's plan focused on two arguments: that he would throw defense workers out of their jobs, and that he would seriously weaken American national security. McGovern's main response was to defend the plan, but in somewhat more general terms and in ways which suggested changes in position. In April he repeated his 1971 Senate proposal for "economic conversion," to redirect defense workers (especially scientists and engineers) to peaceful production without loss of jobs. In October he expanded on this theme to the UAW and the IAM unions, emphasizing government creation of peacetime jobs and provision of adjustment benefits and pension portability.

Similarly, McGovern began to emphasize his long-standing posture as a "disciple of Eisenhower," advocating a "lean and tough" military. He repeated a strong commitment to the defense of Western

Europe, and especially emphasized his commitment to Israel, adding
a special amendment to the Democratic platform and asserting that
he even favored use of U.S. troops if necessary. He campaigned with
Senator Ribicoff in Jewish areas of New York, stressing support for
Israel, and sent Meyer Feldman and Senator Church to Tel Aviv to
reassure the Israelis.

Speaking to the Joint Economic Committee in June, McGovern
declared that he had "not proposed cuts" in the Nixon budget. (This
was technically true, since his program looked ahead to 1975 and
was designed from the ground up rather than in terms of cuts.) He
generally stuck by the Alternative Defense Posture: he admitted that
the tables and labeling at the end of the original paper were "misleading" and offered new details on its costs but kept the same spending totals. In August, to underline the fact that he proposed only
gradual reductions in spending to reach the $54.8 billion figure, Sen-
ator McGovern introduced an amendment to the Military Procurement
Bill limiting 1972–73 spending to $77 billion. (This proposal was
voted down decisively.)

In late August, before the Veterans of Foreign Wars, McGovern
espoused a "hard and tough" military force ("I am deeply committed
to a strong military"), emphasizing the elimination of waste and inefficiency rather than the reduction of force levels. Finally, in late
September he endorsed a report by his national security advisors
which nominally upheld the earlier proposals, but omitted most specifics and in effect blurred his stand. It dropped mention of the $54.8
billion budget figure (or the $30 billion cut), instead speaking of "sig-
nificantly" cutting spending; and it failed to mention the halving of
troops in Europe or the cutting of aircraft carriers from fifteen to six.
Paul Warnke (a former Pentagon official), in announcing the report,
noted that changing defense situations quickly render any specific
budget levels out of date; the intent of the report was to focus on
broad principles.

On abortion, McGovern's shift in position—if any—was a subtle
one. Early in the campaign he had stated his "personal belief" that
abortion should be a matter between a woman and her doctor or anyone else she might choose to consult. Later, however (apparently after
a discussion with Ethel Kennedy), he began to emphasize that this was
a matter for state rather than federal action and that he opposed any

federal liberalizing law; soon he left it at that and ceased mentioning
his personal view at all.

On the Vietnam issue, the pillar of his candidacy and a matter of
strong personal concern, McGovern did not change position at all.
Throughout 1972 he stood by his proposal to stop all U.S. bombing at
once, and, within ninety days, to remove all U.S. troops and get the
U.S. prisoners back. He believed, on the basis of his September 1971
trip to Hanoi, that the prisoners would be released under those conditions, but when pressed as to his reaction if they were not released,
he said he would "entreat" the North Vietnamese, and would not resume the bombing in any event.

Two incidents illustrate how central Vietnam was to McGovern's
supporters. In the autumn of 1971, when McGovern indicated that he
planned to devote more time to discussing domestic economic matters, there was a storm of protest from his supporters—as if even a
decrease in emphasis on Vietnam, let alone a change in position,
amounted to heresy. And in July 1972, at the Democratic convention, a still angrier protest arose when McGovern issued a statement
that he would "retain some military capability in the region,. in Thailand and on the seas," to indicate U.S. firmness about the return of
prisoners of war. This in no way contradicted his pledge to remove
all U.S. forces unconditionally from Indochina. After the uproar, however, he declared: "Upon return of U.S. prisoners of war and a satisfactory accounting of missing in action—a process which I am convinced would be completed in the same time frame as the 90-day
withdrawal of U.S. ground forces—I would, although Thailand is not
a part of Indochina, also close U.S. bases in Thailand and remove all
U.S. Naval forces from waters adjacent to Southeast Asia. . . . I want
to reiterate as strongly as I can that my position on the Vietnam war
has not altered one iota."

McGovern, who had expressed pride in the openness and honesty
of his campaign, took pains to deny that he was changing position on
any issues. In June he denied that he was moving toward the center:
"the center is moving toward us." ". . . I'm not going to betray my
principles or my convictions." "I have no intention of moving left or
right; I'm going to hold to the course I'm on." ". . . [W]e cannot at
this point depart from the principles and the convictions that we've
taken to the people in primaries all across this country."

Yet people perceived changes. By May, columnists and reporters
had noted some shifts in McGovern's positions. In mid-June, *Time*
magazine headlined stories, "McGovern Backpedals—A Bit," and
"McGovern Moves Front, Maybe Center." *Newsweek* noted shifts
under the headline "Back to the Computer."

Just as McGovern's original proposals were less unpopular than
Goldwater's, his changes in position were fewer and less substantial.
Except on guaranteed income (and, to a lesser extent, on defense and
taxes) he did not actually change very much. McGovern did not really
alter his positions on abortion, amnesty, marijuana, Vietnam, or most
other issues. His few shifts were magnified by opponents and the media. As magnified, however, they had some negative effects on his
campaign. One was alienation of his original supporters, some of
whom felt he had betrayed his principles. Echoing McGovern's "Come
Home, America" theme, Tom Wicker wrote, "Come Home, George
McGovern." (Some disillusionment, of course, may have resulted
from symbolic actions like McGovern's attempted reconciliations with
Mayor Daley of Chicago and with Lyndon Johnson, rather than from
policy stands.)

A still more important negative effect damaged McGovern's personal image. His changing and hedging and vacillating on the issues
affected not only what people thought McGovern stood for, but also
what kind of man they thought he was. Particularly because of the
high expectations of candor and principle which the campaign initially inspired, perceptions of McGovern's honesty, knowledge, strength
and stability were bound to suffer when he shifted or seemed uncertain of his stands. Such doubts were crystallized by the Eagleton affair.
In the end (as we will discuss further in chapter 8), negative views
of McGovern's personal characteristics, rather than aversion to his
policy proposals, were probably the strongest factor pushing voters
against him.

As with Goldwater, McGovern's shifts did not silence his attackers
and did not convince voters that he was a centrist candidate. Opponents still labeled him a "radical," and continued to attack his original
proposals. As we saw in chapter 4, the average voter—probably mistakenly—saw McGovern as quite distant from the public on many
issues.

Appealing to Special Audiences

One of the most compelling reasons to expect inconsistency in policy
stands is given by the theory of differentiated appeals: that vote-
seeking candidates will tailor their stands to fit whatever audience
they happen to be addressing. There is, in fact, a great deal of truth
to this prediction. Candidates are skilled at pleasing special audiences.
But they do so, for the most part, without violating the rule of constancy, without creating flagrant contradictions in their policy stands.

There are three main techniques of differentiating appeals. First,
candidates use symbolic words and actions to hint that they are in
sympathy with the outlook of a given audience, leaving the audience
free to interpret this as signifying agreement on policy. Second, candidates sometimes vary nuances and emphases in their policy stands,
when addressing different groups, in ways that imply they favor different policies. Third, and most important, candidates often choose
an especially friendly forum to announce their single, uncontradicted
stand on an issue, in such a way that those likely to oppose their stand
remain unaware of it.

The avoidance of outright contradiction, which was documented in
table 12, can be further illustrated with Nixon's 1968 treatment of
civil rights for blacks. Nixon, allegedly pursuing a "Southern strategy" of trying to win white votes in the South, was no doubt tempted
to advocate policies more tolerant of segregation when he spoke in
the South than when he spoke in the North. On at least one private
occasion—a supposedly secret session with Southern delegates at the
Republican convention—he conveyed such an impression. And once
in public, in a speech made in Charlotte, North Carolina, for use on
regional television, he made a major concession to Southern white
sentiments by indicating that he would not use what had been the
most effective method of enforcing school integration: cutting off
federal funds, under title VI of the 1964 Civil Rights Act, from segregated school districts.

Nixon's Charlotte speech was strongly criticized in the Northern
press, however, and he quickly came up with a slightly different formula. He would use the enforcement powers of title VI, but only to
establish school districts without regard to race. Where a freedom-
of-choice plan was a "subterfuge for segregation," he would withhold

funds, but he would not do so to enforce "integration in a positive way, busing and the like . . . ." Nixon repeated this formula throughout the campaign, and was scrupulously careful to say the same thing North and South, in California, Texas, and in *Education News*. Journalists, who were alert to the possibility of special appeals to the South, remarked on his consistency.

However, using the first of the three techniques mentioned above, Nixon worked to create an impression of special sympathy for the South. In his tours of the region he embraced Southern cultural symbols and identified himself with leading Southern political figures—especially Senator Strom Thurmond of South Carolina. The technique is a familiar one, often involving nothing more subtle than remembering the Alamo in Texas and praising Lincoln in northern Illinois.

Similarly, in 1960, John Kennedy was rather quiet about civil rights during most of the campaign, but shortly before election day he aimed a symbolic appeal at a special audience: he made a sympathetic telephone call to Mrs. Martin Luther King, whose husband was in a Georgia jail. Kennedy offered no public comment on the episode except to declare briefly that Mrs. King was a friend of his and that he was concerned about the situation; but two million copies of a pamphlet about the call were distributed outside black churches on the Sunday before election day, and were thought to play a part in Kennedy's receiving an overwhelming majority of black votes.[16]

When candidates use the second technique, implying different policy stands in speaking to different audiences, the contrary implications sometimes come so close to contradiction that common sense requires us to call them inconsistent, and we did so in table 12. Nixon in 1968, for example, condemned strikes by public employees; he told *U.S. News* that federal law should "stand firmly against" strikes by teachers and others. However, when asked by *Education News* what role the federal government should play to ensure that teachers and school boards bargained in good faith and disputes did not end in strikes, Nixon replied, "I do not think the federal government should intervene with collective bargaining between teachers and school boards."

Nixon was also prone to drop conflicting hints about budgetary questions. He strongly advocated cutting the budget as the chief means of combating inflation; but he realized that while most Americans always want to cut "the budget," they are reluctant to cut specific programs. Except for that orphan program, foreign aid, Nixon was hard put to name items he would cut. After citing one, he sometimes retreated when facing the program's supporters.

Thus even though Nixon had cited the supersonic air transport (SST) as one program that could be deferred or receive less than maximum funding, he gave a contrary impression when he spoke in Seattle, Washington, home of the Boeing Aircraft Corporation—prime contractor for the SST: "If I found that the plane was feasible . . . I want the United States to be first in producing it. . . ."

Similarly, Nixon designated the space program as an area where funds might be cut, but in Houston—site of the manned spacecraft center—he called the program "indispensable and of major importance to our country," and said it must be supported at a level ensuring efficient and steady progress. He repeated this support in Florida, another major center of the space program.

Nixon also vacillated over defense spending, though with less direct relation to audience. He mentioned defense as an area to cut, saying it should not be treated as a "sacred cow"; but on other occasions he said that to cut it would be "blind and reckless economy," and that defense spending might have to go up before it could come down. Similarly, he said that "non-essentials like beautification" must await easier times, after having maintained that appropriations for conservation "should escape the budget knife." Nixon had difficulty with the question of interest rates, too; he implied that they should be raised, asking for new credit policies to stop inflation; but he also said they should be "ease[d]" to help farmers. Most of these opposing implications occurred when Nixon was asked, in face-to-face interviews, to specify just how he would cut the budget or stop inflation.

Humphrey was not above adjusting his pitch to particular audiences, either. Despite his doveward shift on Vietnam, he implied a relatively belligerent position before the Catholic War Veterans of Minneapolis, and declared that if he became president, the people of South Vietnam "won't get a sell-out!" He took a very tough stand against crime—and said less than usual about poverty and injustice—while speaking to the American Legion in New Orleans. Humphrey had endorsed a recommendation for lower farm subsidies, but then said, in Sioux Falls, South Dakota, that he wanted our basic farm programs improved and made permanent, and "adequately funded."

Similarly, John Kennedy in 1960 made his most belligerent foreign policy remarks before the American Legion, the AMVETS, and the VFW.

In all these examples the discrepancy by implication is readily apparent. But it is important also to see that in virtually every case the candidate could argue that his precise language was logically consistent. It is possible that "adequate" funding of the farm program, or "efficient and steady" progress in space, would have been compatible with a lower budget; the United States could perhaps have been "first" to produce the SST, even if the program were "deferred." The rule of constancy has considerable power. In any event, even such contrary implications as we have just quoted are unusual. As we saw in table 12, they occurred in 1968 on only a small fraction (7%) of the issues the candidates discussed, and in only a few of the hundreds of speeches.

Far more common is the third technique, in which candidates take only a single uncontradicted stand but are careful to communicate that stand directly by means of a speech or a special message, to an interested group.

Candidates often talk about farm problems when they address farmers, and about medical care when they speak to doctors. Since the stands enunciated in this way are little reported and rarely reach the general public—and since the candidate may not touch on the same topics in addressing more general audiences—it is often possible to take a stand which pleases a special audience, without offending others.

In 1968, for example, both Nixon and Humphrey, like most presidential contenders in recent years, made strong commitments to aid Israel when speaking to Jewish organizations—Nixon to B'nai B'rith and Humphrey to the Zionist Organization of America. Both suggested that they would protect the textile industry against imports, when they spoke in textile manufacturing areas—Humphrey at Charlotte, North Carolina, and Nixon at Greensboro, North Carolina. In Dallas, Texas, Nixon urged an end to "loopholes" in the legislation restricting meat imports; in Johnstown, Pennsylvania, he sympathized with "temporary measures" to prevent "excessive" imports of steel.

Nixon was particularly adept at selecting favorable, inconspicuous forums for his stands. He set forth his proposal to increase military pay in the *Army Times*. To veterans' groups, he urged legislation to equalize the pay of retired military with that of men with the same

rank on active duty. In Fort Worth, Texas—site of a General Dynamics aircraft plant—he sang the praises of the F-111 (formerly
TFX) warplane, and denied he would end procurement of it. In San
Antonio, Nixon promised to make the F-111 "one of the foundations"
of American air supremacy. At Norfolk, Virginia, a shipbuilding center, he spoke approvingly of nuclear aircraft carriers and submarines,
and promised to restore the goal of a "navy second to none."

Humphrey came out in favor of the farm workers' grape boycott
when speaking to the California AFL-CIO. He advocated organized
farm bargaining in Sioux Falls, South Dakota. Humphrey spoke up
most clearly for civil rights before the African Methodist Episcopal
Church, in Philadelphia and in Detroit. He announced his plan to
"save the Connecticut River" in Hartford, and made his proposals to
expand social security when speaking to a rally of the elderly in Los
Angeles and to a meeting of retired citizens in Detroit.

Nixon was in Texas oil country when he promised to maintain the
oil depletion allowance at its current level. In Miami, Florida, where
many Cuban refugees lived, he proposed his "economic squeeze"
on Castro's Cuba. Similarly, Humphrey promised to "update" the
Robinson-Patman Act (facilitating high drug prices) when he spoke
to a group of retail druggists. He endorsed the controversial Cross-
Florida Barge Canal, pet project of Representative Charles Bennett,
in a visit to Bennett's district.

Nixon used one tactic that Humphrey didn't in order to ensure
appropriate forums for statements: he sent written "messages" or "letters" directly to special groups, without appearing before them himself. Most of these messages were also distributed as press releases,
but were largely ignored by the media, as not being of general interest.
Moreover, a whole series was released simultaneously, at the beginning of October, and was lost in the blizzard of other publicity. Nixon's
most notable selective communication of 1968 was a letter of this type
to the securities industry, which implied he would cut back government regulation of mutual funds and brokers' commissions. This letter
backfired because it was widely publicized, but at the same time Nixon
sent little-noticed messages to military veterans, the air transport industry, federal employees, and the American Vocational Association.

Careful selection of audiences can be found in practically every
campaign. Thus in 1960, when John Kennedy was in Duluth, Minne-
sota, he advocated a depressed areas bill to help the local port and

mines. In a letter to John Kenney of the District of Columbia Democratic committee, he urged home rule for the District. To the National Association of County Officials he emphasized the importance of state and local, as well as federal, problem solving. In *Equity* magazine he favored prompt revision of the tax laws to help artists and writers with fluctuating incomes. In a letter to Representative Santangelo he advocated easing immigration. In a telegram to Senator Sparkman of Alabama he expressed strong support for the Redstone Arsenal.

A discussion of special audiences would be incomplete without mentioning that candidates sometimes deliberately choose unfriendly forums for their policy stands, in order to emphasize the stands, to demonstrate their courage and integrity, or simply to try and defuse opposition where it is most strong. Thus Barry Goldwater in 1964 chose Appalachia to denounce the War on Poverty; Knoxville, Tennessee, to attack the Tennessee Valley Authority; and Fargo, North Dakota, to urge reduction of farm price supports. While enhancing Goldwater's image of integrity, these bold forays probably cost him votes. Carter in 1976 provoked jeers by advocating pardons for Vietnam draft resisters in his speech to the American Legion. More successfully, John Kennedy quieted some vocal opponents when he discussed his Catholic religion with Protestant ministers in Houston. With mixed success, McGovern in 1972 presented his revised tax and welfare program to the conservative New York Society of Security Analysts. Given the mixed results of such ventures, it is not surprising that deliberate choices of unfriendly forums are uncommon.

The reader may well doubt that there is anything sinister about, say, choosing Hartford, Connecticut, as the place to advocate cleaning up the Connecticut River. The point is, however, that by taking stands in inconspicuous and friendly forums, candidates can sometimes win votes by taking positions which would be unpopular if they were widely known. The attention that media and public can or will pay to candidates is limited, and this necessarily permits many quiet stands to slip by without notice. The average taxpayer and consumer may be unaware that he is voting for a candidate who has promised tax loopholes, subsidies, and high tariffs to various special interests.

If carried to the extreme, appeals to special audiences might well take the form of secret deals or corrupt agreements. Our examination of the public side of presidential elections cannot, by its nature, reveal much about such matters. Nor, for that matter, is hard evidence concerning political bribery and extortion easy to obtain, either for scholarly works or in courts of law. But the Watergate and Nixon impeachment investigations, together with other impressionistic evidence, suggest the existence of a subterranean world of electoral politics, in which candidates' representatives trade future "access" or "sympathetic consideration" or even outright policy commitments for campaign money and support.[17]

Even the better documented and less obviously malign forms of special audience appeal can upset the political equality that is basic to democracy. All politicians could be incorruptible men of sterling integrity; bribery could be nonexistent; but money might still succeed in recruiting and electing men who genuinely shared the policy aims of the wealthy and the organized, while being too prudent to make much noise about their beliefs in public. Government policy might then be just as strongly biased away from the public's preferences as if bribery were rampant. Our evidence on special audience appeals gives a glimpse, though only a glimpse, of what may be one of the most important features of elections.

Constancy and Democracy

It is a happy fact, from the point of view of electoral democracy, that neither change nor outright inconsistency in issue stands is common. Voters are spared from coping with the confusion of wildly fluctuating or massively changing stands predicted by some theories. Elections are not lotteries of the extreme sort in which each candidate advocates mutually conflicting policies. Nor are they dynamic processes in which candidates inexorably shift from nomination to general election appeals, or contests of deception in which each group or individual is told exactly what he wants to hear.

The chief exception to constancy, in which insurgent candidates try to move from their early "extreme" stands toward the center of public opinion, is easily understood; the unpopularity of their stands (at least as those stands are perceived by the public) generates considerable pressure for change. Insurgents' efforts to move illustrate the power of public opinion in electoral competition. But their subsequent ill fortune at the polls also illuminates some reasons why, in most campaigns, constancy is the rule.

For one thing, shifts in issue stands tend to alienate a candidate's early supporters, without wholly convincing the new constituencies to which he is trying to appeal. McGovern lost much enthusiasm on the left while middle America continued to think him radical. Such skepticism on the part of voters could be warranted on the principle that it is safer to trust distasteful than appealing information about politicians; voters might also reasonably assume that early stands are more sincere than those taken later to win votes, or they might view the coalition of supporters around a candidate—Goldwater's southerners or McGovern's radical youth—as telling at least as much about his "real" stands as his campaign rhetoric does. Warranted or not, skepticism hurts those who change stands.

Moreover, inconsistency or variation of any sort leads to charges of "trimming" or "waffling," and to negative evaluations of a candidate's personal characteristics. It is seen as incompatible with a high level of knowledge and integrity. The media ensure that blatant changes or contradictions are reported or indeed magnified; in this respect the rise of national media may have had an important impact on electoral politics. Once reported, any flagrant changes or special pleas to different audiences are likely to upset many voters who disagree with one or another of the policy stands, or who simply want candidates to be trustworthy.

At the same time, we have seen that variations in nuance and emphasis, and careful targeting of audiences, permit candidates to accomplish some differentiation of appeals without these negative effects. Candidates can make certain that their precise stands are known to those favoring the stands, but largely unknown to those opposed. Differentiated appeals raise the possibility of corruption or, at least, can seriously interfere with political equality.

Appeals to special audiences are made possible by a fundamental fact about rational man and his political environment: information is costly. No voter can afford to find out everything about a candidate. Indeed, imperfections in the market for information may mean that people do not, on the average, even find out the facts most important to them. This may allow candidates to fool some of the people some of the time, and may permit the election of candidates who do not

maximally suit the voters' policy preferences. It may give advantages
to concentrated interests like producers, who can keep track of policy
stands relevant to them and offer financial and other support to agree-
able candidates, while the diffuse interests of taxpayers and consumers
are less easily protected.[18]

In the next chapter we will further explore the consequences of
imperfect political information, including the fact that limits on information capacity actually lead candidates to reduce the output of information about their policy stands. Politicians turn vagueness and
obscurity into an art.

The Art of Ambiguity

The leading theories of electoral democracy call for clarity and specificity in issue stands. According to responsible party theories, clear stands are needed in order to allow correct perceptions by voters, to permit policy-oriented voting, and to let parties play an educational or persuasive role. Likewise, the economic theory of democracy requires that parties' stands be detailed and specific, so that anticipation of policy voting will force convergence, and the winning stands will precisely represent an aggregation of voters' policy preferences.

In reality, however, neither the prescriptions of these theories nor the predictions of their corresponding spatial models are often met. Although we were able to produce examples of relatively specific policy proposals in previous chapters, such examples are not common. It is simply not the case that candidates spend most of their time talking about policy questions—or that, when they do talk policy, they take clear and detailed stands.

Indeed, the most striking feature of candidates' rhetoric about policy is its extreme vagueness. The typical campaign speech says virtually nothing specific about policy alternatives; discussions of the issues are hidden away in little-publicized statements and position papers. Even the most extended dis-

cussions leave many questions unanswered. In short, policy stands
are infrequent, inconspicuous, and unspecific. Presidential candidates
are skilled at appearing to say much while actually saying little.

Infrequency and
Inconspicuousness of Policy
Stands

In most campaign speeches, much of the verbiage consists of descriptions of problems, promises to attain general goals, criticism of the
opponent's past performance, and lavish praise for the past performance of the candidate's own party. Specific policy stands are uncommon. The charges of ambiguity and evasiveness leveled at Jimmy
Carter in 1976 could just as easily have been applied to Roosevelt,
Eisenhower, Stevenson, Kennedy, Nixon—indeed to all the candidates we have studied; even to those, like McGovern and Goldwater,
most noted for issue orientation.

The infrequency of policy stands can be illustrated by the treatment of the most salient issue of 1968—the Vietnam war—in the
speeches which set forth the main themes of the 1968 campaign:
Nixon's acceptance of the Republican nomination, "I See a Day . . . ,"
and Humphrey's Democratic acceptance speech, "A New Day for
America."[1]

Of the 253 sentences in Nixon's "I See a Day . . . ," only 25, about
10%, were devoted to Vietnam. Even this count is a generous one;
it includes such passing allusions to Vietnam as, "We see Americans dying on distant battlefields abroad"; and sentences about "prevent[ing] more Vietnams" or asking "other nations in the Free World
to bear their fair share of the burden of defending peace and freedom
around this world."

Of the 25 Vietnam-related sentences, at most 6, or about 2% of
the entire speech, concerned future actions and policies. Again the
count is generous; it includes sentences disavowing any promise to
"eliminate all danger of war"; promising "action—a new policy for
peace abroad"; and declaring the aim of preventing "more Vietnams."

Nixon's most specific promises were two: that he would "begin with
Vietnam" in making a "complete reappraisal of America's policies in
every section of the world"; and that "the first priority foreign policy

objective of our next Administration will be to bring an honorable end to the war in Vietnam." The voter could not hope to find much information here—or in the TV spots or stump speeches which echoed the acceptance speech—about what Nixon proposed to do in Vietnam: whether he would "end the war" by massive escalation, by unilateral withdrawal, or by negotiation.

Of the 182 sentences in Humphrey's acceptance speech, only 14, 8%, dealt with Vietnam. Of those only 3, or less than 2% of the speech, said anything about future policy in Vietnam. The first simply mentioned "the necessity for peace in Vietnam. . . ." The second, and most specific, pledged Humphrey would "do everything within my power to aid the negotiations and to bring a prompt end to this war." In the third, he promised to apply to the search for peace in Vietnam the lesson that "the policies of tomorrow need *not* be limited by the policies of yesterday." No one seeking Humphrey's specific stand on Vietnam was likely to be enlightened by these remarks.

In these acceptance speeches the aversion to specifics extended to other issues as well as Vietnam. The attentive listener waited in vain for specific proposals dealing with urban poverty and decay, crime, the arms race, inflation, or indeed any of the major problems facing America. Practically all the talk concerned broad future goals (peace, order, prosperity) and condemnation or praise of past performance. And the acceptance speeches were among the most widely publicized of the campaign; many voters saw no other full-dress presentations by the candidates.

Nor did those exposed to further campaign rhetoric gain much advantage. Nixon built his television advertising campaign around excerpts from the acceptance speech, adding little to it. Both candidates followed the same path of vagueness and low emphasis in their standard speeches to campaign rallies. The rhetoric which Americans were most likely to hear in 1968 had little policy content.

For the 1960 election a more complete collection of speeches and statements is available, allowing more precise measurement of the infrequency with which, in relation to all their rhetoric, candidates talk about policy. From the three-volume government compendium of speeches, 56 pages of Kennedy's rhetoric (containing 1,233 sentences) and 55 pages of Nixon's (with 1,220 sentences), were randomly selected. Each sentence was then classified as dealing with one of nine topics: policy proposals; goals; problems; past performance; praise of people or places; the candidate himself; the candidate's opponent; the campaign or election; and miscellaneous (including greetings, thanks, and requests for support).

Sentences were coded rather liberally as policy-oriented. When Kennedy advocated a higher minimum wage and then went on at length to cite studies on the beneficial effects of past minimum wages, the whole discussion was classified as relating to policy rather than to past performance. Nixon's disquisition on diplomatic "firmness without belligerency," in the course of rejecting Khrushchev's disarmament proposals, was coded as concerning policy rather than goals. Any indications of proposed future action, and any reasons given for the proposals, were included as discussion of policy.

Even by this generous count, however, the candidates allocated only a small proportion of time to policy discussion. Only 16% of Nixon's sentences, and 23% of Kennedy's, were devoted to policy proposals. (The difference between Kennedy and Nixon is statistically significant, but we cannot be sure whether it means that the incumbent party tends to be more ambiguous than the challengers, or that Republicans are more ambiguous than Democrats, or merely that these particular candidates differed.) The bulk of both candidates' rhetoric—about half of the total—concerned goals, problems, and past performance: topics that will be analyzed in chapter 7. The candidates also spent a substantial amount of time praising their hosts, predicting victory, recounting their experiences, and pointing out their opponents' shortcomings (see table 14).

Another way of indicating the low emphasis with which policy stands are conveyed to the public is to consider how often—in what proportion of candidates' speeches—stands on particular issues are taken. It would be possible for candidates to say something brief but specific about practically every issue in each speech. In actuality, however, the frequency of mention is quite low. This can be seen in the 1968 campaign, for which the whole collection of speeches, rather than a sample, was analyzed.

We tabulated the number of speeches from our 1968 collection in which a candidate mentioned policies related to each of the 122 issues on which we have public opinion data. On some topics the candidates were totally silent, perhaps because a stand was implicit

Table 14   Frequency of Policy Discussion, 1960

Topic	Kennedy	Nixon
Policy	23% (281)	16% (195)
Goals, problems, past performance	49% (605)	43% (528)
Praise of people or places	13% (156)	4% (50)
Self or opponent	9% (108)	26% (318)
The campaign and election	3% (37)	6% (78)
Miscellaneous	4% (46)	4% (51)
Total	100% (1233)	100% (1220)

Entries are percentages and numbers of sentences of each type, from a random sample of Kennedy's and Nixon's campaign rhetoric in 1960.

in comments about related matters or because the issue was of little public concern. Neither Nixon nor Humphrey in 1968 explicitly favored or opposed aiding the Arabs in the Middle East conflict, for example; opposition might be considered implicit in their strong support for Israel. (On the other hand, aid to both sides was in fact an established feature of U.S. policy.) The candidates did not mention preventive war against China, but their advocacy of peaceful contacts presumably ruled it out. Neither Nixon nor Humphrey felt compelled to speak out on the item veto, the date of presidential elections, or a particular formula for a conditional Vietnam bombing halt. Both probably felt that some issues on which we have poll data—penalties for drunken driving, for example, or the undergrounding of utility wires—were not subjects for federal decision and did not require comment.

On a few issues of major public concern, too, the candidates remained silent, perhaps because of unusually marked conflicts in views. Nixon said virtually nothing about interest rates, aside from the two inconsistent hints cited in chapter 5; tight money was later to become a part of his anti-inflation program, but was strongly opposed by the public. Humphrey made no mention of strikes by government employees; the public adamantly opposed them, but Humphrey's supporters in organized labor did not.

More prevalent than total silence, however, is infrequency of mention. Even when 122 issues were grouped into 33 broad issue areas, the 1968 candidates were generally found to confine all proposals dealing with a particular area of policy to a handful of speeches and statements. Nixon, for example, spoke about policy on civil rights and integration on only five occasions, 3% of his speeches. He made proposals concerning political protests and riots in only 6% of his speeches, dealt with problems of pollution and the environment in only 3%, and discussed relations with China in 1%. Humphrey proposed environmental policies in only 3% of his speeches; he dealt with foreign aid (military and economic) in only 3%, and the Middle East in 1% (see table 15).

The two candidates differed somewhat in this respect: Humphrey emphasized his positions a little more. For the 33 issue areas of table 15, Humphrey had about a 40% higher frequency of proposals; that is, on the average issue area he made some policy proposal in nearly 6% of his speeches, compared with Nixon's 4%. Further, they stressed different things: Humphrey most often made proposals concerning Vietnam and criminal justice, followed by international negotiations (chiefly the nonproliferation treaty), income maintenance, and aid to education. Nixon most frequently proposed policies concerning criminal justice (particularly Supreme Court decisions), and then foreign aid, economic policy, and Vietnam. But even on these most favored issue areas, the candidates mentioned specific proposals in only 10% to 20% of their speeches. The voter who heard or read reports of only a few speeches would likely learn nothing at all about the candidates' stands on most issues.

Even these low figures may give a somewhat inflated impression of how much candidates say about policy. Many of these "policy stands" were one-line allusions to positions taken in more detail elsewhere. Often the same few items were repeated in several deliveries of The Speech, in order to lend it some illusion of concreteness. Thus Nixon repeatedly called for a "new Attorney General" with a new attitude; for "restor[ing] the balance" which the courts had upset between criminal forces and peace forces; and for cutting the budget. Humphrey again and again demanded ratification of the nonproliferation treaty, and called for a 50% increase in Social Security payments. Repetition of these few proposals helped the candidates appear to talk policy more than they did.

Table 15 Frequency of Policy Stands by Issue Area, 1968

Issue Area	Nixon	Humphrey
Foreign aid (Items 2, 3, 4, 5, 6)	11% (17)	3% (4)
Military intervention (7)	6% (9)	2% (2)
United Nations (8, 9)	0% (0)	8% (9)
Vietnam (10, 11, 12, 13, 13a, 14, 14a, 15, 16, 17, 18)	9% (14)	18% (22)
Alliances (19, 20)	4% (6)	3% (4)
Negotiation with communists (21, 22)	5% (8)	17% (20)
Trade with communists (23)	1% (2)	3% (3)
China (24, 25)	1% (2)	3% (3)
Cuba (26)	2% (3)	1% (1)
Czechoslovakia (27, 28)	2% (3)	3% (3)
Middle East (29, 30, 31, 32, 33, 34, 35, 36, 37, 38)	1% (2)	1% (1)
Urban problems (39a, 40, 40a, 41)	7% (11)	9% (11)
Jobs (42, 43, 44, 45)	8% (13)	8% (10)
Income support (46, 47)	7% (11)	14% (17)
Education (48, 49, 50)	6% (10)	13% (16)
Medical care (51, 52, 53, 54)	6% (9)	7% (8)
Housing (55, 56, 56a, 57)	4% (6)	6% (7)
Inflation (58, 59, 60, 61)	9% (14)	12% (14)
Unions (62, 63, 64, 65)	2% (3)	3% (3)
Strikes (66, 67, 68, 69, 70, 71, 72, 73, 74, 75)	4% (6)	2% (2)
Civil rights (76, 77, 78, 79, 80)	3% (5)	8% (10)

Table 15—*continued*

Issue Area	Nixon	Humphrey
Protest and disorder (81, 82)	6% (10)	9% (11)
Law and courts (83, 84, 85, 86)	12% (20)	18% (22)
Gun control (87, 88, 89)	2% (4)	6% (7)
Selective service, military pay (90, 91, 92, 93, 94, 95, 96, 97)	2% (3)	3% (3)
Environment (98, 99, 100, 101)	3% (5)	3% (3)
Transportation (102, 103)	3% (5)	2% (2)
Space exploration (104, 105)	4% (6)	1% (1)
Farming (106)	5% (8)	2% (2)
Electoral system (107, 108, 109, 110, 111)	2% (3)	3% (3)
Congressmen's finances (112, 113, 114)	0% (0)	0% (0)
Drivers' drinking (116)	0% (0)	0% (0)
School prayers (117)	0% (0)	0% (0)
Average issue area	*4.2% (6.6)*	*5.8% (6.8)*

Entries are percentages and numbers of speeches in which explicit policy stands were taken concerning each issue area, based on 162 speeches and statements by Nixon, and 120 by Humphrey.

The issue item numbers, referring to the Appendix, are illustrative of topics included in issue areas.

In addition Humphrey and Nixon, like other candidates, studded The Speech with references which seemed to portend significant policies and which in this study have been counted as policy statements but which had little or no explicit content. Humphrey's favorite tactic was to proclaim programs with impressive names like "Heritage Riverways" and "Save Our Shores," without ever saying exactly what they would involve. Even his "Marshall Plan for the Cities" had some of this character. Nixon often used vague phrases to refer to policy, calling for an "era of negotiation"; "building bridges" to Eastern Europe; "strengthen[ing]" NATO; and getting people off the welfare rolls and onto payrolls.

Nixon also made some proposals which sounded quite specific, but which would have trivial or unknown consequences, as in the case of his frequent plea for a computer "job bank" to bring together employers and employees. The job bank had the ring of innovation and high technology, and would not cost much—no matter that it could be expected to have little impact on unemployment. Seeing that he had a good thing, Nixon also proposed a data bank on voluntary activities.

Similarly, Nixon made many proposals to call conferences and set up study groups, institutes, and commissions. Each of these suggestions shared the attractive features of the computerized job bank. It sounded specific and innovative, it would cost practically nothing, and the direction of policy that would come out of it—if any—was completely unclear. Who could disagree? Thus in 1968 Nixon called for a National Institute for the Educational Future; a National Mental Retardation Information and Resource Center; a White House Conference for Mexican-Americans; a White House Conference on the aged; a study of the role of financial institutions in the economy; a national skills census; a National Law Enforcement Council (together with nationwide town hall conferences on crime, and a National Coordination Center to fight crime); a task force for religious affiliated schools; a Congressional Committee on Organized Crime; and a Commission on Government Reorganization. Such proposals inflated the apparent frequency of policy discussion and gave an illusion of specificity.

The average campaign speech, then, may include a reference to one of the handful of important proposals which candidates regularly repeat; it may include some pat phrases alluding to policy, or some minor proposals of an organizational or informational sort; but it does not present the candidates' stands on many policies or in any great detail. The infrequency with which candidates discuss policy is a major factor preventing most Americans from learning what the stands are. This problem, in turn, is compounded by the fact that the most specific stands are often taken in inconspicuous places and go virtually unreported by the media.

"Position papers" are distributed to newsmen, who may report their existence but seldom their contents. Speeches before special organizations are sometimes reported, but rarely in detail. In 1968, not many consumers heard about Humphrey's speech to the National Association of Retail Druggists, where in effect he advocated higher drug prices. Speeches and statements to small local audiences hardly penetrate the national media at all. How many voters learned of Nixon's remarks about nuclear desalination, near the Oak Ridge Laboratories, or his statement on prison reform, in Moline, Illinois? About Humphrey's stand concerning the New Haven Railroad, delivered in Hartford, Connecticut?

Some of candidates' most specific stands (as will be seen in table 16) are taken in magazines and journals. Few voters ever read *Medical Economics* (1968 circulation 187,955), *Medical World News* (244,078), *Merchandising Week* (38,515), *Business Week* (578,600), *Education News* (87,070), or the *AOPA Pilot* (141,736)—to say nothing of the *Waterways Journal* (5,329), the *American Abroad, Highway Highlights, Missiles and Rockets, Musical America, Rural New Yorker,* or the *Keystone Catholic Veteran,* several of which are too small to be listed in the standard reference works. Yet Nixon and Humphrey placed policy statements in all these publications and in others equally obscure. Candidates in other years have followed the same practice. The "Joint Appearances" volume of Kennedy's and Nixon's 1960 speeches includes statements in more than 40 specialized magazines and newspapers.

Inconspicuousness of policy stands is not wholly the candidates' fault. Sometimes they would no doubt like to reach a wide audience, but are frustrated by poor media coverage. Humphrey in 1968, for example, repeated his most detailed proposals about criminal justice on two main occasions, and summarized them frequently, but they were still little reported. Ultimately he set forth the details in a paid television address. Poor coverage, in turn, is not necessarily a sign of bias or editorial whim. Newspapers and TV news programs have limited time and space, which they are naturally tempted to devote to whatever sells newspapers and products, not to the cause of political enlightenment. Whether free enterprise media satisfy social needs is a

complicated question. Information channels are limited and political
news must compete for space with everything else; it could be argued
that if voters wanted more information, they would demand and get it.

On the other hand, candidates' stands on many significant issues are
nearly invisible for reasons which cannot entirely be attributed to the
media or the public to which media cater. Whether initial statements
are reported or not, candidates seldom repeat the details of their
positions. Much inconspicuous presentation, too, is plainly deliberate.
This is most obvious in the case of appeals to special audiences. As
we saw in Chapter 5, Nixon's statements in 1968 on restricting imports of steel, meat, and textiles, as well as his support of the oil
depletion allowance and the space program, were delivered in places
where they would reach friendly audiences but would not be seen by
most of the consuming and taxpaying public. So were Humphrey's
stands on the California grape boycott, textile imports, and the en-
vironmentally damaging Florida Barge Canal.

Lack of Specificity

The infrequency and inconspicuousness of policy stands make it difficult for the ordinary voter to find them. But even the most diligent
and successful seeker after information is frustrated by the fact that
stands on policy, once found, turn out to be quite unspecific. This is
true not only of the brief allusions to policy we have just described,
but also of the most detailed issue discussions which candidates offer.

Nixon in 1968, for example, delivered his major speech on inflation, "To Make a Dollar Worth a Dollar," over CBS radio. But he
spent virtually the whole of it bemoaning the evils of inflation and
criticizing the Democrats' past policies for having caused it. Only at
the end did he come close to a policy proposal: he promised a "responsible fiscal policy," without increasing unemployment or institut-
ing "un-American" price controls. This presumably meant cutting the
budget, though Nixon disclaimed any allegiance to "mechanical bal-
ancing" of the budget every year, and did not explicitly mention cuts.
Only by implication did he oppose the "massive step-up" in spending
which he claimed Humphrey stood for.

Nowhere in the speech did Nixon indicate what level of spending
would be "responsible"; nowhere did he suggest what part of the
budget might be cut. (Indeed throughout the whole campaign Nixon

dropped only a few inconspicuous and sometimes contradictory hints about how he would cut the budget: at a press conference in Anaheim, California; a locally televised interview in Seattle; a regional panel in Dallas; and in response to questions from *Business Week.* In each case, he merely suggested one or two areas where cuts might be made.) Nowhere in the speech—or, for that matter, at any point in his campaign, except in the conflicting implications to farmers and businessmen noted in chapter 5—did Nixon say anything, one way or another, about interest rates. The most specific point in the inflation speech, ironically, was opposition to wage and price controls, which he later put into effect as president.

In another of Nixon's 1968 radio speeches, "Time to Save NATO," he recited the ills of the alliance, particularly the fall of allied troop contributions below prescribed force levels. He advocated bringing forces up to prescribed strength, but offered no suggestions for U.S. action to accomplish that aim, except that we should begin "paying Europe more attention" and should have "free and far-ranging discussion of all problems" with our allies, and specifically with President de Gaulle of France. He said nothing about how many U.S. troops or how much equipment should be committed (though he made a passing reference to "poorly equipped" American troops in Germany); nothing about arms sales or aid to allies; nothing about allied contributions to the maintenance of American troops; nothing about how to reverse the withdrawal of French forces from NATO.

Humphrey was generally a little more specific than Nixon, but only a little. In his major statement on civil rights, he praised the progress which had been made by current laws, saying nothing, however, about how he would enforce them—ignoring the controversy over title VI of the 1964 act, which authorized fund cutoffs from discriminatory programs. He asserted that the new objective was "to build *real* equality . . ." in terms of education and jobs, but mentioned no specific measures for attaining those aims. Indeed Humphrey devoted much of his main civil rights speech to attacks on "extremists" of both left and right.

The vagueness of candidates' policy stands can be underscored by pointing out how they deviate from an ideally clear policy proposal. A clear proposal would state an intention; specify the time when action would be taken; chart the direction of action; and delimit the magnitude of action. In these respects—intention, timing, direction, and magnitude—candidates' proposals almost always fall far short of clarity.

Intention. Candidates often mention a proposal without actually stating that they intend to carry it out. Sometimes support is conditioned on some vague contingency. Thus Nixon in 1968 favored producing the SST *if* it proved "feasible." He advocated providing Phantom jets to Israel *if* they were needed to provide a "margin of superiority." Both Humphrey and Nixon made a Vietnam bombing halt conditional on action by the North Vietnamese.

In other cases a proposal is brought forward merely as something to think about. Nixon said the states should "carefully consider" the eighteen-year-old vote. Humphrey urged "consideration" of a national primary, and of the educational recommendations of the Association of American Universities. He wanted to "explore" the possibility of revenue sharing with the states. He asked for presidential "authority" to remove restrictions on trade with communist countries, without saying he would use it. Such statements give the impression that candidates are taking a specific stand, without firmly committing them to anything.

Timing. Candidates sometimes state a reasonably clear intention to pursue a policy, but leave vague just when they will do so. Nixon in 1968 talked about reaching a limitation on armaments "one day"; he ruled out admitting China to the UN "at this time"; he favored repealing the income surtax "as soon as possible." Both candidates were vague about when they would begin Vietnam troop withdrawals.

Direction. Some candidate proposals give little or no indication of what direction policy would actually take. In 1968 Nixon favored "clear guidelines" to deal with conglomerates, but did not even hint at what they would provide. He said he would "completely reappraise" the Taft-Hartley Act, to ensure a proper balance between business and labor. Nixon undertook to "re-evaluate" the farm program. Humphrey promised "orderly regulation" of the textile trade.

Similarly, Nixon's many proposals for commissions, institutes, conferences, and the like gave no indication of what sort of policy would be carried out.

Nature and magnitude. A number of the policy stands we discussed in previous chapters included a fairly clear statement of intention, some indication of timing, and a general idea of what direction the policy would take. But virtually all were vague about the exact nature and magnitude of policy. Candidates practically never make clear exactly how much of anything they favor.

It is especially rare for candidates to mention dollar figures, which are open to technical challenge. Virtually the only exceptions in 1968 were Nixon's claim that his all-volunteer army could cost only $5–7 billion a year (an estimate disputed by many analysts), and Humphrey's proposal to spend $620 million under the Safe Streets Act. Other programs, including Humphrey's apparently ambitious Marshall Plan for the cities and his programs for income maintenance and aid to education, went without price tags—except those that Nixon tried to pin on them. McGovern's defense proposal early in 1972 stands alone among recent campaigns in its presentation of detailed budget figures, and his problem with charges of computational errors illustrates why the example is seldom emulated. Most policy proposals lie in vague realms of "more," or "much more," or "less." Often the statement of magnitude is not even that definite; Humphrey in 1968 wanted to fund the farm program "adequately"; he favored "selective American assistance" to Southeast Asia.

The same is true of other magnitudes as well as dollar expenditures. On interest rates, neither candidate in 1968 specified a desired percentage figure, or even a range; Humphrey simply did not want to rely "too heavily" on tight money. Nixon did not specify numbers of U.S. troops when he advocated "revitalizing" NATO. Neither candidate indicated how many U.S. troops would come out of Vietnam each month under his withdrawal plan, or whether any would be left as a residual force.

Scarcely any of the proposals quoted in chapters 3, 4 or 5 above, which were the most specific that could be found, included more than a vague notion of the shape and size a program would assume. The reader may want to reexamine some of them with this point in mind. Even if a voter somehow waded through the whole flood of campaign rhetoric, even if he found policy proposals in their inconspicuous and obscure locations, he would only discover that the candidates' proposals were far removed from the concreteness and specificity of legislation.

Variations in Ambiguity

We cannot speak with complete confidence about the degree of ambiguity in elections other than those of 1960 and 1968, since the

collections of speeches and statements from other years are not sufficiently complete. Findings about frequency of mention require at least
a representative sample of speeches, and definite findings about the
limits of specificity require a complete collection. Yet the available
speeches and the accounts of observers indicate that considerable
ambiguity has been characteristic of practically all elections and candidates.

Franklin Roosevelt in 1932, for example, devoted most of his efforts
to decrying the Depression and blaming the Republicans for it, and
to setting forth general goals for the future. Much to the frustration
of Tugwell and other brain trusters, Roosevelt would not spell out his
recovery program, barely hinting at a federal role in relief, in planning,
and in supporting farm incomes. Roosevelt was also ambiguous about
other major issues, saying practically nothing about Prohibition (repeal being advocated in the platform), fuzzing over the question of
the League of Nations, and dealing with the tariff only by reference
to reciprocal trade negotiations.[2]

Dewey in 1948 was either silent or very general about most social
welfare questions. Even though he favored changes "where necessary"
in the Taft-Hartley Act, he left open the possibility that none were
needed; and he gave no indication of what direction changes might
take—whether they would be harder or easier on unions.

Adlai Stevenson, while always an eloquent speaker, was not very
specific in proposing policy. His 1952 proposal to "repeal" Taft-Hartley was something of a mirage, since his outline of a substitute looked
remarkably similar to the old law; Stevenson later remarked that the
method—repeal or amendment—was less important than the nature
of the changes, but he was far from clear about what he would change,
except to imply opposition to the eighty-day injunction. On compulsory arbitration he said only that "if Congress sees fit to direct the
President to intervene in a labor dispute," it should give the authority,
among other things, to refer the dispute to arbitration. On "tidelands"
oil, he opposed "giving away" such national assets to the states, but
favored an unspecified "fair and equitable" division of the proceeds,
without indicating how much the states would get. Stevenson's endorsement of public power and reclamation projects said nothing
about what projects, or how many, or how much spending he had in
mind.

In 1956 Stevenson was, if anything, less definite. His suggestion about ending the military draft was vague as to when or under what conditions action would be taken: "ultimately," or "in the foreseeable future." His national health insurance proposal merely called for "some form" of federal aid to make voluntary insurance available to everyone, without specifying either the means or the amount. His "Program Paper" on education—a rather thoughtful document—advocated aid for teachers' salaries and construction, but (after noting the different sizes of Republican and Democratic bills) just declared that "[w]e must decide" how much of the burden should be borne by the federal government, and how much by the states. It recommended only that we "probably explore at least on an experimental basis" help for college students, leaving open whether it would be by scholarships or loans, and saying nothing about amounts.

Jimmy Carter in 1976 followed the same pattern. Advocating the general idea of "tax reform" to benefit low- and middle-income taxpayers, he refused to specify what provisions he would change and said it would take at least a year of study to decide. Criticizing high unemployment rates, he favored public service employment but would not say how much, declining fully to endorse the Humphrey-Hawkins bill. He accepted the idea of national health insurance but did not indicate which variant he favored or when it could fit into the budget. Carter strongly opposed nuclear proliferation but did not say how it could be prevented; he urged "openness" in foreign policy without explaining how it could be accomplished.

Although noted for unusual specificity early in their campaigns, both Goldwater in 1964 and McGovern in 1972 gradually retreated to more ambiguous stands. McGovern replaced his detailed Alternative Defense Posture of January 1972, by the September report which spoke only of "significantly" cutting spending. He dodged the abortion issue on grounds that it was for states to decide. His income redistribution plan, and the $1,000 example, gave way in August to a mixture of New Deal programs of unspecified size.

Goldwater's final stand on the farm program—that he would not end supports "until something better has been developed that can be gradually substituted for it," left unclear what such a substitute might be, and when (or whether) it would be developed. On civil rights, Goldwater said virtually nothing except in one speech, and there did not spell out the policy implications of his declaration that "government should not discriminate," or the meaning of his advocacy of freedom of association. Goldwater never did make clear exactly what measure of control over nuclear weapons, under what circumstances, he wanted to give to the NATO commander. His belated support of making Social Security "stronger" did not specify what benefit increases he wanted.

Thus we must add yet another qualification to the conventional wisdom that insurgent candidates offer clear choices. In addition to the fact that they are not necessarily very far from the public's views (McGovern in chapter 3) and that they tend to shift toward the center (chapter 5), their campaign rhetoric, like that of other candidates, is often ambiguous. Both the public perceptions (chapter 4) and the realities of choice have more to do with insurgents' past actions and past statements, and with their association with ideological movements of activists, than with what they actually say in the autumn presidential campaigns.

The responsible party arguments about relatively distinct choices on party cleavage issues must be qualified in the same way. As many of our examples indicate, ambiguity extends to cleavage as well as noncleavage issues. In particular, a party whose activists and money givers hold opinions opposed by most of the general public (as has often been true of the Republican party on social welfare questions) tends to put forth candidates who fudge over their stands on those questions. Nixon, Eisenhower, and Dewey all hinted at pro-social welfare stands but shrouded those issues in an especially high degree of ambiguity. This tendency makes party identification all the more necessary as a voting cue, since campaign rhetoric only weakly reflects the underlying party differences.

The policy positions of incumbent presidents raise some special difficulties for the analysis of ambiguity. In one sense we would argue that the most ambiguous campaign rhetoric of all comes from incumbents, who generally stay aloof from the campaign. They try to win votes by "being president," rather than talking about what policies they propose for the future. Perusal of the *Public Papers of Presidents of the United States* for Ford in 1976, Nixon in 1972, Johnson in 1964, and Eisenhower in 1956 indicates that during the autumn of an election year presidents issue the usual greetings for foreign dignitaries, general statements upon the signing or vetoing of bills, and occasional messages proposing legislation to Congress; but nothing comparable to the position papers or study reports of nonincumbent candidates. Presidents rarely discuss either present or future legislation in detail. (Harry Truman, as we have seen, was an exception.)

The burden of campaigning, in fact, is generally left to vice-presidents, cabinet officials, and prominent senators of governors of the president's party: those who were called "surrogates" for Nixon in 1972, and those whom Goldwater in 1964 called Johnson's "curious crew of camp followers." The surrogates expend most of their energy attacking the president's challenger, and defending the incumbent's record in general terms, rather than proposing new policies.

There is something of a paradox here, however, for in another sense a president's issue stands would seem to be revealed in more detail than a challenger's ever are. The incumbent, after all, has *acted*; he has proposed or signed some pieces of legislation and opposed or vetoed others, and has promulgated executive orders and participated directly in foreign affairs. Does this refute the argument that incumbent presidents take ambiguous stands?

It does not, for two reasons. First, to whatever extent a president's past actions are clear, they need not determine his future plans, which may remain entirely unstated. But second, even if we grant that what a president will do can be inferred from what he has done, the latter is by no means always clearly presented to the public. Much legislation and executive action is virtually invisible to the voters. Who, after all, reads the *U.S. Code* or the *Federal Register*? Moreover, the president's relation to legislation is often murky. He may request a particular sort of bill from Congress; his agency heads may provide testimony and draft legislation that differs; the president and his aides may even work behind the scenes to scuttle a proposal that they had publicly favored. Signing a bill can represent reluctant compromise or enthusiastic endorsement. A veto can mean inalterable opposition or pressure for concessions or merely a symbolic gesture intended to be overridden. Furthermore, much of foreign policy is carried out in secret. It is not always easy for journalists or scholars to know what presidents are trying to do, and it is all the more difficult for citizens who must rely on fragmentary news reports.

Even incumbent presidents, therefore, are surrounded by a cloud of vagueness. Some of this results from the costs of transmitting information through the media and the costs of citizens receiving it, and some results from deliberate efforts to be vague. The average voter has a good idea of how well a president has been performing, as indicated by the state of the economy and the world situation; he also has some notion of what general things the president has been trying to do; but he does not get very much information about exactly what policies the president has favored or what he proposes for the future. It is possible, in fact, that the heightened media attention to politics that comes with an election campaign makes the proposals of challenging candidates more widely known than those of incumbents.

Just as more precise policy stands may be transmitted by the non-incumbent who is campaigning than by the incumbent who is not, so does a rise in specificity of policy proposals correspond with the historical rise of political campaigning itself. If we consider presidential elections over the broad sweep of two centuries, it becomes obvious that the candidates of today are more specific and more visible in their policy stands than were those of the past.

Campaigning is a relatively recent innovation. In the early years of the United States it was thought unseemly for a presidential candidate to make any personal effort on his own behalf. Instead, he simply sent a message to his party caucus or convention, accepting the nomination (and perhaps endorsing the platform), and then stayed quietly at home or at work while others organized rallies and torchlight parades. This gave voters very little information about policy stands.

The first campaign tour with speeches by a presidential candidate (setting aside the "noncampaign" of Winfield Scott in 1852) was that of Stephen Douglas, in 1860; he argued that preservation of the Union was important enough to justify a breach of decorum. Campaigning on a large scale did not appear again until 1896, when William Jennings Bryan whistlestopped around the nation. Subsequently, with Democratic candidates leading the way, it became common practice for presidential contenders actively to seek votes and to give some indications of what policies they favored. Even as late as 1920, however, Warren Harding conducted a "front porch" campaign in Marion, Ohio, giving no formal speeches and making only a few comments to the delegations which came to visit him.[3]

Before the invention of the telegraph and telephone and the development of newspaper wire services, there was no guarantee that whatever statements a candidate did make would be disseminated around the country. The rise of national communications media helped to ensure that what candidates said would be conveyed in some form to citizens, but on into the early twentieth century voters had to rely upon newspaper accounts of candidates' statements, with little assurance of accuracy. Radio, and then television, made it possible for the first time for the average citizen to hear candidates' words directly. The development of press conferences, debates, and other interactive settings finally put candidates in a position where there was pressure on them to say something fairly specific, and what they said was transmitted directly to the voters. For all the ambiguity of present-day candidates, then, their stands are clearer and more accurately communicated than were those of the past.

There are variations in ambiguity within contemporary campaigns, as well. One type we have already noted: typically the early rhetoric is more general and the later somewhat more specific, as issues staffs and task forces complete their work and position papers are released. (The campaigns of Goldwater and McGovern, with their movements away from specificity, were exceptional in this respect.) A second type of variation in ambiguity is related to the particular format or kind of rhetoric being used. This can be illustrated with evidence from the 1960 campaign, based on a random sample of what the candidates said in different situations.

Kennedy and Nixon did not much talk about policy in casual remarks to campaign rallies: only 9% of Kennedy's sentences, and 4% of Nixon's, concerned policy proposals. In formal prepared speeches they devoted more attention to questions of policy, but still less than one-fifth of their sentences: 19% for Kennedy, and 14% for Nixon. In written statements for magazine forums and the like (often obscure or inconspicuous to the general public), the candidates discussed policy much more often; indeed, about half their sentences were devoted to policy. Finally, in interactive settings involving personal confrontations—press conferences, interviews, and debates—Nixon again spent half his time talking about policy. Kennedy was much less policy-oriented than Nixon in such settings—just why is not clear—but he still talked about policy more often than he did in remarks or speeches (see table 16).

Apparently personal questions and requests for written statements carry some pressure to say something about policy, whereas candi-

Table 16 Frequency of Policy Discussion in Different Formats, 1960

Type of Rhetoric	Kennedy	Nixon
Remarks	9% (34)	4% (25)
Speeches	19% (88)	14% (51)
Statements, magazine forums, letters	51% (119)	48% (89)
Press conferences, interviews, question and answer sessions, debates	26% (42)	49% (45)

Entries are numbers of sentences dealing with policy proposals, as percentages of all sentences of the given type. The data are based on a random sample of 1,233 Kennedy and 1,220 Nixon sentences.

dates are able to be more vague in remarks and speeches, where the subject matter is under their own control. We should recall, from table 11, that the formats conducive to vagueness are used much more frequently than the specific ones.

What Are Candidates' "Real" Policy Stands?

The pervasiveness of ambiguity raises difficult questions about how to conceive of and measure candidates' policy stands. We have proceeded, up to this point, on the understanding that issue stands consist of what candidates say about future policies. This is a commonsense definition and generally a correct one: it is appropriate to examine explicit policy statements in order to assess the validity of electoral competition theories and ideas of democratic control through elections, and to decide what the objective stands of a particular candidate are.

Yet we have seen that even "explicit" statements are not usually very emphatic or specific, and are not communicated clearly to the average voter. Voters are forced to rely on a variety of other clues in guessing what candidates stand for. We must consider the argument that these—rather than explicit statements—should be taken for some purposes as constituting candidates' "real" policy stands.

One such clue involves politicians' past behavior. It is tempting to assume that whatever influenced previous actions (legislative voting records or administrative behavior) will continue to do so in the future.[4] Even though Lyndon Johnson said little about the War on Poverty in the campaign of 1964, his earlier record of proposing and signing antipoverty legislation seemed to imply that he would continue or expand it; Goldwater's vote against the Civil Rights Act that year appeared to portend continued opposition to federal civil rights measures. Similarly, the records of established public figures like Nixon and Humphrey might seem to locate them firmly with respect to future policy.

As we suggested in discussing incumbents' ambiguity, however, straight-line extrapolations from the past are not always reliable predictors. In looking at someone's history it is difficult to judge whether he will next say "more of the same," "enough," or "let's redress the balance." Nor is it necessarily the case that past actions are easy to learn about in detail. We would argue that information about the past is more accessible and useful in assessing the *results* of governmental performance, in the retrospective fashion we will discuss in chapter 7, than it is for making projections about the details of future policy.

Another possible indicator of policy stands is the nature of a candidate's allies and supporters. It might seem reasonable to assume that the policy preferences of supporters reflect the likely future course of a politician, both because they may have reasons for their adherence based on close acquaintance with the candidate or commitments from him, and because support itself may give later leverage over action. Even though McGovern disclaimed any intention to legalize marijuana, his youthful backers created the impression that he was relatively favorable to legalization. Although Nixon in 1968 said nothing at all about banks or investment houses, one might have inferred from bankers' generous financial contributions that he would pursue monetary and fiscal policies desired by them. Jimmy Carter's popularity among blacks in 1976 suggested a commitment to civil rights going beyond any specific proposals he made. Such inferences, however, are not free of pitfalls. It is not unthinkable for followers to be betrayed or given only symbolic benefits. Nor is it easy to translate observations about a candidate's backing into precise positions on policy.

Still another sort of clue may be found in a candidate's actions during a campaign. McGovern's sacrifice of the women's challenge to the South Carolina delegation in 1972 might have been taken as an indication that he was not so keen on women's rights after all. Similarly, the choice of vice-presidential candidates is sometimes considered a sign of sympathy to the policies desired by particular groups or regions—Agnew in 1968 for conservative white ethnics, Johnson in 1960 for the South, Mondale in 1976 for Northern liberals. Campaign tours through the South have often been seen as signalling "go slow" on civil rights, while campaigning in black ghettos is taken as an indication of favoring civil rights and antipoverty measures, regardless of explicit policy statements. But these signs, too, are subject to varying interpretations.

Finally, clues can be sought in a candidate's rhetoric about problems, goals, and past performance, or in his presentation of his own character. Strong emphasis on a particular problem area (e.g., Nixon on street crime) might be taken as showing willingness to spend resources on it; endorsement of a goal might imply acceptance of the most straightforward means of attaining it. Personal vigor like that of John Kennedy might foreshadow activism, while aloofness might augur governmental restraint. Expressions of general sympathy, like Carter's recitation of his impoverished upbringing and his boyhood closeness to blacks, could be taken as signs of policy intentions. But it is hard to know how seriously to take such signals, and they can at best give only rough indications of the direction of future policy. The various indicators do not, of course, always point in the same direction.

In order to decide what "real" stands are we must distinguish among different conceptions of policy stands, as well as different measures. Which we choose must depend upon our purposes. One conception of policy stands concerns what a politician would like to do— what his own policy preferences are. A second is what he is most likely to do in office; a third, what impression he tries to create among the public about what he will do; a fourth, what impression his own words and actions in fact give; and a fifth, what total impression the public actually gets. No two of these are necessarily the same. Which one we attend to depends largely on whether we are most interested in the relation of likely future policy to voters' policy preferences; or in the determinants of candidates' strategic behavior; or in what affects voters' attitudes and behavior.

To discern what is truly in a politician's heart, what he himself would like to do, is probably a hopeless undertaking, since candidates have been reluctant to undergo lie detector tests or hypnosis. Inadvertent comments and gestures no doubt shed at least as much light on the inner man as do position papers and voting records, but inferences from them are little more than guesses. Fortunately, for most of our purposes such speculation is irrelevant: we are chiefly interested in what politicians do, not in what they think.

To predict politicians' future actions is perhaps more feasible: explicit policy stands do not on the whole seem to be terribly bad predictors, and they offer considerably more detail than do alternative measures.

The impressions that candidates try to present and those they *do* present to the voters, on the other hand, plainly involve past records and symbolic actions as well as explicit proposals. At the same time, it is no easy matter to know how important each element is or how to combine them into a single measure of a candidate's stand. For ease in measurement it is tempting to use average public perceptions (drawn from survey data) as indicators of candidates' policy stands, and we have cautiously done so on occasion. But it would be most unfortunate to confuse perceptions with reality: we are concerned with perceptions mainly as dependent variables, as something to be explained by the behavior of candidates and others. One should exclude from the definition of a candidate's stands, for example, any false characterizations spread by his opponents, even if, as argued in the case of McGovern, such characterizations affect his public image. It should be left as an empirical question (an important one, for which we have tried to suggest some answers) just what factors among the words and deeds of candidates and others have how much effect on perceptions of candidates' policy stands.

Our own focus on explicit policy statements has followed from the fact that they are, compared to other indicators, relatively specific; they are objective, not mediated by anybody's guess as to what they mean; they represent deliberate behavior of the sort envisioned in electoral competition theories; and they bear some relation to what politicians do in office, as well as constituting a substantial part of the information about policy stands which is made available to voters. That is, they provide good measures of the particular conceptions of candidates' stands which are of most interest in this study. From time to time, however, other indicators have been mentioned, both in order fully to understand public perceptions and in order to judge what the most reasonable predictors of a candidate's later actions would have been. In later chapters, as we move beyond the investigation of policy stands to consider past performance, candidates' personal character-istics, and the like, in their own right, we will have still more reason to examine actions and rhetoric of a broader sort, as well as some stimuli not generated by candidates at all.

Since there is no unique or noncontroversial definition of candi-dates' policy stands, some confusion about "real" stands is unavoid-able. Indeed, one of the main points is precisely that there is no escape from the fact of ambiguity. If one scorns explicit policy statements, he must face the fact that other indicators of stands are at least equally ambiguous, and usually more so. If it was hard to tell from McGov-ern's statements how he would feel about federal legislation or a court decision legalizing abortion, it would have been even riskier to base a guess on his treatment of the South Carolina challenge. Whether a politician who shakes hands in the ghetto will really do anything for blacks—and, if so, what—is no easy question.

Why Politicians Are Vague

Why is ambiguity so prevalent? The short answer, we would argue, is that politicians have incentives to be ambiguous; they win more votes through vagueness than they would by taking clear policy stands. To spell out precisely how and why vagueness wins votes, however, is not so straightforward. A leading attempt to specify the reasons is Ken-neth Shepsle's *lottery theory*.

Shepsle worked with a formal spatial model, but dropped the usual assumption that candidates always take a single clear stand on each issue. Instead, he postulated that they can take "lottery" stands, in which they attach definite probabilities to a variety of contradictory policies. Candidate A might, for example, convey the impression that there was half a chance he would spend $150 billion on defense, and half a chance he would spend $50 billion. Shepsle showed that in uni-dimensional competition, if voters used an expected utility rule of decision making, and if a majority were risk-acceptant (in the techni-cal sense of having increasing marginal utility for policies: that is, the closer to a favored policy they were, the happier they would be with a given increase in closeness), then a candidate who took a lottery stand with expected payoff at the median could defeat one who took a single clear stand at the midpoint of public opinion. If the average voter favored spending $100 billion on defense, for example, our candidate A with his lottery stand could defeat candidate B who flatly favored spending $100 billion.[5]

If we could identify ambiguity with lottery stands, therefore, and if the assumption of expected utility decision making held, and if most voters were risk-acceptant, then the lottery theory would seem to offer an explanation of candidates' ambiguity.

Unfortunately, however, there is some doubt about exactly what the lottery theory predicts. The existence of an equilibrium stand—an optimal lottery—is not guaranteed, and, in fact, it has been shown that under certain assumptions a nondegenerate lottery stand *cannot* be optimal: if some lottery can defeat a single stand at the midpoint, then there always exists another single stand which can defeat that lottery; but the new single stand can be defeated by the midpoint and so on in an endless cycle.[6]

Thus in electoral competition with lotteries there is in general no winning strategy and hence no prediction of what stand a vote-seeking candidate will take. Shepsle's result depends upon his further premise that one candidate—the incumbent—is stuck at a midpoint position and is unable to move. Yet we have pointed out that incumbents' stands are not known with certainty; it is neither necessary nor (according to the theory) desirable for an incumbent to cling to the midpoint. And of course there is not always an incumbent in the race.

Moreover, there are indications that neither of the crucial assumptions of the lottery theory—risk acceptance and expected utility decision making—is met among the voters.[7]

Finally, lotteries do not fully represent the sorts of candidate ambiguity we have described. They do allow for nonspecificity: vagueness, together with conflicting hints about policy, could permit voters to make their own rough guesses about the probability that a candidate favors various different policies. But lotteries do not take account of low emphasis—infrequent mention and inconspicuous placement—of policy stands; they do not allow for variations in emphasis at all. In a curious sense, the lottery theory is a perfect information theory of ambiguity. It assumes that voters know exactly what probabilities a candidate attaches to each alternative policy; all voters agree on the probabilities; and they pay attention to nothing but policy (with fixed salience weights) in making their voting decisions.

A different and perhaps more satisfactory account of the causes of ambiguity, which we call the *emphasis allocation theory*, follows from further consideration of the effects of imperfect information. Information costs entail a different model of man than that of most spatial models or even the lottery theory: man who can pay only limited attention to politics, who is not altogether sure of his policy preferences, and who uses a variety of shortcuts (involving a candidate's party affiliation, his personal characteristics, his general goals, his party's past performance) in assessing which candidate he would rather have in office. Moreover, the voter varies the weight he puts on each factor, depending on what the candidates emphasize.

Because voters' attention, the transmission capacity of media, and the time and energy of candidates are all limited, candidates must allocate their communication efforts among policy stands and other sorts of appeals. Specific policy proposals turn out to be relatively ineffective in winning votes. Candidates therefore devote most of their efforts to projecting a favorable personal image and making other productive appeals; policy stands are left ambiguous, with very low emphasis.

The heart of this emphasis allocation theory is simply the observation that opinions differ on specific policy questions but that there is widespread consensus on general goals and on what attributes of leaders are desirable. A candidate who takes a specific policy stand is bound to alienate those who disagree; but a candidate who promises peace, progress, and prosperity, and projects an image of warmth and honesty, is likely to please almost everyone.

Low emphasis requires vagueness and nonspecificity as well, for candidates cannot completely control the criteria by which they are judged. A detailed and specific stand on an important policy matter, even if issued quietly, might be picked up and publicized by opponents and news media, and the candidate would then find himself constantly answering charges (like McGovern on income redistribution) and devoting his energy to policy rather than to more consensual and productive appeals.

At the same time, candidates cannot get away with ignoring policy altogether, since ambiguity itself is not held in high regard by voters;

forthrightness and specificity play a part in evaluations. Hence we find Nixon in 1968 taking pains to claim that he had enunciated stands on 227 specific issues, and putting out a book to prove the point.[8] For the same reason, candidates regularly repeat stands on some specific issues (chosen to be as consensual as possible), and—when directly confronted by a question about policy—they feel compelled to make some answer. That is why they make an art of ambiguity, rather than falling into total silence about policy.

Information, Perceptions, and Democracy

Candidates' ambiguity has a number of important effects. Because most policy stands are obscure and ill-defined, for example, it is difficult for voters to perceive them clearly. Confusion and misperception are greatest for the most vague issues and candidates.

In 1972, a year for which good data on perceptions are available, some 10–20% of the population admitted that they did not know where Nixon stood on each of the issue scales used in the CPS survey; for the lesser known McGovern, "don't know" responses more often ran 20–30% and even higher. On such salient issues as the Vietnam war, job assistance, and aid for minority groups, where the candidates took relatively emphatic stands, more citizens were willing to place candidates on the scales—especially in postelection interviews, after they had received all the information the campaign had to offer. But on little-discussed issues like rights of the accused, legalization of marijuana, women's rights, and government health insurance many people felt unable to locate the candidates. On health insurance, which the candidates scarcely mentioned at all, the proportion of "don't know's" reached 33% for Nixon and 38% for McGovern. Inability to locate candidates can be caused by conflicting information, as well as by lack of information; thus on issues like taxation, marijuana, and women's rights, where McGovern had shifted position, many voters declined to place him on an issue scale (see table 17).

"Don't know's" tell only part of the story, however. Some respondents feel an obligation to give some answer to interviewers' questions, even if they have to guess, so we cannot infer from table 17 that 80–90% of Americans in 1972 knew exactly where the candidates stood on most issues. In fact, the perceptions of those offering them were quite scattered, and here the effect of ambiguity is even more apparent. On issues upon which a candidate took a relatively clear, consistent, and emphatic stand, most voters perceived it. Thus 88% of the voters who placed McGovern on the Vietnam scale put him to

Table 17   Nonperception of Candidates' Stands, 1972

Issue	Don't know Nixon's stand (%)	Don't know McGovern's stand (%)
Pre-election		
Health insurance	33	38
Marijuana	26	34
Tax rate	25	29
Women's rights	24	33
Busing	18	32
Pollution	17	29
Jobs	15	20
Inflation	11	31
Vietnam	8	13
Post-election		
Tax rate*	20	26
Rights of accused	15	23
Campus unrest	12	19
Minority aid	11	17
Urban unrest	10	18
Jobs*	10	17
Inflation*	8	29
Vietnam*	7	12
Liberalism/ conservatism	5	10

Entries are "don't know" responses as percentages of the number of respondents asked to place a candidate on a given issue scale.

*Item repeated from preelection survey.

he dove side of the midpoint (only 4% put him to the hawk side), and nearly two-thirds placed him on the extreme "immediate withdrawal" point. Similarly, 75% saw McGovern as left of center on jobs and living standards (only 13% saw him to the right), and large majorities knew Nixon was opposed to legalization of marijuana and firm on campus unrest (see table 18).

Where candidates' stands were especially infrequent, inconspicuous, or nonspecific, however, the public's perceptions were dispersed all along the issue scales. On many issues Nixon was seen as standing at every possible point by some sizable fraction of voters. On unemphasized subjects such as health insurance and rights of the accused, people simply could not agree where either candidate stood. Forty-four percent thought Nixon stood to the "stop crime" side of the midpoint on rights of the accused, but 29% thought he stood on the "protect rights" side; with McGovern there was less confusion, but 16% saw him on the "stop crime" side, as opposed to the 55% who thought he was more concerned about protecting the rights of the accused (see table 18).

As we have seen, the Vietnam issue of 1968 offered a classic case of candidate ambiguity: both Nixon and Humphrey mentioned Vietnam policy infrequently, and were unspecific when they did. As a result (accentuated by the fact that the Vietnam policy comments the two candidates did make were quite similar) voters were confused about what differences, if any, there were between the candidates. Fifty-seven percent saw little or no difference (zero or one point on the seven-point scale); 26% thought Nixon substantially more hawkish than Humphrey, but 17% saw Humphrey as substantially more hawkish than Nixon (see table 19). By way of contrast, confusion was less in perceiving the relatively clear dovish Vietnam stands of Eugene McCarthy and Robert Kennedy, and even in seeing that Ronald Reagan and George Wallace had definitely hawkish inclinations.[9]

It would of course be wrong to conclude that all confusion or error in perceptions results from candidate ambiguity. Even if every issue stand were clear and emphatic, some citizens would undoubtedly fail to perceive some of them, since politics must compete with other aspects of life for people's attention. The roles of limits in citizens' attention, access to media, and cognitive skills are suggested by the fact that perceptions by voters with a high level of formal education

| Table 18 | | | Scattered Perceptions of Candidates' Stands, 1972 | | | |

Issue and Candidate	Perceived Position (%)					
Vietnam*						
Nixon	4	7	12	26	22	15	15
McGovern	64	16	8	7	2	1	1
	Immediate withdrawal					Complete military victory
Jobs and standard of living*						
Nixon	7	7	13	23	20	15	14
McGovern	32	23	20	12	5	2	6
	Government see to it					Each person on his own
Health insurance						
Nixon	8	5	12	20	19	16	19
McGovern	29	23	16	17	7	3	5
	Government insurance					Private insurance
Rights of the accused*						
Nixon	10	8	11	27	19	13	12
McGovern	19	18	18	19	8	4	4
	Protect rights					Stop crime

Entries are percentages of respondents placing a candidate at a given position on a seven-point issue scale. "Don't know's" omitted.

*Postelection data; all other data are preelection.

Table 19   Perceptions of Differences Between
                        the Vietnam Positions of the Major
                        Party Candidates, November, 1968

				Amount and Direction of Difference
Humphrey more hawkish	17% (152)	1.0% (8)	6	Humphrey much more hawkish
		0. (2)	5	
		1. (13)	4	
		6. (52)	3	
		9. (77)	2	
Difference slight or nonexistent	57% (523)	11. (104)	1	
		29. (260)	0	No difference
		18. (159)	−1	
Nixon more hawkish	26% (236)	14. (128)	−2	
		9. (79)	−3	
		2. (18)	−4	
		0. (4)	−5	
		1. (7)	−6	Nixon much more hawkish

Entries are percentages of those voters locating both candidates on the 7-point Vietnam scale who saw a given
amount of difference between the two. The amount and
direction of difference in perceptions is the arithmetic difference between the scale scores given the two candidates.

are generally somewhat less scattered than the perceptions by those
with less education. But the variations we have observed—the rather
accurate perceptions of McGovern's Vietnam stand in 1972, for example, as contrasted with confusion about Humphrey and Nixon in
1968—suggest that when the stimulus is clear, most people are able
to perceive it, and that much of the prevailing confusion in perceptions results from ambiguity. Low emphasis (inconspicuousness and
infrequency) raises information costs for everyone; nonspecificity
thwarts even the most attentive and diligent searchers for information.

Moreover, as we have argued, the very limits on voters' attention
—together with other factors beyond candidates' control, such as limited communication channels and finite resources for communicating
—are themselves causes of ambiguity, since they compel candidates
to devote resources to more consensual and more easily understood
appeals, rather than to policy stands. It is a case of positive feedback.
Ambiguity, resulting from inherent limits on information, in turn reduces the information about policy stands which is available for voters
to obtain.

In the face of ambiguity, citizens are forced to guess where candidates stand, using a variety of clues: hints that candidates drop; the
allies they embrace (or enemies they make); their social, regional or
religious background; their apparent sympathy with various social
groups. In addition, the voter may be influenced by his own opinion
on an issue, together with his overall evaluation of a candidate. He
may guess that a candidate he favors, who agrees with him on most
things (for example, the candidate of his own party), probably also
agrees with him on the issue in question. That is, the voter may "selec-
tively perceive" the candidate's stand, or "project" his own opinion
onto the candidate. Similarly, he may guess that the opposing candidate stands far from him on the issue.

Thus, in 1972, Republicans tended to see Nixon as standing wherever they themselves did on an issue, and McGovern as standing somewhere away from them. (The corresponding effects on perceptions by
Democrats were less marked, not necessarily because they were less
prone to project, but because many of them were neither sufficiently
favorable toward McGovern nor unfavorable toward Nixon to moti-
vate projection.) On rights of the accused, for example, where (in
post-Watergate contrast to 1968) Nixon had said virtually nothing,

Republicans treated the task of locating him on a seven-point scale virtually as a projective test. If they were quite concerned with protecting civil liberties, they attributed the same concern to Nixon; if they were eager to stop crime regardless of infringements on rights, they thought Nixon's stand was the same. About half of the Republicans, in fact, thought that Nixon's stand on the seven-point scale was exactly the same as their own, whatever that was (see table 20).

The interpretation of table 20, like many findings concerning attitudes or self-reported behaviors, is complicated by uncertainty about what causes what: it is theoretically possible that citizens chose to be Republicans because their own opinions agreed with whatever they heard was Nixon's stand on rights of the accused, or that Republicans brought their own opinions into line with what they thought Nixon stood for, rather than bringing perceptions into harmony with opinions. Any of these three processes, or a mixture of them, could give rise to the relationship found in our table. But the alternatives attribute a great deal of causal importance to inputs of information about Nixon's stand on an issue upon which he scarcely took a stand at all, and a low salience issue at that. It is more plausible to infer that citizens used their own opinions and their own rather stable party affiliations to guess at Nixon's stand.

This tendency to project was strongest on issues upon which Nixon was most ambiguous, like rights of the accused (gamma = .73), and urban unrest (.71), and pollution (.66); it was weakest where his stand was most clear, as on aid to minorities (.47), racial busing (.42), and general liberalism/conservatism (.37). But uncertainty about all of Nixon's stands was great enough to produce some projection or selective perception on every issue. The same was true of both Carter and Ford in 1976.

It has been usual—for example in the work of Berelson and associates—to understand projection as reflecting inner needs, such as a need for cognitive consistency, satisfied at the expense of instrumental behavior.[10] We would argue, instead, that projection can be an entirely rational response when information about a candidate's stand on an issue is difficult or impossible to obtain. A calculation based on the candidate's agreement or disagreement with the voter on other issues is likely to serve the voter better than a purely random guess. The blame for confused perceptions lies with candidate ambiguity and with the high costs of transmitting and receiving and processing information, not with the "irrationality" of voters.

When ambiguity confuses perceptions, it necessarily interferes with policy voting as well, for citizens cannot vote their policy preferences with any confidence if they do not know where candidates stand. There is every reason to expect that ambiguity generally depresses the extent of policy voting (this, we have argued, is in fact the purpose behind

Table 20   Republicans' Perceptions of Nixon's Position on Rights of the Accused, 1972

Perception of Nixon's position	*Respondent's Opinion*							
	Protect rights (1 on scale)						Stop crime (7 on scale)	
Protect rights (1 on scale)	58	0	0	4	1	0	1	8
	(30)	(0)	(0)	(3)	(1)	(0)	(1)	(35)
	14	72	28	7	3	0	0	10
	(7)	(21)	(7)	(6)	(2)	(0)	(0)	(43)
	10	10	28	11	8	8	4	9
	(5)	(3)	(7)	(9)	(6)	(5)	(4)	(39)
	15	14	40	55	32	19	10	27
	(8)	(4)	(10)	(46)	(23)	(12)	(10)	(113)
	0	3	0	16	50	21	21	20
	(0)	(1)	(0)	(13)	(36)	(13)	(21)	(84)
	2	0	0	7	4	46	22	15
	(1)	(0)	(0)	(6)	(3)	(29)	(22)	(61)
Stop crime (7 on scale)	2	0	4	0	1	6	41	11
	(1)	(0)	(1)	(0)	(1)	(4)	(40)	(47)
	12	7	6	20	17	15	23	100
	(52)	(29)	(25)	(83)	(72)	(63)	(98)	(422)

Entries are percentages (numbers) of respondents with a given opinion on the 7-point scale, who perceived Nixon as standing at a given point on the scale. Based on Republicans only, excluding independents who lean Republican. Postelection data.

Tau B = .63; Gamma = .73.

candidates' ambiguity), and that policy voting is especially reduced on issues upon which the candidates are most ambiguous.

We are handicapped in testing these expectations by the previously discussed difficulties in assessing the extent of policy voting, but the best available evidence tends to confirm our expectations. The Vietnam war in 1968, for example, was a highly salient issue: more than half the American people judged it the "most important problem" facing the country, and many had intense policy preferences. But, as we have seen, Nixon's and Humphrey's positions on the war were highly ambiguous and similar to each other; as a result, people could not in any systematic way cast major party votes on the basis of Vietnam policy. "Doves" and "hawks" were almost equally apt to vote for Nixon or Humphrey (see table 21). Yet people were able and willing to vote on the basis of Vietnam policy, if given the chance. When candidates with more clear and distinct stands were paired in mock elections—Eugene McCarthy against Ronald Reagan or George Wallace—the choices of hawkish and dovish citizens differed substantially.[11] Similarly, Vietnam policy preferences were more closely related to the vote in 1972 than in 1968.

Some phenomena formerly attributed to the inadequacies of voters, therefore—misperceptions or nonperceptions of candidates' stands, and infrequent issue voting—result at least in part from the behavior of candidates. Or, more precisely, they result from the sorts of candidates cast up by the electoral system, and the incentives with which those candidates find themselves. As V. O. Key argued, the people's choice is an echo of what they are offered. The electorate behaves rationally, given the clarity of the alternatives presented to it and the character of the information available to it.[12]

The most important consequences of ambiguity have to do with obstruction of democratic control. It is plain that if voters are prevented from deciding on policy grounds, a responsible party sort of control is—in its full form—made impossible; only the attenuated version in which party identification is used as a substitute for issue voting can function. Further, ambiguity makes a mockery of the idea that parties educate and persuade voters about policy alternatives.

Similarly, ambiguity would seem to thwart democracy of the kind envisioned in the economic theory. The reduction in issue voting lowers pressure for convergence to popular stands; and vague stands cannot, one would assume, represent a perfect summation of voter's preferences.

. We must, however, deal with two objections which arise from the economist's way of thinking. First, is it not possible—as Zeckhauser has argued—that the public may *want* ambiguous stands? That the optimal social choice may be a lottery, preferred by a majority of voters to any definite set of single policy stands?[13] Second, perhaps

| Table 21 | Vietnam Policy Preferences and the Major Party Vote, 1968 |

	Opinion on Vietnam		
Vote	Pull Out Entirely	Keep Soldiers, Try to End Fighting	Take Stronger Stand, Even if it Means Invading North Vietnam
Nixon	51% (88)	47% (174)	62% (180)
Humphrey	49% (86)	53% (194)	38% (109)
	100% (174)	100% (368)	100% (289)

Note: Tau b = .10 Correlation ratio (eta) = .018.
Pearson correlation (r) = .10 r^2 = .012.

	Opinion on Vietnam						
Vote	Immediate Withdrawal 1	2	3	4	5	6	Complete Military Victory 7
Nixon	42% (46)	51% (38)	51% (39)	52% (139)	59% (60)	64% (47)	59% (83)
Humphrey	58% (63)	49% (36)	49% (37)	48% (130)	41% (42)	36% (26)	41% (57)
	100% (109)	100% (74)	100% (76)	100% (269)	100% (102)	100% (73)	100% (140)

Note: Tau b = .10 Correlation ratio (eta) = .015.
Pearson correlation (r) = .11 r^2 = .012.

the mere reduction in pressure for convergence is irrelevant; so long as politicians are seeking to win every possible vote, won't they still be forced to converge on the most popular policies? After all, an economist might point out, no one imagines that all consumers are perfectly informed about the quality of different brands of automobiles, yet a degree of ignorance (so long as it does not vary systematically with preferences, or if it can be overcome by repeated decisions) need not stand in the way of optimal manufacturing decisions which produce just the automobiles that consumers want. Perhaps competition in both the political and the economic markets is not sensitive to limited information and social choices remain optimal. It could be argued, similarly, that a responsible party process could function in a low information environment. The party standing for the more popular policies might always win despite voters' confusion over party stands, so long as that confusion was self-canceling, with as many voters erring in one direction as in another.

It is not a sufficient rejoinder to the optimal lottery claim to recall that theorists have shown that under broad conditions lotteries *cannot* be strictly optimal: that if some lottery can be found which defeats the most popular single stand, there will generally exist some other single stand to defeat the lottery. This point does not rehabilitate the argument that ambiguity obstructs democracy; instead, it casts doubt on the possibility of defining or obtaining a democratic outcome when people like lotteries, since every possible outcome is considered by a majority to be inferior to at least one other outcome. Instead, the answer must be that the available evidence indicates citizens are not risk acceptant and do not like lotteries.[14] The concept of a popular lottery outcome in any event requires that definite probabilities, known by all citizens, be attached to specific policy alternatives. No such precision is found in ambiguous stands, and no such consensus exists among voters about what the probabilities are. It must be added that even if lotteries did represent the most popular electoral outcomes, they would eventually have to be translated into specific policies, and in that translation democratic control would be tenuous indeed—who would ever know whether the policies carried out had been chosen honestly (by chance) from the preelection probabilities? Until presidents begin holding lottery drawings on inauguration day, we are justified in doubting that candidates' ambiguous stands promote democratic control.

The second objection, too, fades in the face of closer examination. While it is true that a blurring of issue voting need not in itself upset electoral competition or a responsible party outcome, this saving clause can operate only if the effects of information costs are neutral—if no group of voters with a particular set of policy preferences is systematically disadvantaged in finding out who best represents them. Such neutrality may not exist. Every citizen has one vote, but not all have equal access to information. Money, organization, and other unequally distributed resources are useful in learning what candidates stand for —and also in informing (or misinforming) other voters. Thus the monied and the organized may have more than an equal voice in electing a candidate whose policy stands please them, and in providing pressure for convergence at stands they favor. Information costs, in other words, may go far to upset the political equality of one-man-one-vote, and to award political power in unequal portions corresponding to the inequalities of money and organization.

We have earlier encountered some of the specific effects of imperfect and costly information. Politicians need money for the media and other channels of communication; that need, together with the necessity to attract activists who will defray voters' transaction costs in registering and turning out to vote, causes candidates to respond to party cleavages—to the preferences of the activists and money givers of their parties—rather than only to public opinion. Thus information costs give those activists and contributors—organized labor for the Democrats, and business for the Republicans, for example—a disproportionately strong voice in electoral outcomes. Similarly, imperfections in the transmission of information permit politicians, without fear of being overheard by ordinary voters, to make corrupt bargains with and special appeals to groups which have money or organization to offer.

Information and transaction costs involved in voting favor those best able to pay them: the well educated, the wealthy, organized groups, large corporations. They introduce class biases into the electoral system, so that those who are on top in terms of wealth and other resources also come out on top in terms of political influence. Despite formal democracy, electoral systems can accommodate unequal political power.[15]

Candidate ambiguity, which raises information costs, is one contributing cause of these problems. The explanation of ambiguity in terms of the incentives facing candidates indicates that this is one of the cases in which Adam Smith's vision falters: pursuit of individual self-interest does not lead to maximization of the common good. Candidates have good reason to be ambiguous, and yet ambiguity is harmful to the workings of electoral democracy. Individual rationality leads, if you will, to collective irrationality.

What could the reformer do about it? As Stanley Kelley points out, the discovery that politicians have incentives to be vague should not cause us to despair; the point is to change the incentives.[16] One approach might be to persuade voters to be more risk-averse: to put an increased value on candor and specificity, even when it disagrees with their policy views. Just how such persuasion could be accomplished is not obvious, however, and it would entail manipulating the very preferences to which the electoral process is supposed to respond. A more promising tack would be to use legal requirements to put candidates into settings where there is direct questioning about policy. As we saw in table 16, ambiguity is discouraged under such circumstances.

We must bear in mind, however, that some of the barriers against having a highly informed electorate stem from limits inherent in channels of communication and in the amount of attention which it is reasonable for citizens to pay to politics. Imperfect information, and therefore inequalities in political power, may be persistent characteristics of all political systems.

7

Electoral Reward and Punishment

The Record and the Promise

Presidential candidates do not often discuss specific policies. What they do talk about most of the time, as indicated in table 14, are goals, problems, and past performance. Challengers describe problems that need solving, and condemn the incumbents' failure to deal with them. Candidates of the incumbent party point with pride to their real or imagined accomplishments. Both incumbents and challengers enunciate broad goals and conjure up visions of the glorious society which their future administrations will bring into being.

Such behavior is not exactly inconsistent with spatial models, but it falls largely outside their purview. It has certain features which are not well handled by them.

A first point that is sometimes urged against spatial models, however, is not very compelling. True, questions of goals and performance, unlike policy alternatives, often do not admit of a wide range of conflicting opinions. While citizens may disagree about how much money should be spent on education and defense, they almost unanimously prefer peace to war and prosperity to depression. On such "valence issues,"[1] practically everyone's preferences are found at the same end of the continuum. But this does not alter the logic of spatial competition;

192

it merely makes obvious the point at which a vote-seeking candidate should try to locate himself. It really just alters calculations concerning ambiguity, within the spatial setting. Candidates need not fear that they will offend anyone by coming out clearly in favor of peace and prosperity. There are no incentives to deemphasize or to be vague about valence issues. Instead, candidates strongly emphasize boasts and promises and accusations which associate themselves with desired end-states and their opponents with the undesirable.

A second distinction, however, fundamentally affects the way in which spatial competition is supposed to work. In dealing with end-states, candidates often do not have the perfect mobility assumed in spatial models. They are not free to choose whatever stand they want. They are constrained by the accusations of opponents, and by the facts (or voters' beliefs) about feasibility: people know that not every goal or combination of goals can be attained. They are also constrained by the facts of past performance. If the country is beset by riots, few will believe claims of domestic tranquillity. A party with a history of presiding over depressions will not get far with promises of prosperity. The objective state of the economy and the world enter into voters' decisions.

Similar constraints undoubtedly interfere with competition over policy stands, too, as when candidates have trouble convincing people that they favor policies contrary to those they previously espoused, or when candidates (like McGovern) are tagged by their opponents as favoring unpopular policies. But the constraints imposed on claims about results and performance are generally stronger. Even if one prefers to put it that candidates are free to say whatever they want about goals and performance but that the voters won't always believe them, the result is the same: in this realm the winning of votes and the outcomes of elections do not depend solely upon factors which candidates can freely control.

The third point is perhaps even more important. Candidates do not only "take a stand" on these issues; they also analyze and discuss them. They touch upon causal relationships, chains of means and ends by which they claim they would (or did) attain desired ends, or by which their opponents will (or did) fail to do so. They discuss responsibility for past disasters and ways of attaining future bliss. Such talk is foreign to spatial models because it does not involve locations in a space of coequal policy alternatives. It concerns *hierarchies* of actions and outcomes, some of which are desired as ends and others only as means; some of which entail others as consequences.

The emphasis on goals and problems and performance, and discussion of hierarchies of means and ends, involves a different model of man than that of perfect information theories in which all know and agree upon the consequences of alternative policies and have fixed policy preferences. It follows from the fact that information is imperfect and costly.[2] Voters aren't sure of their policy preferences because they don't know, and can't easily find out, just what the effects of alternative policies would be. But they do know their basic goals and values, and can rather easily in their daily lives get some information about whether times are good or bad in terms of those values. Candidates, in turn, have incentives to emphasize goals and performance, because voters are responsive to such appeals and because the consensual nature of many basic values makes them more productive of votes than divisive policy stands could be. Further, there is room for disagreement and discussion of just what means produce what ends.

These aspects of the electoral process do not fit very well either with the responsible party theory or with what we have called the economic theory of democracy. As we will see, however, they are consistent with a different sort of democratic theory: that of electoral reward and punishment.

The Exploitation of Discontent

One common type of political rhetoric is that which points out unsolved problems and condemns the failures of opponents. It is most enthusiastic and effective when times are bad, due to war, depression, or civil unrest; the voters are discontented, and a challenger attacks the performance of the incumbent president and his party. In such cases, in fact, the reality of bad times speaks largely for itself, and the job of the challenger is simply to draw attention to it, to fasten the blame securely on the incumbents, and to promise that things will be better under his administration.

In 1932, for example, the Great Depression provided an ideal setting for attacks on past performance, and offered abundant ammunition for Franklin Roosevelt to fire—or to lob, in a genteel fashion—at Herbert Hoover and the Republicans.

In his "forgotten man" radio address of early April 1932, Roosevelt began with a recitation of American success in the World War, and proceeded to contrast the Republicans' reactions to the Depression: "In my calm judgment, the Nation faces today a more grave emergency than in 1917. . . . The present administration in Washington . . . has either forgotten or it does not want to remember the infantry of our economic army . . . the forgotten man at the bottom of the economic pyramid."[3]

In his "concert of interests" speech later in April, Roosevelt sought to allay the fears of those on top that the "forgotten man" was about to shove them aside, by invoking Jefferson on the community of interests, North and South, rich and poor. He then offered another mild allusion to the economic crisis:

> Two weeks ago I said that we were facing an emergency today more grave than that of war. This I repeat tonight.
> That a great fear has swept the country few can doubt. Normal times lull us into complacency. We become lazy and contented. Then with the coming of economic stress we feel the disturbing hand of fear. This fear spreads to the entire country and with more or less unity we turn to our common Government at Washington.
> In meeting this appeal, what has the present Republican administration done and what is the policy and spirit that has guided it?[4]

The guiding policy, Roosevelt charged, was in the Hamilton tradition espoused by Governor Meyer of the Federal Reserve Board: to remove fear from the strong institutions, so that they could conduct business as usual. To proceed from the strong to the weak.

> And what has the Administration provided to meet the situation?
> First, an appeal to charity. Second, the moratorium declared after a hesitation and delay of months and without calling the Congress into session. Third, the creation of the Emergency Finance Corporation, the spirit of which, I submit, is well embodied in Governor Meyer's words just quoted. Finally, unscientific, belated —almost frantic—economy in Government.
> Compare this panic-stricken policy of delay and improvisation with that devised to meet the emergency of war fifteen years ago.

In closing, Roosevelt took note of warnings not to swap horses crossing a stream (or toboggans while sliding downhill), but made the plea that "[i]f the old car in spite of frequent emergency repairs has been bumping along downhill on only two cylinders for three long years, it is time to get another car that will start uphill on all four."

In his acceptance speech in July, Roosevelt elaborated somewhat on why the Depression had occurred, why it was the Republicans' fault, and how Hoover had erred in recovery efforts. He declared:

> It will not do merely to state, as do Republican leaders to explain their broken promises of continued inaction, that the depression is worldwide. That was not their explanation of the apparent prosperity of 1928. The people will not forget the claim made by them then that prosperity was only a domestic product manufactured by a Republican President and a Republican Congress. If they claim paternity for the one they cannot deny paternity for the other.[5]

Roosevelt recounted recent history and some "simple economics": there had been a vast cycle of building and inflation in the 1920s; enormous corporate surpluses had built up, which went into new and unnecessary plants that "will now stand stark and idle," or into the call-money market of Wall Street. Consumers and workers were ignored.

> Then came the crash. You know the story. Surpluses invested in unnecessary plants became idle. Men lost their jobs; purchasing power dried up; banks became frightened and started calling loans. Those who had money were afraid to part with it. Credit contracted. Industry stopped. Commerce declined, and unemployment mounted.
> And here we are today.

Washington had ignored the interdependent credit structure of people in industry, in agriculture, and small investors and depositors, Roosevelt said. He proceeded to a skimpy description of some policy stands, and then returned to the theme of performance.

> For years Washington has alternated between putting its head in the sand and saying there is no large number of destitute people in our midst who need food and clothing, and then saying the States should take care of them, if there are. Instead of planning two and a half years ago to do what they are now trying to do, they kept putting it off from day to day, week to week, and month to month, until the conscience of America demanded action.

I say that while primary responsibility for relief rests with localities now, as ever, yet the Federal Government has always had and
still has a continuing responsibility for the broader public welfare.
It will soon fulfill that responsibility.

Roosevelt closed his acceptance speech by pledging "a new deal for
the American people."

At the end of July, Roosevelt discussed the Democratic platform at
some length in a radio speech; he began by reading the platform's
preamble.

> In this time of unprecedented economic and social distress, the
> Democratic Party declares its conviction that the chief causes of
> this condition were the disastrous policies, pursued by our Gov-
> ernment since the World War, of economic isolation fostering the
> merger of competitive businesses into monopolies and encouraging
> the indefensible expansion and contraction of credits for private
> profit at the expense of the public.
> Those who were responsible for these policies have abandoned
> the ideals on which the War was won and thrown away the fruits
> of victory. . . . They have ruined our foreign trade, destroyed the
> values of our commodities and products, crippled our banking sys-
> tem, robbed millions of our people of their life savings and thrown
> millions more out of work, produced widespread poverty and
> brought the Government to a state of financial distress unprece-
> dented in times of peace.
> The only hope for improving present conditions . . . lies in a
> drastic change in economic and governmental policies.[6]

Throughout the 1932 campaign, Roosevelt continued to note the dismal state of the economy—but never painting such a bleak picture as
to rule out hope, and always presenting himself as calm, competent,
and optimistic. He blamed Republican policies for America's troubles; he emphasized the goals of restoring employment and purchasing
power and a measure of prosperity; and he cited a few policies (never
very specific) for attaining those goals.

Dwight Eisenhower in 1952 found himself with an opportunity not
unlike that of FDR twenty years earlier. The country and the Democratic incumbents were in trouble because of an apparent world trend
toward communism and a costly, stalemated war in Korea; economic
stringency and price controls at home; and allegations of corruption

and of communists in government. President Truman's popularity was
at a low ebb and discontent was widespread. Eisenhower, like Roosevelt, exploited the situation by attributing these problems to poor performance by the incumbents. He acted as if his opponent were Truman rather than Stevenson. Eisenhower's approach was akin to that
of the present day in its aggressive style and in the use of television.

Accepting the Republican nomination, Eisenhower declared: "Our
aims—the aims of this Republican crusade—are clear: to sweep from
offices an Administration which has fastened on every one of us the
wastefulness, the arrogance and corruption in high places, the heavy
burdens and anxieties which are the bitter fruit of a party too long
in power."[7]

The plan of Eisenhower's campaign was drafted by Robert Humphreys, public relations director of the Republican National Committee. Humphreys maintained that Eisenhower should seek the votes
of some forty-five million "Stay-at-Homes—those who vote only
when discontent stirs them to vote against current conditions." The
recommended strategy was "Attack! Attack! Attack!"

Mildly at first, and with greater vigor as the campaign unfolded,
Eisenhower attacked. He concentrated on the themes which Humphreys' plan cited as the Democrats' weak points: Korea, communist
infiltration of government agencies, corruption, high prices, high taxes,
and centralization of government. He attacked the Democrats' performance in those areas, while reassuring voters in general terms that
the New Deal would not be repealed. Eisenhower charged, "This
Washington mess is not a one-agency mess or a one-bureau mess or
a one-department mess—it is a top-to-bottom mess. . . . Stirred into
this sorry brew are all the facts you have learned and many none of
us will ever hear about—of Washington waste and extravagance and
inefficiency; of incompetence in high places and low places; of corruption such as makes us hang our heads in shame; of bungling in our
affairs at home; of fumbling in the life and death matter of war and
peace."[8]

Eisenhower repeated much of this language about corruption
throughout the campaign. The "scandal-a-day Administration," the
"top-to-bottom mess," and the need for a "new broom" became campaign slogans. He struck out at men "who cheered the blithe dismissal
of the Alger Hiss case as a 'red herring.' " He promised, ". . . we will

find the pinks; we will find the Communists; we will find the disloyal," but did not propose any concrete changes in Truman's loyalty security program.

On foreign policy, Eisenhower did not disagree with Truman's decision to intervene in Korea, nor with his refusal to bomb China, but he asserted that "really terrible blunders" had caused the war. "We are in war because . . . there was a failure to build up adequate strength in Korea's own defense forces. We are in that war because the Administration announced to all the world that it had written off most of the Far East as beyond our direct concern."[9] Eisenhower's proposals for the future were few and vague. He called for manning the front lines with Korean troops; he climactically promised, "I shall go to Korea," without saying what he would do there. He undertook —providing a model for Nixon's handling of the Vietnam issue sixteen years later—to review and reexamine every course of action, with one goal in view: "To bring the Korean War to an early and honorable end."

Eisenhower's 1952 campaign was the first in which national television played an important part, and was a triumph for the new profession of public relations. Discontent was exploited through hard-hitting visual methods.

The Republicans hired two advertising agencies (one of them the well-known BBDO) to execute their media campaign. Six cartoon films were prepared for use by local clubs and businesses: "Korea—The Price of Appeasement"; "America's Creeping Socialism"; "Inflation, or Our Fifty Cent Dollar"; "Taxes"; "Scandals"; and "Ticket to Freedom." The Democratic party was put on televised "trial" by Republican congressional leaders and professional actors. Eisenhower's speeches were televised. At the end of the campaign, an elaborate "Report to the General" on the campaign "crusade" showed ordinary people campaigning for Eisenhower in many cities, intermingled with film sequences of cash registers ringing up higher costs; of Alger Hiss; of the Rosenbergs; of the Korean War.

The brief, high-impact messages of campaign advertising tell even less about policy than do candidates' speeches, and they rely even more heavily on symbols of government success or failure. A Republican campaign comic book in 1952, entitled *From Yalta to Korea*, featured Owen Lattimore and Alger Hiss along with Dean Acheson, and

implied that high American officials had "bungled" and conspired
against their own country. Another Republican pamphlet said a vote
for the Democrats was a vote for "corrupt government," "higher
taxes," "more spending," "higher living costs," "fumbling in foreign
affairs," and "more socialism—communism."

Eisenhower's television spot announcements brought his campaign
themes, in capsule form, into millions of living rooms.

Voice: It was extra tough paying my income tax when I
                    read about the internal revenue tax collectors being
                    fired for dishonesty.

Eisenhower: Well—how many tax payers were shaken down, I
                    don't know. How many crooks escaped, I don't
                    know. But I'll find out after next January.[10] . . .

Voice: General, the Democrats are telling me that I never
                    had it so good.

Eisenhower: Can that be true when America is billions in debt,
                    when prices have doubled, when taxes break our
                    backs, and we are still fighting in Korea? It is tragic.
                    It is time for a change.[11]

The election of 1968, when the United States was deeply involved in
Vietnam and was suffering from inflation and civil unrest, brought
another high point for attacking government performance. Richard
Nixon dwelt upon the problems of America and the faults of past
Democratic leadership (including, by implication, Vice-President Humphrey) in his acceptance speech, his stump speeches, and the media
campaign. Often his language was stronger and more aggressive than
Roosevelt's or even Eisenhower's. He emphasized the negative rather
than analyzing why things had gone wrong or what could be done. His
acceptance speech, in particular, was a classic of this genre.

After thanking the convention for his nomination, alluding to Eisenhower's hospitalization with a football metaphor (". . . I say let's win
this one for Ike!"), and calling for a united and victorious Republican
party, Nixon asked his audience to look at America and listen to
America.

    As we look at America, we see cities enveloped in smoke and
    flame. We hear sirens in the night. We see Americans dying on

distant battlefields abroad. We see Americans hating each other; fighting each other; killing each other at home. And as we see and hear these things, millions of Americans cry out in anguish. Did we come all this way for this? Did American boys die in Normandy, and Korea, and in Valley Forge for this?[12]

Nixon spoke with praise of "the great majority of Americans, the forgotten Americans—the non-shouters; the non-demonstrators": black and white, native born and foreign born, who work, save, and pay taxes. "They give lift to the American Dream. They give steel to the backbone of America." Not America's people, but America's leaders had failed.

When the strongest nation in the world can be tied down for four years in a war in Vietnam with no end in sight; when the richest nation in the world can't manage its own economy; when the nation with the greatest tradition of the rule of law is plagued by unprecedented lawlessness; when a nation that has been known for a century for equality of opportunity is torn by unprecedented racial violence; and when the President of the United States cannot travel abroad or to any major city at home without fear of a hostile demonstration—then it's time for new leadership for the United States of America.

Nixon promised "action—a new policy for peace abroad; a new policy for peace and progress and justice at home." Concerning Vietnam:

Never has so much military and economic and diplomatic power been used so ineffectively. And if after all of this time and all of this sacrifice and all of this support there is still no end in sight, then I say the time has come for the American people to turn to new leadership—not tied to the mistakes and the policies of the past. That is what we offer to America.

And I pledge to you tonight that the first priority foreign policy objective of our next Administration will be to bring an honorable end to the war in Vietnam.

Without specifying the nature of an "honorable end" to the war, and without saying how he would achieve it, Nixon went on to the question of U.S. prestige.

For five years hardly a day has gone by when we haven't read or heard a report of the American flag being spit on; an embassy

being stoned; a library being burned; or an ambassador being insulted some place in the world. And each incident reduced respect
for the United States until the ultimate insult inevitably occurred.
    And I say to you tonight that when respect for the United States
of America falls so low that a fourth-rate military power, like North
Korea, will seize an American naval vessel on the high seas, it is
time for new leadership to restore respect for the United States of
America.

Nixon declared that it was time for the United States to start acting
like a great nation and to restore prestige and respect. The place to
begin was at home. "[L]et us have order in America . . . ." As to domestic social welfare: "For the past five years we have been deluged
by government programs for the unemployed; programs for the cities;
programs for the poor. And we have reaped from these programs an
ugly harvest of frustration, violence and failure across the land. . . . I
say it is time to quit pouring billions of dollars into programs that have
failed in the United States of America. . . . [W]hat we need are not
more millions on welfare rolls—but more millions on payrolls . . . ."
    Nixon called up a vision of America, eight years hence, in the second term of the next president: Americans again proud of their flag,
the president honored and respected; every child with a chance for
the best education and an equal chance to rise high; rural America
attracting people; "massive breakthroughs" in solving the problems of
slums, pollution, and traffic; freedom from fear; the nation at peace.
This would take the "total commitment" of the American people.
    Television spot advertisements are poorly suited for complicated
discussions of policy, but they are highly effective at damning past
performance. In Nixon's 1968 campaign, a thirty-minute version of
the acceptance speech was rebroadcast a number of times during August. Later, in brief TV spots, Nixon read passages from the speech
while sequences of still photographs (and sometimes film) illustrated
his words.
    While Nixon spoke of failing leadership, dying Americans, and
sirens in the night, the television screen showed a riot in a city, with
flaming buildings; Vietnam combat, and a G.I. slumping dejectedly;
riot and fires; fire engines; and a montage of urban and rural decay.
As Nixon spoke of the great majority of Americans, "non-shouters"
and "non-demonstrators," the screen showed Americans creating and

contributing, in busy factories and farms; then scenic views of ocean, desert, and mountains, while Nixon said, "What America needs are leaders to match the greatness of her people."[13]

Several Nixon spot announcements emphasized problems of crime and civil disorder. In one, the video showed a lonely policeman at a call box, and then scenes of explosive criminal actions, ending with an image of a bullet-shattered automobile window. Next appeared a rifle and a hand holding an open jack-knife; then the faces of anxious Americans; pictures of drug sales, a mugging, youths fighting police, capture of a robbery suspect; and finally a line of handcuffed criminals. Along with the pictures Nixon's voice intoned, "In recent years crime in this country has grown nine times as fast as the population. At the current rate, the crimes of violence in America will double by 1972. We cannot accept that kind of future."[14]

In another TV spot, an announcer declared that crimes of violence had almost doubled in recent years; that a violent crime was committed every 60 seconds—a robbery every 2½ minutes, a mugging every 6 minutes, a murder every 43 minutes. On the screen a woman walked alone at night in the city, along a deserted sidewalk; as it grew darker, the viewer felt sure she would be mugged at any moment.

In still another, scenes of urban rioting, crowds taunting the police; a flaming apartment house, and police patrolling a deserted street; perplexed faces of Americans; people moving past destroyed shops and homes, were accompanied by the voice of Nixon:

> It is time for some honest talk about the problem of order in the United States.
> Dissent is a necessary ingredient of change. But in a system of government that provides for peaceful change there is no cause that justifies resort to violence. There is no cause that justifies rule by mob instead of by reason.[15]

Foreign policy was handled in much the same way. While Nixon's voice complained, "Never has so much military, economic, and diplomatic power been used as ineffectively as in Vietnam," the video showed a fast-paced helicopter assault, wounded Americans and Vietnamese, and soldiers and civilians with perplexed expressions. As Nixon declared, ". . . if after all of this time and all of this sacrifice and all of this support there is still no end in sight, then I say the

time has come for the American people to turn to new leadership. . . .
we will have an honorable end to the war in Vietnam," the camera
showed proud faces of Vietnamese peasants and the face of a GI, with
"LOVE" painted on his helmet. ("LOVE" was removed from later show-
ings as too controversial.)

George Wallace as a third-party candidate in 1968 offered a still
stronger version of the rhetoric of discontent. His attacks on government performance had a bitter and sometimes violent tone. Wallace's
appeals were aimed mainly at the South: at Southern whites' resentment of civil rights enforcement for blacks, and at lower-middle-class
resentment against Eastern intellectuals and wealthy liberals.

Wallace declared in North Carolina that the leaders of both major
parties had joined in the movement that

> took away the schools from the people of North Carolina; they've
> joined in the movement that took over the seniority of apprentice-
> ship lists of labor unions in this state, the apportionment of your
> legislature, they take over your hospitals, your businesses, and other
> institutions, and just about two or three weeks ago all the candi-
> dates for the Republican nomination and Democratic nomination
> join with other leaders in Congress and pass a bill that would put
> you in jail without a trial by jury, if you didn't want to sell or lease
> your home or property to someone that they think you ought to
> lease it to.
>
> So, you can tell your national Republican friends in North Caro-
> lina, what difference does it make? There's not ten cents worth of
> difference between the national Republicans and the national Dem-
> ocrats in the state of North Carolina.[16]

The elite sneered at ordinary people:

> Now, let me say also I'm sick and tired of some preachers, I say
> some, and some editors and some judges and some professors, look-
> ing down their nose at the people of this state—the textile workers,
> the aircraft workers, and the tobacco workers, the beauticians, the
> barman, the policeman, and the fireman—and saying you folks
> don't know where to send your child to school. Or who ought to
> teach your child, and don't know who you ought to sell your prop-
> erty to. "We folks are going to write you a 'guide line' and we are
> going to tell you." So I say that the average North Carolinian
> doesn't need anybody to tell him when to go to bed at night and
> get up in the morning.

Wallace's treatment of blacks' civil rights blended into a discussion of crime:

> The President's Crime Commission report says that we must pay a ransom to this group not to burn our country down. We got to pay law violators, we got to raise our taxes and buy out ransom for safety in our country. And then they want to say that all the American people are sick because of the breakdown of law and order. . . .
> . . . [I]f you walk out of this building and someone knocks you in the head, and the person who knocks you in the head is out of jail before you get to the hospital, and on Monday morning they're telling the policemen about it.
> . . . And the Supreme Court of this country has handcuffed the police and makes it impossible today to convict someone who is self-proved or confessed murderer of five or more people. And you can't walk the large city streets or the parks without fear of your life or your limb. And that's a sad commentary on this supposedly most civilized country in the world.

Wallace was wary of the Vietnam issue because many of his supporters backed the war while others wanted out. He turned his fire on a safe target.

> . . . [W]e should stop the morale buildup for the communists in our own country. Today we have some professors on the college campuses throughout the country who speak and say, as one did in Berkeley, let us organize a freedom brigade and go fight the Americans, the imperialist soldiers. They printed that in the Communist capitals and it makes the Communist soldiers think that half the American people want our own service men killed and maimed in Southeast Asia.
> And when you say why don't you fire those folks, they say academic freedom, they say free speech. . . . And if I get to be the President of our country, I'm going to ask my Attorney General to seek an indictment against every professor in this country who calls for a Communist victory and see if I can't put him into a good jail somewhere.
> I'm sick and tired of seeing these few college students raise money, blood, and clothes for the Communists and fly the Vietcong flag; they ought to be dragged by the hair of their heads and stuck into a good jail also.

Roosevelt, Eisenhower, Nixon, and Wallace all had the advantage of challenging the incumbent party at a time of widespread discontent; they had only to fan the flames. But challengers try to point out problems and condemn past performance even when times are not so obviously troubled. Sometimes their appeals fall flat, as McGovern's did in 1972; sometimes they are able to create or at least accentuate a measure of discontent with the incumbents.

In 1960, for example, John Kennedy played on Americans' unease following the Russian launching of the Sputnik space satellite and Castro's coming to power in Cuba. He warned of dangerous foreign adversaries:

> . . . [T]he enemy is the Communist system itself—implacable, insatiable, unceasing in its drive for world domination.
>
> When I visited the Soviet Union in 1939, it was barely emerging into the 20th century, isolated in its godless tyranny, devoid of allies and influence. Today, 21 years later, the Kremlin rules a ruthless empire stretching in a great half circle from East Berlin to Vietminh —with outposts springing up in the Middle East, Africa, Asia, and now, only 90 miles from our shores, in the fretful island of Cuba.
>
> The products of their once-backward educational system have surpassed our vaunted science and engineering in launching rockets to the moon and outer space. The growth of their once-backward economy now progresses at rate nearly three times as fast as our own.[17]

Under the Republican administration (Kennedy rarely mentioned Eisenhower by name), the United States had fallen behind. The Republicans had let communism establish a foothold in Cuba: "After doing nothing for 6 years while the conditions that gave rise to Communism grew . . . . Mr. Nixon and the Republicans . . . now attempt to make up for this incredible history of blunder, inaction, retreat and failure, by cutting off several million dollars worth of exports in a move which will have virtually no effect by itself in removing Communist rule from Cuba."[18]

Kennedy quoted military men and Republican politicians on the existence of a "missile lag" or "missile gap" which put the United States in "mortal danger"; the fault was the Republicans'. Kennedy would not forget ". . . the tragic mistakes of the last 8 years: the cutbacks in our budget for research and development, the slashes in Army personnel, the impounding of funds voted by the Congress, the silencing of critics, the consistent overriding by the Budget Bureau of the requests made by our Service Chiefs for the funds they knew they needed to carry out the missions assigned to them."[19]

The "image" of the United States as the most vigorous, vital, and powerful country in the world had begun to dim, Kennedy said. A Gallup poll showed that people abroad expected the Soviet Union to be first, militarily and scientifically, in 1970. American prestige was down. Khrushchev was threatening to "bury" the United States. "The implacable Communist drive toward world domination now reaches to within 90 miles of our shores—on the once-friendly island of Cuba —and Communism is on the march in Asia, and Africa and the Near East."[20]

According to Kennedy, the world struggle had a domestic dimension: only an America that was strong at home could be strong abroad. At home, too, the problems were serious and the Republicans had failed. The United States had the lowest rate of economic growth of any modern industrialized society. America had fallen behind in the education of young people, and was short of classrooms, short of teachers, short of scientists and engineers.

> Ten years ago we in the United States graduated 52,000 engineers from our universities while the Russians graduated 28,000. Last year they graduated 106,000, more than twice as many as our 47,000. Ten years ago Russians were already spreading their new colonialism throughout Asia and Africa and working hand in glove with the Red Chinese. To this day few American universities teach the Chinese language and the African tongues that soon will fall every day on Western ears. But we must improve our education, not only to compete with the Russians but for the sake of education itself.[21]

Farm income was down—this was the "number one domestic problem." Unemployment was high; Kennedy predicted a "hard, cold winter" for many in 1961.

Kennedy's speeches were especially notable for the coherence with which his statement of problems, analysis of causes, setting of goals, and prescription of policies all fitted together in a general world view. Whether he was right or wrong is another question. With hindsight his analysis sounds less persuasive, and the militant anticommunism is rather alarming. But he did link together relations of means and ends into a general statement of where the country had been and why, and how it could get where people wanted to go.

Different world views, with varying degrees of development, appear in the rhetoric of other candidates as well: Roosevelt's conceptions of economic collapse and recovery in terms of ordinary workers and consumers, and government action; or, as we will see, Eisenhower's vision of America with boundless private energies, which only needed to be unleashed from government interference; or Johnson's affluent America, strong and safe against foreign threats, able to help the underprivileged at home. In each case the point was not just to "take a stand," but to convey an understanding of the world which entailed a need for the candidate and his policies.

In 1976 the country had recently suffered the damage of the Vietnam war, Watergate scandals and the Nixon resignation, the OPEC oil embargo, and a deep recession combined with rapid inflation from which it was only then emerging. Jimmy Carter, in an approach more like Roosevelt's than Kennedy's, chose not to belabor the obvious misfortunes of the past. He put his greatest stress on the positive, on hopes for the future, of the sort we will discuss in the next section. But as a prologue to his vision of the future, Carter reminded voters of the time of troubles. In his acceptance speech, lumping together Ford and Nixon, he declared:

> We have been shaken by a tragic war abroad and by scandals and broken promises at home. Our people are seeking new voices, new ideas and new leaders. . . .
>
> . . . [I]n recent years, our nation has seen a failure of leadership. We have been hurt and disillusioned. We have seen a wall go up that separates us from our own government. . . .
>
> We have suffered enough at the hands of a tired, worn out Administration without new ideas, without youth or vitality, without vision, and without the confidence of the American people.[22]

The autumn of 1972, on the other hand, was a particularly unpromising time to condemn government performance—Nixon had just journeyed to Peking and Moscow, the recession was over, and peace was "at hand" in Vietnam. Still, George McGovern attacked the Nixon administration as the "most corrupt" in American history. Several times he catalogued the charges that later became so familiar, concerning the ITT antitrust settlement; the milk price rise; $10 million in secret campaign contributions; profiteering on the Russian wheat deal; the Watergate burglary; campaign espionage and sabotage; harassment of the press.[23] But people didn't want to believe it and didn't demand an accounting. Much of the evidence was concealed until after the election.

Most criticisms of performance are aimed by challengers at the party of the incumbent president. But an unusual twist on the exploitation of discontent was tried in 1948 by Harry Truman, the incumbent. He vigorously—some would say viciously—attacked the "do nothing" Republican-controlled 80th Congress. "This Republican Congress has already stuck a pitchfork in the farmer's back. They have already done their best to keep the price supports from working." The Republicans had begun to "tear down the whole western development program." The Republican Congress "tried to choke you to death in this valley" by cutting off appropriations for publicly owned electric power lines. The Republicans "have begun to nail the American consumer to the wall with spikes of greed." He predicted "a headlong dash toward another depression" if a Republican president as well as Congress were elected. He declared that John Taber of the House Appropriations Committee had "used a butcher knife and a saber and a meat axe on . . . every forward-looking program" that had come before Congress.[24]

Gerald Ford tried the same thing in 1976: he complained of the "vote-hungry, free-spending congressional majority" of Democrats, which had forced him fifty-five times to veto "extravagant and unwise legislation"; which had refused to act on tax reform, school busing, or a crackdown on crime; and which had "slashed" the defense budget for a decade.[25] But Ford was much less successful than Truman in shifting blame. By far the strongest and most effective attacks on the past have come from candidates of the "out" party, during bad times, as in 1932, 1952, and 1968.

Glories of the Past
and Visions of the Future

For the most part, members of the incumbent party accentuate the positive side of the past, and promise more and better things to come. Candidates of the out party cannot get away with merely complaining about problems and condemning past performance; attempts to do so would lead to charges of negativism and "running down America." They too set forth goals for the future.

Statements of goals were intertwined with discussions of performance in several of the examples of the previous section. Eisenhower in 1952, for example, while condemning the "blunders" that led to the Korean war, promised to seek an "honorable end" to it. Nixon in 1968, besides bemoaning the futility of years of Vietnam involvement without an end in sight, espoused the same goal as Eisenhower had: an "honorable end" to the war.

Roosevelt in 1932 urged that the Depression be ended by restoring the purchasing power of Americans, and especially farmers; he sought increased security for homes and farms against mortgage foreclosures; he wanted more adequate relief payments, and more foreign trade.

Eisenhower in 1952 sought an end to corruption in government, elimination of security risks, control of inflation, and reduction of taxes.

Nixon in 1968 urged that the crime rate be reduced; that an understanding be negotiated with the communists; that respect for American foreign policy be restored; and that poor Americans be given jobs rather than welfare.

Carter in 1976 called for a fair tax system, welfare reform, arms limitation, and openness in government.

It is characteristic of these goals—at least at the level of generality with which they were expressed—that practically everyone could agree with them. Almost no one wanted the Depression, or the Korean or Vietnamese wars, to drag on; everyone favored peace and prosperity, even if they differed about how to attain them. Vote-seeking candidates have every incentive to emphasize their commitment to consensual goals. But it is incumbent presidents and candidates of the incumbent party who usually devote most of their campaign energy to invoking such shared values as peace, property, and progress. They claim that they have made great strides in achieving them, and promise even more of the same in the future. Such claims are most effective, of course, when times are good.

Such was the mood in 1956. Despite the year-end Suez and Hungarian crises, neither the United States nor the Soviet Union was involved in armed conflict anywhere in the world, and the American economy was relatively healthy. In his campaign for reelection, Eisenhower emphasized these facts, and offered some analysis of why his administration deserved the credit. In his acceptance speech, he claimed that the Republican party was the "Party of the Future," because it followed principle, not expediency; because it looked to the facts and issues of tomorrow, not yesterday; because it drew people together, rather than driving them apart; because it used the free creative energies of individual people, steering clear of paternalistic government interference; and because it was dedicated to peace. Within that appealing framework, he cited achievements of the past and challenges of the future.[26]

On the farm issue, Eisenhower said the Republicans had rejected the expedient course of doing something in a hurry that would multiply price-depressing surpluses and make the problem twice as bad next year. "We are . . . determined that farm prices and income, which were needlessly pushed down under surpluses—surpluses induced first by war and then by unwise political action that was stubbornly and recklessly prolonged, shall in the coming months and years get back on a genuinely healthy basis."

According to Eisenhower, the Republicans had turned away from the expediency of dealing with labor disputes by getting injunctions, seizing steel mills, or knocking heads together. Instead, principle said that free collective bargaining without government interference is the cornerstone of the American philosophy of labor-management relations. "The results: For the first time in our history a complete steel contract was negotiated and signed without direct government intervention, and the last three and a half years have witnessed one of the most remarkable periods of labor peace on record."

It might be easy to plan, finance, and direct all major projects from Washington, Eisenhower said, but only at the price of a "swollen, bureaucratic, monster government in Washington, in whose shadow our state and local governments will ultimately wither and die." The Republicans had "stemmed the heedless stampede to Washington," built up state activities, state finances, and state prestige. "[T]he world has moved on from the 1930's: good times have supplanted depression; new techniques for checking serious recession have been learned and tested. . . . The present and future are bringing new kinds of challenge to federal and local governments: water supply, highways,

health, housing, power development, and peaceful uses of atomic energy . . . , urban organization and redevelopment . . . , education . . . ."
The Republicans had made progress on civil rights. (Eisenhower
did not actually mention the words "Negro," or "black," or "civil
rights.")

> . . . [A] wide range of quietly effective actions, conceived in
> understanding and good will for all, has brought about more gen-
> uine—and often voluntary—progress toward equal justice and op-
> portunity in the last three years than was accomplished in all the
> previous twenty put together. Elimination of various kinds of dis-
> crimination in the Armed Services, the District of Columbia, and
> among the employees of government contractors provides specific
> examples of this progress.

Without peace, Eisenhower declared, there would be no future.

> . . . [T]he United States proposed its Atoms for Peace Plan in
> 1953, and since then has done so much to make this new science
> universally available to friendly nations in order to promote human
> welfare. We have agreements with more than thirty nations for re-
> search reactors, and with seven for power reactors, while many
> others are under consideration. Twenty thousand kilograms of nu-
> clear fuel have been set aside for the foreign programs.
>   In the same way, we have worked unceasingly for the promotion
> of effective steps in disarmament . . . .

One of the requirements of peace, Eisenhower said, was maintaining
our own national strength: "During the past three and one-half years,
our military strength has been constantly augmented, soberly and
intelligently. Our country has never before in peacetime been so well
prepared militarily." A second imperative of peace was collective
security. And the third imperative was to actively try to "bridge the
great chasm that separates us from the peoples under Communist
rule." "Now, at last, there appear to be signs that some small degree
of friendly intercourse among peoples may be permitted. We are beginning to be able—cautiously and with our eyes open—to encourage
some interchange of ideas, of books, magazines, students, tourists,
artists, radio programs, technical experts, religious leaders and government officials."

As peace gradually comes about, Eisenhower concluded, young people could dream of a "brave and new shining world": one in which backbreaking toil and longer hours will not be necessary.

> Travel all over the world, to learn to know our brothers abroad, will be fast and cheap. The fear and pain of crippling disease will be greatly reduced. The material things that make life interesting and pleasant will be available to everyone. Leisure, together with educational and recreational facilities, will be abundant, so that all can develop the life of the spirit, of reflection, of religion, of the arts, of the full realization of the good things of the world. And political wisdom will ensure justice and harmony.

When things are going well, the glories of the past can be celebrated with slogans, posters, banners, and campaign hoopla. In 1956 the song, "Ike for Four More Years" ("three cheers/Give us what we like/What we like is Ike") rang out at rallies. "I like Ike" buttons were everywhere, and pictures of Eisenhower's smiling face summarized the mood of euphoria.

In 1964, too, times were propitious for satisfaction about the past and hope about the future. The Vietnam war was at that time only a far-off skirmish; student unrest and black urban riots were yet to come. The incumbent Lyndon Johnson could point to some solid achievements and set forth an uplifting agenda. In his acceptance speech, Johnson asked everyone to rededicate himself to "keeping burning the golden torch of promise which John Fitzgerald Kennedy set aflame." The Democrats, he said, had written a proud record of accomplishments. "We are in the midst of the largest and the longest period of peacetime prosperity in our history. And almost every American listening to us tonight has seen the results in his own life."[27]

But prosperity for most, according to Johnson, had not brought prosperity to all. Those who had received the bounty of this land must not turn away from the needs of their neighbors.

> Our party and our Nation will continue to extend the hand of compassion and the hand of affection and love to the old and the sick and the hungry. . . .
> Most Americans want medical care for older citizens. So do I.
> Most Americans want fair and stable prices and decent incomes for our farmers. So do I.

Johnson continued the litany with respect to "a decent home in a
decent neighborhood for all"; "an education for every child to the
limit of his ability"; "a job for every man who wants to work"; "victory in our war against poverty"; and "continually expanding and
growing prosperity."

In order to reach our goals in our own land, Johnson said, we must
work for peace among all lands. Strength and courage and responsibility are the keys to peace.

> Since 1961, under the leadership of that great President, John F.
> Kennedy, we have carried out the greatest peacetime buildup of
> national strength of any nation at any time in the history of the
> world. . . .
> I report tonight as President of the United States and as Com-
> mander in Chief of the Armed Forces on the strength of your coun-
> try, and I tell you that it is greater than any adversary. I assure you
> that it is greater than the combined might of all the nations, in all
> the wars, in all the history of this planet. And I report our supe-
> riority is growing.

Weapons do not make peace; men make peace. And, Johnson said,
President Kennedy brought a treaty banning nuclear tests in the atmosphere. Other agreements were reached for the purpose of world
peace. There is no place in today's world either for weakness or for
recklessness; we cannot act rashly (alluding to Goldwater) with the
nuclear weapons that could destroy us all.

At home, Johnson said, one of our greatest responsibilities was to
ensure fair play for all people, equal justice under law. But those who
create disorder, whether in the North or the South, must be caught
and brought to justice. The law must be respected and violence must
be stopped.

Johnson asked the American people for "a mandate to begin."

> We seek a nation where every man can find reward in work and
> satisfaction in the use of his talents. We seek a nation where every
> man can seek knowledge, and touch beauty, and rejoice in the
> closeness of family and community.
> We seek a nation where every man can, in the words of our old-
> est promise, follow the pursuit of happiness—not just security—
> but achievements and excellence and fulfillment of the spirit.

Johnson asked his audience to join him in rebuilding the cities, in starting a program to protect the beauty of the land and the air we breathe, in starting a program to give every child the best education he could take. "So let us join together in giving every American the fullest life which he can hope for." This is the true cause of freedom. "Let us be on our way."

Gerald Ford in 1976 had a harder time defending the record. Besides attacking the Democratic Congress, he claimed that he had brought the nation back from the depths:

> Tonight I am proud to stand before this convention as the first incumbent president since Dwight D. Eisenhower who can tell the American people: America is at peace.
>
> Tonight I can tell you straight away—this nation is sound. This nation is secure. This nation is on the march to full economic recovery and a better quality of life for all Americans. . . .
>
> Together, out of years of turmoil and tragedy, of wars and riots, assassinations and wrongdoing in high places, Americans recaptured the spirit of 1776. We saw again the pioneer vision of our revolutionary founders and of our immigrant ancestors.[28]

Against all odds, Ford tried to dissociate his performance from that of Nixon. Two years before, he declared, anger and hatred had driven friends and families apart; the economy was in the throes of runaway inflation, taking us headlong into the worst recession since Franklin Roosevelt took the oath of office. Ford, at his inauguration, had promised that the long national nightmare was over. And America had made an incredible comeback.

> Two years ago, inflation was 12 per cent. Sales fell off, plants shut down, thousands were being laid off every week. . . . Inflation has been cut in half. Payrolls are up, profits are up, production is up, purchases are up. . . .
>
> Two years ago, America was mired in withdrawal from Southeast Asia. A decade of Congresses had shortchanged our global defenses and threatened our strategic posture. Mounting tension between Israel and the Arab nations made another war seem inevitable. . . .
>
> Today America is at peace . . . . Not a single American is at war anywhere on the face of this earth tonight.

Our ties with Western Europe and Japan, economic as well as military, were never stronger. Our relations with Eastern Europe, the Soviet Union, and mainland China are firm, vigilant, and forward-looking. . . .

Israel and Egypt, both trusting the U.S., have taken an historic first step that promises an eventual just settlement for the whole Middle East. . . .

Two years ago, people's confidence in their highest officials, to whom they had overwhelmingly entrusted power, had twice been shattered. . . .

From the start, my administration has been open, candid, forthright. . . . I have demanded honesty, decency, and personal integrity from everybody in the executive branch of the government.

Ford insisted that from August 1974 to August 1976 "the record shows steady upward progress toward prosperity, peace, and public trust." He then declared that he had no intention of standing on the record alone.

We will continue winning the fight against inflation. We will go on reducing the deadweight and the impudence of bureaucracy. We will submit a balanced federal budget by 1978.

We will not abandon our cities. . . . We will make sure that the party of Lincoln remains the party of equal rights.

We will create a tax structure that's fair for all our citizens. . . .

We will ensure the integrity of the Social Security system and improve Medicare. . . .

We will create a climate in which our economy will provide a meaningful job for everyone who wants to work and a decent standard of life for all Americans.

Ford promised to reduce the growth and the cost of government; to ensure a useful education and a proud career for all young people; to assure fair farm prices, full production, and an easing of hunger; to build a safer and saner world through patient negotiations and dependable arms agreements; and to build an America rich in spirit as well as worldly goods. "God helping me, I will not let you down."

But apparently not enough voters shared Ford's rosy assessment of his accomplishments. As a Republican he naturally incurred some blame for the disasters of the Nixon administration, and perceptions of Ford's complicity were no doubt increased by his pardon of Nixon.

It has already been noted that challengers, as well as incumbents, pay some attention to the future. They paint a bright picture of how much better things can be compared to the dismal past. John Kennedy and Jimmy Carter provide leading examples.

In 1960 Kennedy regularly followed up his condemnations of Republican performance with an outline of his hopes and aims. Always the leading theme was U.S. strength in foreign affairs: we must keep the peace; be strong—not with words but with weapons; rebuild our prestige; raise the standard of freedom abroad; provide the "ultimate and impregnable" defense needed for peace.

> I want to see in the next 10 years people around the world begin to wonder what the United States is doing, not merely what Mr. Khrushchev or Castro are doing, but what we are doing in this country, the most powerful and productive country in the world— a country which represents and stands for freedom.
>
> If we move ahead here, if we are first in space and first in defense and first in the things which catch people's imaginations, then I think we can demonstrate to the people of Latin America and Africa and Asia that they don't have to follow Mr. Khrushchev or Mr. Castro, that they can come with us and meet their problems and also live in freedom.[29]

Kennedy cited domestic goals as well—sometimes as ends in themselves, but often as a means for attaining foreign policy objectives. He particularly emphasized the importance of education, "a decent education for all Americans."

> We pledge ourselves to seek a system of higher education where every young American can be educated, not according to his race or his means, but according to his capacity.
>
> Never in the life of this country has the pursuit of that goal been more important or more urgent. For our universities have become the research and training centers on which American defense and industry and agriculture and the professions depend. . . .
>
> And our universities are not only essential to a strong society here at home, they are vital to the cause of freedom throughout the world.
>
> Our universities are our hope for success in the intense and serious competition for supremacy in ideas, in military technology, in space, in science, and in all the rest in which we are now engaged

with the Soviet Union. Other nations will look to us for leadership, our prestige will rise only if we are a vital and progessing society.[30]

Kennedy went on to say that our universities must train men and women to bring the benefits of modern technology to the developing nations of the world, and must serve as centers in which the youth of other lands can acquire knowledge to run the factories, schools, and governments of their own countries. American universities are also a great catalyst of the democratic way of life, giving opportunity to men and women of all backgrounds. "And that is why," Kennedy said, "we intend to work until a college education is available to every young man and woman with the talent to pursue it."

Kennedy's objectives were encapsulated in his often repeated slogans, "We must move forward," "Get America moving again."

Jimmy Carter, the challenger in 1976, also offered hope for the future:

> There is a fear that our best years are behind us, but I say to you that our nation's best is still ahead.
> Our country has lived through a time of torment. It is now a time for healing.
> We want to have faith again!
> We want to be proud again!
> We just want the truth again![31]

It is interesting to contrast Carter's rhetoric with that of his opponent Gerald Ford, which was described above. Some of Carter's general goals closely resembled those of Ford. Carter, too, promised to strip away secrecy in government, to eliminate waste, to provide tough management. He called economic competition preferable to regulation. He said he was determined to see a balanced budget. Carter, like Ford, spoke in general terms of world peace; he called for shaping "an international framework of peace within which our own ideals gradually can become a global reality."

At the same time, however, some of Carter's aims differed notably from Ford's. The differences are characteristic of Democratic as opposed to Republican candidates, and can be seen in a number of examples in this chapter; they are linked to party cleavages on policy. In other words, not all appeals to broad values are purely consensual. Some are aimed at particular groups or classes in society which may be in conflict with others, and may be found predominately in one party coalition.

More than Ford, Carter stressed government action to help ordinary citizens.

> We should make our major investments in people, not in buildings and weapons. The poor, the weak, the aged, the afflicted must be treated with respect and compassion and love. . . .
>
> It is time for a complete overhaul of our tax system. It is a disgrace to the human race. . . . It is time for universal voter registration. It is time for a nationwide, comprehensive health program for all our people. It is time to guarantee an end to discrimination because of race or sex. . . .

Carter, in a fashion that would have been unthinkable for a Republican candidate, declared that too many had suffered at the hands of "a political and economic elite who have shaped decisions and never had to account for mistakes nor to suffer from injustice. When unemployment prevails, they never stand in line looking for a job. When deprivation results from a confused welfare system, they never do without food or clothing or a place to sleep. When the public schools are inferior or torn by strife, their children go to exclusive private schools."

He alluded to a major Republican-Democratic difference, concerning macroeconomic policy:

> Any system of economics is bankrupt which sees value or virtue in unemployment. We simply cannot check inflation by keeping people out of work. . . .
>
> I believe that anyone who is able to work ought to work—and have a chance to work.

Carter closed his acceptance speech on an upward note.

> I see an America on the move again, united, a diverse and vital and tolerant nation, entering our third century with pride and confidence—an America that lives up to the majesty of our Constitution and the simple decency of our people.
>
> This is the America we want.
>
> This is the America we will have.
>
> . . . And once again, as brothers and sisters, our hearts will swell with pride to call ourselves Americans.

Democracy by Anticipation
of Reward and Punishment

In certain ways the campaign rhetoric we have been discussing is not unrelated to the economic and responsible party theories of democracy. Discussion of problems and goals and past performance can imply policy stands. Republican and Democratic candidates do tend to emphasize different aims and accomplishments which articulate with party cleavages on policy and thereby contribute to a relatively distinct choice along responsible party lines. Just as Ford and Carter expressed some differing objectives, Roosevelt's concern for the forgotten man and Johnson's call for more government action to help people contrasted with Hoover's and Eisenhower's emphasis on individualism and freedom from government interference.

Moreover, such rhetoric can contribute to the educational side of responsible parties. A proclamation of goals can be uplifting, appealing to the best in people, to their generosity and creativity. Analysis of problems can be instructive. If the discussion is factual, it can inform citizens about the state of the world and explain to them why particular policies are necessary to attain shared goals.

As the passages quoted above suggest, however (and the selections have by no means been atypical of or unkind to the candidates), campaign rhetoric, while occasionally inspiring, is rarely very enlightening. It seldom goes beyond superficial promises and accusations. Furthermore, talk about goals or performance provides only weak and unreliable hints about which policies will be pursued. It takes up communication effort which, according to the economic and the responsible party theories, ought to be devoted to clear and specific policy stands. Reality appears to fall far short of these hopes.

It is possible, however, to set forth a different kind of democratic theory which is somewhat more consistent with the electoral behavior we have observed and more compatible with considerations of limited information.

We have argued that information costs make it difficult for citizens to vote on the basis of policy preferences, or even to have firm preferences. It is hard for people to know the details of alternative policies or to figure out which politicians stand for what. Above all, it is hard to know exactly how particular policies would affect their lives. Citizens do have beliefs about political causes and effects, and they do try to judge policies as helping or hurting their desired ends; but it would be irrational for most people to invest the time and energy necessary to be sure of these things and to have a full understanding of policy alternatives and their consequences. The average person cannot, for example, easily learn the differences among possible government or private health insurance programs, or calculate which proposed peace settlement in the Middle East would ensure equity among the parties and give the best chance of peace, or assess how various mixtures of monetary and fiscal policies and public job programs would affect unemployment and inflation.

What people do know very well is what they need in their own lives, and what conditions they want in the nation and world, such as good health, jobs, a high income, peace at home and abroad. These fundamental needs and values are not subject to much uncertainty.

Further, the average citizen can usually figure out how things are going in terms of his values. Are paychecks up or down? What about grocery bills? Are friends and relatives prosperous, or unemployed? Are sons and nephews living their lives in peace, or have they been drafted to fight in some jungle or desert? Is the TV news full of American riots and war casualties? Such information, together with opinions about the actual and desired scope of government action, permits an evaluation of the results of government performance. The citizen can then cast his vote retrospectively, on the basis of past performance: reward the incumbents if they have done well, and punish them if they have done badly.[32]

This is a sensible shortcut for voters to take, and is compatible with democratic theory, because of the effect it has upon politicians' actions. Most presidents and other high-level politicians want to stay in office, or at least (if ineligible for reelection) to go down in history as successful and pass power on to others in their own party. They have strong incentives, therefore, to *anticipate the reactions* of the public. If they can determine what the people value, they will try to produce the appropriate results, in order to maximize votes at the next election. The outcome of this process should be a government that accomplishes just what its citizens want, with some flexibility about the means employed so long as the results are good.[33]

This electoral reward and punishment theory of democracy has several attractive features. For one, it orients government responsiveness toward fundamental needs and values of the people rather than toward ephemeral or weakly held policy preferences. In that respect it is quite different from social choice theories, which (as usually interpreted) call for government to respond at every moment to its citizens' preferences on policy. Yet it is also populistic, weighting citizens equally.

The reward and punishment theory asks little of voters: none of the burdensome analysis of policy stands called for (unrealistically) by the economic and the responsible party theories, but only reliance on evidence that is close at hand. Indeed the theory could work even though voters knew little about the causes of bliss or misfortune, and simply attributed everything to incumbents. Even if the Great Depression and lack of recovery were not at all Hoover's fault—and arguments about his responsibility can become rather technical—it could make sense to punish him in order to sharpen the incentives to maintain prosperity in the future. Even if crop failures of the early 1970s resulted from bad weather, and oil price rises were due to OPEC, why not blame the American president and his party? To err on the side of forgiveness would leave voters vulnerable to tricky explanations and rationalizations; but to err on the draconian side would only spur politicians on to greater energy and imagination in problem solving. Presumably fears of unfair ouster would be overcome by the pleasures of power, so that we would not run out of politicians willing to run the risk.[34]

By the same token it would make sense for the public to judge performance on a party basis. Even if Adlai Stevenson in 1952 had nothing whatever to do with corruption in Washington, or the war in Korea, or the "loss" of China, it was appropriate to punish him and other Democratic candidates in order to create incentives for all members of the governing party—whether in or out of national office—to put pressure on their fellow partisans to make things work. Similarly, it was reasonable to hold Humphrey accountable for Johnson's performance in 1968, and Ford for Nixon's in 1976.

Moreover, the electoral reward and punishment theory allows for a division of political labor, in the manner envisioned by such theorists as John Stuart Mill.[35] Citizens dictate the ends of government and judge the results, but leaders specialize in designing policies to accomplish those ends. Incumbent officials are given some time between elections in order to devise solutions, to experiment, and even to try out unpopular policies, so long as the results please the public. In this way legislative and executive expertise play an important and appropriate part in democratic policy making.

Still another appealing aspect of this theory of electoral democracy —which it shares, in some measure, with the economic theory and with certain versions of responsible party ideas—is that it rests upon the self-interest of power-seeking politicians. It does not require from them any unlikely degree of altruism or any impulse to be honorable and keep campaign promises. Politicians are forced to serve the people in order to serve themselves.

The historical record suggests that a process of electoral reward and punishment does in fact occur. When times are good, incumbent politicians are usually returned to office; when times are bad, the rascals often get thrown out. The Republicans were ousted in the midst of depression, in 1932; the Democrats were turned out of office with the Korean war in 1952 and Vietnam in 1968; Eisenhower was triumphantly returned to office in the relatively prosperous and tranquil year 1956, and Johnson in 1964.

Survey data reinforce this impression, indicating that individual voters who are unhappy about government performance tend to vote against the incumbent party, even when they themselves identify with that party. In 1968, for example, Democratic voters who thought that the incumbent Democrat, Lyndon Johnson, had handled problems poorly or only fairly well, were much more likely to vote for the Republican Nixon (running against Hubert Humphrey), than were Democrats who thought Johnson had done a good job. This was a very strong tendency, involving differences as high as 60 percent, and gammas from .46 to .73, among groups of Democrats and independents (see table 22).

Similarly, in 1976, those who disapproved of Gerald Ford's handling of his job were much more likely to vote for Jimmy Carter than were those who approved. Again evaluations of performance were colored by party loyalty—Democrats disapproved Ford's performance more often than Republicans did—and party had some effect on the vote regardless of evaluations—many Democrats voted against Ford even though they approved of his performance. But within each category of party identification, those who disapproved Ford's handling of his

Table 22	Vote by Party and Evaluation of Lyndon Johnson's Performance, 1968		
	Johnson's Handling of Problems		
Party Identification	Poor or Very Poor	Fair	Good or Very Good
Strong Democrat	40% (10)	11% (44)	5% (146)
Weak Democrat	70% (23)	34% (70)	23% (98)
Lean toward Democrat	83% (6)	42% (31)	23% (35)
Independent	100% (14)	74% (31)	45% (20)
Lean toward Republican	100% (29)	91% (33)	100% (23)
Weak Republican	92% (38)	89% (70)	87% (40)
Strong Republican	98% (41)	98% (55)	94% (18)

Entries are percentages voting for Nixon as against Humphrey. The number upon which each percentage is based—the number of major party voters within each category of party identification and evaluation—is given in parentheses.

job were much more likely to vote for his opponent than were those who approved. As in 1968, these differences were quite large, ranging from 31% to 75%. The chief difference between the two years was that more people disapproved of Johnson's performance than Ford's, so that the Democrats' advantage in number of identifiers was overcome in 1968 (and was just barely sufficient in 1976), and the incumbent party narrowly lost both elections (see table 23).

There is also a tendency for voters who are upset about any particular aspect of government performance to vote against the incumbents. This has been true, in a number of election years, of those who reported that their family's financial situation had worsened, or who had lost confidence in their party's ability to keep the United States out of war, or who were discontented about some other aspect of foreign or domestic events. In 1952, for example, Democrats who blamed the United States for the "loss" of (that is, the communist revolution in) China were substantially more likely than those not blaming the U.S. to defect from their party and vote for Eisenhower (see table 24).

Similarly, in 1976, voters who thought the government had done a poor job of dealing with inflation were less likely to vote for President Ford (see table 25). This tendency was even stronger when it was translated into a relative judgment about which party could handle inflation better in the future (see table 26). To be sure, few Republicans went so far as to say that the Democrats could do a better job with inflation, but those who did—and those who saw no difference between the parties—were more likely to vote for Carter.

Table 23	Vote by Party and Evaluation of Gerald Ford's Performance, 1976	
Party Identification	Ford's Handling of his Job	
	Approve	Disapprove
Strong Democrat	32% (61)	1% (179)
Weak Democrat	42% (176)	6% (149)
Lean toward Democrat	45% (73)	11% (92)
Independent	78% (100)	15% (50)
Lean toward Republican	91% (149)	50% (15)
Weak Republican	89% (193)	14% (29)
Strong Republican	98% (183)	64% (7)

Entries are percentages voting for Ford as against Carter. The number upon which each percentage is based is given in parentheses (weighted data.)

Table 24   Vote by Party and Perception of U.S.
                                 Responsibility for China Going
                                 Communist, 1952

Party Identification	Assessment of Government Responsibility	
	Our Fault	Nothing We Could Do
Strong Democrat	31% (52)	12% (161)
Weak Democrat	60% (52)	33% (157)
Lean toward Democrat	41% (39)	34% (62)
Independent	78% (23)	76% (25)
Lean toward Republican	96% (47)	91% (22)
Weak Republican	97% (58)	92% (75)
Strong Republican	99% (82)	97% (65)

Entries are percentages voting for Eisenhower as against Stevenson. Within parentheses is the number upon which each percentage is based: that is, the number of major party voters of a given party identification with a given assessment of U.S. responsibility.

While more remains to be learned about exactly which categories of voters, under what circumstances, react to performance of what sorts, the available survey data broadly support the notion that citizens vote retrospectively, on the basis of results: that they reward success and punish failure.[36] Electoral punishment can of course take other forms besides voting for the "out" party: abstaining, casting a third party vote, or changing campaign participation.

At the same time, the survey evidence cannot be taken as conclusive, since cross-tabulation tables (and regressions or other techniques using cross-sectional data) can be interpreted in more than one way.

We cannot be sure about the direction of causal influence: whether evaluations of past performance actually cause voters to defect from their party; or whether those evaluations are rationalizations, caused by some other factor which leads voters to defect from their party; or whether declared party loyalties are themselves affected by evaluations of performance;[37] or whether some combination of these things occurs.

Fortunately, the survey findings are reinforced by evidence based on changes over time in objective conditions and changes in the proportion of the vote won by the incumbents. Such aggregate data are largely free of the possibility of rationalization or reciprocal causation. They indicate that evaluations of past performance are sufficiently strong, and usually push so heavily in one partisan direction in any

Table 25	Vote by Party and by Evaluation of the Government's Handling of Inflation, 1976		
Party Identification	Government's Job with Inflation		
	Good	Fair	Poor
Strong Democrat	56% (13)	11% (123)	2% (128)
Weak Democrat	72% (16)	29% (229)	10% (119)
Lean toward Democrat	56% (9)	24% (120)	17% (56)
Independent	90% (25)	60% (88)	34% (51)
Lean toward Republican	93% (36)	85% (107)	83% (26)
Weak Republican	87% (39)	83% (162)	46% (42)
Strong Republican	98% (46)	97% (128)	96% (22)

Entries are percentages voting for Ford as against Carter. The number of respondents upon which each percentage is based is given in parentheses (weighted data.)

Table 26   Vote by Party and by Judgment of
                                Which Party Can Handle Inflation
                                Better, 1976

| Party | Which Party Can Handle Inflation Better | | |
Identification	Republican	No Difference	Democratic
Strong Democrat	85%	16%	3%
	(7)	(70)	(175)
Weak Democrat	81%	30%	6%
	(34)	(180)	(140)
Lean toward Democrat	55%	33%	2%
	(10)	(111)	(54)
Independent	80%	63%	10%
	(26)	(106)	(24)
Lean toward Republican	95%	82%	25%
	(75)	(86)	(6)
Weak Republican	89%	80%	12%
	(94)	(122)	(13)
Strong Republican	97%	97%	63%
	(114)	(74)	(4)

Entries are percentages voting for Ford as against Carter.
The number upon which each percentage is based is given
in parentheses (weighted data.)

given election, that they often determine electoral outcomes, even if
they don't account for the behavior of a very high proportion of voters.

This is seen most clearly in congressional elections. Changes in real
per capita income, together with the level of presidential or candidate
popularity, almost totally determine how the outcome differs from a
normal division of the two-party vote.[38]

For presidential voting the evidence is less direct and less conclusive. Outcomes are heavily influenced by voters' reactions to candidates' personal characteristics. But the popularity of incumbent
presidents, which in turn affects voting for both congress and the
presidency, is itself strongly influenced by the balance of good or bad
news about government performance.[39] Evaluations of presidential
performance apparently give much weight to foreign affairs, while

electoral punishment of congress rests heavily on domestic policy matters, much of which is summarized by changes in personal income.

We cannot be sure to what extent this retrospective voting behavior represents a proclivity of citizens, and to what extent it is brought about by candidates' rhetoric and other stimuli of the political world. Probably there is some truth to both explanations, and the two reinforce each other. On the one hand, candidates may accentuate predispositions to vote on the basis of past performance by talking so insistently about whether things are going well or poorly, while inhibiting policy voting through the ambiguity and similarity of their policy stands. On the other hand, we have suggested that voters may in any case prefer to judge on the basis of the past, and that—in the face of information costs—it is rational for them to do so.

In any event, the behavior both of voters and of political parties is largely consistent with the electoral reward and punishment version of democratic theory. Often the most real choice in elections is that between the "in" and the "out" party, based upon objective facts of past performance, and voters respond to this choice. The rhetoric of presidential candidates, too, fits the theory, with its emphasis upon goals, problems, and past performance. To what extent incumbent politicians actually anticipate reward or punishment, and are thereby subjected to democratic control, is a harder question, which must be answered with data on policy making as well as the electoral process.

At the same time, it is well to consider some possible defects of this version of electoral democracy.

1. To some degree candidates may be able to confuse or distort the public's judgments of the state of the world. The "missile gap" of 1960 never materialized. (Kennedy loyalists later argued that the Russians *could* have got ahead on delivery systems if they had tried.) Kennedy's picture of a militant expansionist Soviet Union, gobbling up the world, was overdrawn. The "security risks" and communists in government in 1952 were mostly figments of red-baiting imaginations. Nixon in 1972 managed to convey an impression of honest and efficient administration, concealing most of the evidence of spying and corruption until after the election.

2. Incumbents can sometimes manipulate reality, on a temporary basis, so that the voters are pleased at election time. The economy regularly improves in election years. Nixon timed the 1970 recession

—deliberately induced in order to slow inflation—so as to ensure a return to prosperity by 1972. In 1964, Johnson kept his hands clean as the candidate of peace (while displaying "firmness" in the Gulf of Tonkin) even though plans for large-scale American intervention in Vietnam were well advanced. Election year tax cuts, spending sprees, and the like, at which Nixon excelled,[40] can temporarily obscure the state of the economy and blunt the edge of electoral punishment.

Secrecy, false information and the manipulation of reality, then, may reduce public control and thereby permit unequal influence upon policy making by interest groups and politicians. On the other hand, economic reasoning raises some questions about such a conclusion. In the long run, perhaps, voters can be expected to catch on to these tricks, to penetrate falsehoods and to give no credit for illusory gains. Certainly people are harder to fool about conditions that affect them directly than about, say, complex policy questions. Much depends upon the nature of the political market, particularly on whether there are systematic and continuing biases in the acquisition of information; and on how long "the long run" is: whether increasing public alertness actually catches up with reality, or whether politicians are clever enough to invent new tricks which keep them a step ahead and ensure lengthy or permanent disequilibrium of the control system.

3. Divided party government can confuse responsibility and upset the incentive system for politicians. The congressional leadership may find it profitable to sabotage the economy or foreign relations, with the expectation that in our president-centered system, the president of the opposite party will be blamed. Ford complained in 1976 about such sabotage by the Democrats. Or, of course, the president may try the same thing on Congress, as perhaps Truman did in 1948.

4. Failures in foresight by leaders can frustrate the control process. Even if presidents know what results the people want, and try to attain them, they may not know how to do so. Hoover had no Keynesian or post-Keynesian economics to help him figure out what to do about the Depression. Johnson had no idea of the tenacity of the Viet Cong; victory in Vietnam (which—for better or worse—most Americans would have applauded if it had been quick) always seemed just around the corner, and Johnson thought that perseverance would bring the desired results.

Indeed, the very evidence we have cited, showing that Americans punish incumbents in bad times, is also evidence of the *failure* of that part of the electoral punishment model of democracy that involves anticipated reactions. In each case of punishment, the incumbents had failed to bring about the desired results, usually because they could not control events or could not foresee the consequences of their actions. The same leeway for leadership that allows for innovative (even unpopular) measures, for the sake of producing results, also leaves room for error and failure. Of course this should be taken more as a limitation on human knowledge than as a defect of this model of democracy; and again economic reasoning suggests the possibility of movement toward the equilibrium of perfect knowledge by leaders.

It appears, then, that the workings of electoral reward and punishment can, at best, ensure only a rather limited sort of democratic control. It pressures politicians to achieve relative peace and a reasonably balanced economy; to avoid major disasters like unsuccessful wars, civil disorder, or depression. The pressure is not foolproof, and even when it applies there is no guarantee that politicians can perform. But the measure of democratic control achieved in this way is more reliable than that promised by other democratic theories.

Character and the Presentation of Self

In a presidential system like that of the United States, where a single individual is directly elected to the highest office, the personal traits and characteristics of candidates play a critical part in voters' decisions and in the outcome of elections.[1] Electoral choices involve not only what candidates stand for, but also what they *are* or what they seem to be. Political parties give close attention to personality in deciding whom to nominate, and candidates, aided by media specialists, devote much effort to presenting themselves in the best possible light.

This emphasis on matters of personality is somewhat foreign to spatial models of the electoral process, since in this respect the mobility of candidates (and even parties) is not unlimited—they cannot, chameleonlike, appear to be precisely what the voters want at any given moment. It is also foreign to some conventional notions of rationality, in which the voter is seen as entirely policy-oriented. Pursuing our reasoning about the consequences of costly information, however, many personal characteristics of candidates are relevant to skills or styles of governing, and therefore to voters' calculations about what outcome would benefit them most. Indeed it may be that, in an age of nuclear weapons, no aspect of electoral outcomes is more important than the personality of the president, which might well determine how the United States would react in an international confrontation. Moreover, we contend that voters are relatively skillful at judging personal traits; that they can do so at little cost, on the basis of readily available information; and that voting on the basis of candidates' personality can therefore be quite rational.[2]

Parties' and voters' attention to personality also conflicts with the usual policy-focused theories of democracy. Again, however, as in the case of electoral reward and punishment, it is possible to outline a rather different theory of electoral democracy, which is more consistent with observed behavior. This theory, which we will call "selection of a benevolent leader," offers only an attenuated kind of control over government action, but in combination with other processes it can make a significant contribution to popular sovereignty.

In assessing what sorts of people are nominated for president, how candidates present themselves, and what effect this has on voters, we face at the outset the problem of specifying categories. We are concerned here with a broad array of personal traits, from superficial aspects of style, to matters of social and cultural background, to deeply rooted characteristics of individual psychology. To discuss them in a coherent and theoretically grounded way, or even to group them sensibly, requires a general theory—or at least a typology—of style and personality, together with a congruent theory of how persons are perceived. But psychologists are far from agreement on such matters; both theory and evidence are murky.

The approach here is to draw categories from several sources. We begin with the configuration of knowledge, experience, and competence; it is of great political importance, but refers more to skills and abilities than to underlying psychological dispositions. We then turn to three categories—warmth, activity, and strength—which are prominent in certain general theories of personality and person perception. Finally, we discuss some traits such as candor, dignity, and stability, which fall near the boundaries between style and personality and which lack grand theoretical underpinnings but appear to be important in voters' decisions. Also treated is candidates' religion, which can be considered a blend of philosophy, style, and ascriptive status.

Even after the category problem is resolved, there remain, as we will see, a good many uncertainties in measuring candidates' behavior and voters' responses. For all its importance in the electoral process, candidate personality is a topic about which impression and speculation are easier to come by than evidence.

Knowledge, Experience, and Competence

Astronauts, movie stars, and other nonpolitical or antipolitical types have had some startling successes in winning elective office in the United States. For the presidency, however, the American people have generally insisted on leadership experience. Most of the earliest presidents previously served in the executive branch, often as secretary of state; other successful candidates have been governors, senators, and leaders of the House of Representatives. A number of military heroes have also been elected president: Washington, Jackson, W. H. Harrison, Taylor, Grant, Theodore Roosevelt, Eisenhower. In some cases the personal appeal of the hero has enabled a minority (usually conservative) party to win.

Experience generally involves high public visibility—not only name recognition, but concrete information which reduces voters' uncertainty about what sort of president a candidate would be. Beyond that, successful experience may bespeak knowledge of public affairs, and competence at particular aspects of leadership: organizational ability, a talent for persuasion, adeptness at interpersonal relations, and the like. Of course these attributes are not always found together or drawn from the same sorts of experience. Military eminence, for example, ordinarily tells little about knowledge of public policy, but it implies a high level of leadership skills, as well as energy, toughness, and patriotism.

Thus Eisenhower in 1952 was seen not only as the avenger of the "out" party, punishing the incumbents for their failures, but also as a conquering hero who had led the allies to victory over Germany. Eisenhower, in fact, had run one of the largest and most complex organizations in history. In 1947 and 1948 his appeal cut across party lines; indeed, Democrats were more prone than Republicans to favor Eisenhower for president. In 1952, perceptions were colored by party loyalties, with Republicans more favorable than Democrats, but Eisenhower's experience and his qualities of leadership were still heavily

approved by all sorts of voters.[3] His promise to go to Korea carried
real weight because of his experience.

The overriding importance of experience in the public mind gives
a special advantage to incumbent presidents running for reelection.
Other things being equal—that is, so long as times are reasonably
good—people would rather stay with proven leadership than try someone new. As we have noted, most incumbent presidents—Ford in
1976, Nixon in 1972, Johnson in 1964, Eisenhower in 1956, Roosevelt in 1936, 1940 and 1944—have campaigned mainly by "being
president." They continue to meet with foreign dignitaries, to sign bills,
to preside over the executive branch. The pomp and majesty of office
are used for maximum contrast with the lesser known challenger, who
has to scurry about the country after votes. Trips abroad, which draw
media attention and cast the president as representative of all Americans, are particularly helpful: Nixon's trips to Peking and Moscow
in 1972 emphasized his experience and put him in a favorable light.
Foreign policy crises at election time, fortuitous or arranged, also accentuate the president's mastery of the office, and carry with them an
unspoken plea for continuity of leadership. Eisenhower in 1956 and
Johnson in 1964 were clear favorites for reelection without Suez or
Tonkin, but those incidents certainly did not shrink the incumbents'
margins of victory. Nor did the Cuban missile crisis harm the Democrats' congressional vote in 1962.

Some indication of the incumbent's advantage is given by table 27.
In 1956 and 1964, when the SRC (now CPS) asked voters what they
liked and what they disliked about the candidates, there were many
positive references to Eisenhower's and Johnson's general ability and
experience. Fewer voters mentioned these traits in connection with the
challengers, Stevenson and Goldwater, and those who did were nearly
as often negative as positive. The frequent perceptions of Stevenson
as unusually intelligent made up only part of the experience deficit.

Next to an incumbent president or a military hero, a vice-president
has perhaps the greatest advantage in presenting himself as experi-
enced. Richard Nixon and John Kennedy in 1960 give us examples
of how this can be done, and how an opponent can respond.

Nixon, who had served as vice-president under Eisenhower, talked
almost as if he had been the incumbent president. He repeatedly
pointed out the need for "tough," "firm" men who knew the Soviets

Table 27	Incumbency and Evaluations of Experience, 1956 and 1964			
	Eisenhower, 1956		Stevenson	
	Pro	Con	Pro	Con
Experience and ability (codes 010–099)	502	89	167	141
Information, education, intelligence (231, 240)	37	7	115	8
Total responses	1320	789	794	862
	Johnson, 1964		Goldwater	
	Pro	Con	Pro	Con
Experience and ability (codes 010–099)	373	30	45	44
Information, education, intelligence (231, 240)	34	6	9	18
Total responses	1153	687	619	1113

Entries are numbers of respondents who mentioned a given trait in their first responses to open-ended questions concerning what they liked or disliked about each candidate.

and wouldn't be taken in by them. Again and again he asserted that he and his running mate, Henry Cabot Lodge, were such men:

Both Cabot Lodge and I have been part of that record. For 7½ years we have worked with the President of the United States. We have sat in the meetings of the Cabinet. We have sat in the meetings of the National Security Council. I have participated in the discussions on the great decisions on Quemoy and Matsu and Lebanon and the others that the President has made during these last 7½ years. And you know the record of Cabot Lodge in the United Nations.[4]

Nixon frequently referred to his travels—the fact that he had represented the president and the American people in fifty-five countries abroad. He took particular pleasure in recounting his recent tour of Poland.

. . . on that Sunday afternoon there were a quarter of a million Poles on the streets of Warsaw. They were cheering, as you have cheered tonight, but they were doing more than that. They were shouting at the top of their voices, "Niech Zyje America"—"Long

live America"—and then when the cars stopped in the middle of the
town, they threw flowers into our car, hundreds and hundreds of
bouquets of flowers, and I looked into their faces, and lots of them
were smiling and laughing, in joy, but over half of them, men and
women, grown men and women, were crying, with tears streaming
down their cheeks.[5]

Although Nixon attributed this reception to the Poles' love for
American moral and spiritual ideals, rather than to his own fame,
the anecdote had the effect of emphasizing his foreign policy experience and his role as representative of America, as well as associating
him with cheers and flowers.

The main thrust of Nixon's claim was that he and Lodge had had
specific experience that would be useful in dealing with that "ruthless,
fanatical man, whose object is not Quemoy and Matsu . . . but the
world"—Nikita Khrushchev. Nixon reminded listeners of the "kitchen
debate" in Moscow. He asserted ". . . we have been tried. We have
been tested. We have been through the fire of dealing with this man
and his colleagues."

> We both know Mr. Khrushchev. We both have sat down across
> the conference table from him. We both have had the opportunity to
> know what kind of man he is, that he is ruthless, that he does not
> follow the rules of the game that people in the free world would
> follow. . . . There will be no woolly, fuzzy, softheaded thinking
> about Mr. Khrushchev in this next administration.[6]

Implicit in Nixon's praise of himself and Lodge was criticism of Kennedy as inexperienced. On occasion, particularly toward the end of
the campaign, the contrast was made explicit. Claiming that Kennedy's
domestic program ignored economic realities by promising benefits
without increased taxes or inflation, Nixon likened Kennedy to a
"Pied Piper," or a "modern day medicine man": only an "economic
ignoramus" could make such promises. He referred to Kennedy's
"innocent, little boy manner." On foreign policy—especially Quemoy
and Matsu—he accused Kennedy of "shooting from the hip," "talking
off the top of his head." The Democrats, he asserted, were offering
"[u]ntried, rash, impulsive leadership." If Kennedy had been president
at the time of the crises over Quemoy and Matsu, or Cuba, because
of his inexperience "he would have made a fatal error that might have
led to war or surrender of territory or both."

Thus, in 1960, John Kennedy had a problem. Neither his Senate career nor his brief run for the vice-presidential nomination in 1956 had brought him anything like the national renown resulting from Nixon's service as vice-president and his foreign travels. Kennedy's youthful appearance did not help. In mid-1960 a Gallup poll showed substantial pluralities of Americans preferring Nixon over Kennedy for dealing with Russia's leaders, keeping the United States out of World War III, and representing the United States at the next summit meeting.[7]

Kennedy dealt with this discrepancy in several ways. At times, he approached the subject lightly. Speaking of Nixon: "I do not believe that this is the kind of experience this Nation will want to reward with the White House. As Otto Kerner can tell you, no judge is impressed by the experience of a driver whose record is full of accidents." Or: "The big news story of the past 7 days was not Mr. Khrushchev or the presidential campaign; it was the news out of Boston that Mr. Ted Williams had retired as an active ballplayer for the Boston Red Sox. It seems that at 42 he was too old. It does show that perhaps experience doesn't count."

More seriously, Kennedy made it a major task of his campaign to convey an impression of expertise and knowledge, particularly in foreign affairs. Just as Nixon relied on his ties with the Eisenhower administration, so Kennedy identified himself with great statesmen of the past: with Lincoln, who, Kennedy said, had also faced a time of crisis; with Churchill, who in Missouri warned against Soviet strength and intentions; with Theodore Roosevelt, who "met the issues." One or more of their names appeared in practically every speech.

Kennedy also mentioned his own experience on the subcommittee on Africa of the Senate Foreign Relations Committee, and his work on area redevelopment legislation and other specific domestic programs—often referring to Democratic originators or backers as "we."

In order to lend more weight to his analyses of foreign affairs, Kennedy invoked many authorities. On the insignificance of Quemoy and Matsu, he cited Secretary of State Christian Herter, General Ridgway, General Collins, Admiral Spruance, John Foster Dulles, General Maxwell Taylor and even President Eisenhower, as all agreeing with his judgment and disagreeing with Nixon's. Similarly, on U.S. military vulnerability and the existence of a "missile gap," he cited the Gaither

Committee report to President Eisenhower; the Rockefeller Brothers'
report and Nelson Rockefeller himself; Robert Lovett; Robert Sprague;
Lieutenant General James Gavin; General Maxwell Taylor; and the
American Legion.

Kennedy frequently demonstrated his knowledge by rattling off a
barrage of facts. His discussions of past performance (though not of
future policy) were unusually detailed. He would list Democratic
accomplishments—the Social Security Act, minimum wage laws, the
FHA, the REA, guaranteed bank deposits, TVA—even when his audiences could not be expected to be familiar with all the alphabetical
agencies. He gave lengthy accounts of Democratic bills and Republican vetoes, on depressed areas, farm price supports, pollution control
and the like. He listed countries or regions of the world (especially
Africa) as posing particular problems. He recounted the details of
specific incidents in foreign policy, such as a minor foul-up in a U.S.
invitation for a visit by African students.

Kennedy's favorite device for conveying an image of expertise was
the citation of statistics:

> Under Governor Williams' leadership, you here in Michigan have
> moved promptly to take advantage of the meager benefits for the
> elderly under new Federal legislation. But the Federal program is
> wholly inadequate—in Michigan it will cover only 60,000 new
> people, only one-seventh of the number that would have been cov-
> ered under the Democratic bill that tied medical care to social
> security without a pauper's oath.
>
> Here in Michigan you have led the Nation in your educational
> programs. But you are still short an estimated 10,000 classrooms
> and 7,000 fully certified teachers. And every year tens of thousands
> of new children are entering your public schools. . . .
>
> Ten years ago we in the United States graduated 52,000 engineers
> from our universities while the Russians graduated 28,000. Last
> year they graduated 106,000, more than twice as many as our
> 47,000.[8]

In the televised "Great Debates," Kennedy mentioned facts and numbers much more often than Nixon did. His display of virtuousity was
made possible in part by a cram session, using flash cards provided by
his Harvard brain trust.[9] Kennedy, aided also by his vigorous appearance and Nixon's makeup problems, was widely seen as having done

a better job in the debates, especially the first; his image of expertise improved markedly, and a number of doubtful voters were converted to his cause.[10]

By election day, Kennedy had made up much of the experience deficit. To be sure, in the SRC open-ended questions asking why people liked or disliked the candidates, Nixon's experience (particularly in foreign affairs) was mentioned very often and very positively. In fact, of all the positive comments about Nixon, covering party and issues as well as personal characteristics, almost exactly half concerned his experience and ability. He got very few (about one-eighth as many) negative mentions of that type. Positive comments on Kennedy's experience and ability were less frequent and were nearly balanced by negative feelings about his inexperience. But many voters saw Kennedy as "intelligent," "well educated," or "well informed." These comments were overwhelmingly positive, and greatly outnumbered comparable perceptions of Nixon (see table 28).

When government performance has been poor, of course, incumbency gives no advantage (see chapter 7); experience in federal government may be a hindrance. In 1976, when many people were cynical about government institutions, Jimmy Carter made a virtue of inexperience: he ran as an "anti-Washington" candidate, an outsider

Table 28	Evaluations of Candidates' Knowledge and Experience, 1960			
	Kennedy		Nixon	
	Pro	Con	Pro	Con
Experience and ability (codes 010–099)	179	121	485	37
Information, education, intelligence (230, 231, 240)	162	3	53	11
Domestic experience and ability (410–411)	0	0	3	0
Foreign policy experience and ability (601)	2	18	111	34
Total responses	1136	1022	1188	770

Entries are numbers of respondents who mentioned a given trait in their first responses to four open-ended questions concerning what they liked or disliked about each candidate.

untainted by any service in the nation's capital. At the same time, however, Carter—like Kennedy before him—had to establish his own skills and qualifications. This he did by citing his accomplishments as Georgia governor; by pointing to his scientific and technical skills, and emphasizing the need for efficiency in government; and (like Kennedy) by quoting statistics and displaying detailed knowledge of facts.

Carter's autobiography, *Why Not the Best?*, was a carefully designed campaign document. In discussing his early life on his family's farm, it devoted much space to the technical details of farming: just what crops were planted when, how they were cultivated and harvested, what prices they brought.[11] After the reader had absorbed Carter's accounts of making cane syrup, mopping cotton against boll weevils, and plowing with mules, he was likely to be convinced that young Jimmy was a diligent lad and that Carter had a good grasp of farming techniques and an excellent memory for detail.

The autobiography also recounted Carter's achievements at Annapolis as an eager student of gunnery, seamanship, navigation, astronomy, engineering and naval tactics, and his training at New London in the intricacies of submarines. Carter wrote proudly of his selection for the nuclear submarine program, especially the interview with Hyman Rickover which produced the title of the book, and he noted his study of mathematics, nuclear physics, and reactor technology.

The autobiography described how, after leaving the navy, Carter rapidly updated his knowledge of farming, and how, as a freshman state senator, speed-reading techniques enabled him to keep a campaign promise and read every one of the 800–1,000 bills he voted on, often spotting technical errors and mistakes. It mentioned his part in a county planning and development commission, and his meticulous organization of the successful campaign for governor. It emphasized his achievement, as governor, of reorganizing the Georgia state administration—abolishing 278 of 300 agencies, centralizing the computer systems, rewarding employee suggestions which led to savings, making bank deposits by competitive bid.

In his campaign speech making, Carter continued to stress these themes of skill, experience, and competence. He frequently referred to himself as "a farmer, an engineer, a planner, a businessman, a nuclear physicist, a naval officer. . . ." He underlined his commitment to efficiency: the party platform should emphasize the need for "a *streamlined, efficient* government, without the incredible red tape, duplication, and overlapping of functions which has hamstrung the effectiveness of government and deprived the American people of the benefits of many of its programs." He called for zero-based budgeting, long-term planning budgets, reducing the number of federal agencies, increased program evaluation, and a policy making machinery that transcended narrow perspectives.

Using Kennedy's technique, Carter demonstrated his knowledge of government by citing statistics. This was most impressive in the televised debates, when he spoke without notes. In the first debate Carter declared:

> The present tax structure is a disgrace to this country. It's just a welfare program for the rich. As a matter of fact, 25 percent of the total tax deductions go for only 1 percent of the richest people in this country, and over 50 percent of the tax credits go for the 14 percent of the richest people in this country. . . . And in January of 1975, [Ford] asked for . . . a $5.6 billion increase on low- and middle-income private individuals, a $6.5 billion decrease on the corporations and the special interests. In December of 1975 he vetoed the roughly $18 to $20 billion tax reduction bill that had been passed by the Congress and then he came back later on in January of this year and he did advocate a $10 billion tax reduction, but it would be offset by a $6 billion increase this coming January in deductions for Social Security payments and for unemployment compensation.[12]

In condemning the Republicans' economic performance, too, Carter packed his indictment with facts and figures.

> . . . We had last year a $65 billion deficit—the largest deficit in the history of our country—more of a deficit spending than we had in the entire eight-year period under President Johnson and President Kennedy.
> We've got 500,000 more Americans out of jobs today than were out of work three months ago and since Mr. Ford's been in office in two years, we've had a 50 percent increase in unemployment from five million people out of work to 2½ million more people out of work and a total of 7½ million.[13]

While some viewers may have lost the point in these outpourings of statistics, Carter did succeed in removing much of the bite from charges of ignorance or inexperience. The Ford campaign, worried about the intelligence issue, began advertising the president's standing in his Yale Law School class.

Warmth

While experience, competence and knowledge are uniquely relevant to qualifications for leadership, warmth and its opposite, coldness (or positivity and negativity), are more general characteristics, basic to human personality and to the way in which all people are perceived. Psychologists have found, using factor-analytic techniques, that positivity/negativity, together with activity/passivity and strength/weakness, constitute the major dimensions along which people and other objects are perceived and evaluated.[14] The same dimensions are central to some typologies of human personality.[15]

Ambiguity is inherent in the category "warmth"—a quality which could refer to a person's feelings about himself, about other people, or about his job. The three need not be the same. A man can be highly warm and positive about people and yet feel ambivalence toward politics or the presidency, as Eisenhower did; or one can enjoy the powers of the presidency but be uncertain or negative about people, as Nixon was.

At the same time, as James David Barber has suggested, different sorts of warmth or positivity tend to cluster together and to be seen as one. A man who has high regard for people often feels happy about his work and about himself. In Barber's view, warmth and positivity are not immune to events—failure can sour the sweetest disposition—but they are rather deeply rooted in psychological development. Abundant affection received in childhood tends to produce high self-esteem throughout the individual's life. The full acceptance of self then frees emotional energy for affection toward people and enthusiasm about activities.

Be that as it may, Americans generally seek personal warmth in their presidents, and most especially so after traumatic times of civil discord or foreign failure. Then they want reassurance and normalcy, they want the president to "bring us together." There may perhaps have been times when the public mood was receptive to a cool, aloof president like Calvin Coolidge, for the sake of legitimacy; the Eugene

McCarthy appeal in 1968 partook of this quality. As best we can tell
from the survey evidence of recent years, however, most Americans
most of the time want warmth and emotional out-goingness in their
chief executive.

Voters have good cause to seek positivity in their leaders, not
merely for symbolic reassurance, but for the instrumental reason that
a president who cares about his fellow citizens is more likely to carry
out policies that benefit them. In addition, it is sometimes argued that
high self-esteem and positivity are important aspects of emotional
health; that individuals with flawed self-esteem, like Richard Nixon
and Woodrow Wilson, have compulsive tendencies which lead to rigid
behavior; and that the election of such men to the presidency can
bring unsuccessful and even disastrous administrations.[16]

In any event, both parties try to find men who have warmth and
positivity. The supply of politicians with desirable traits is limited,
however, and chance plays a part in what choices the electorate is
actually offered. Certainly it is an enormous stroke of luck to the party
and/or country when either party can come up with a genuinely be-
loved and loving personality.

A classic example is Dwight Eisenhower. "I Like Ike" in 1952 and
1956 came to mean that people really cared about their hero, and
thought he cared about them. Much of this relationship was visual and
verbal: cold print cannot convey the effect of that enormous, ear-to-
ear grin, and the warm feeling it inspired that America was in good
hands. In the SRC election surveys, voters do not often explicitly
mention candidates' warmth or coldness; instead, perceptions of those
qualities spill over into other traits including "sincerity." Nineteen
fifty-six, however, was exceptional; more than one-tenth of all the
many positive comments about Eisenhower concerned his warmth
and likeability (see table 29).

Franklin Roosevelt, too, gave an impression of really caring about
the "forgotten man," the ordinary citizen. His fireside chats, his tours
among the people, and his speeches projected warmth toward everyone but the "malefactors of great wealth." Jimmy Carter in 1976
spoke often of "love" and "compassion," and of his "intimate" relationships with people of all sorts, including blacks. Few have matched
Eisenhower or Roosevelt, but most presidential candidates—at least
those subsequent to Coolidge and Hoover—have displayed warmth

and friendliness in one way or another: Gerald Ford, in the manner of a kind, earnest neighbor; Lyndon Johnson (before the bitterness of Vietnam) with gusto; John Kennedy, engagingly, while retaining a degree of aristocratic aloofness; Harry Truman, being just plain folks. Much of American political campaigning, with its smiling, handshaking, and baby kissing, and with festive crowds and music, is an exercise in demonstrating the candidates' warmth and personal appeal.

Table 29	Evaluations of Candidates' Warmth and Likability, 1956 and 1968			
	Eisenhower, 1956		Stevenson	
	Pro	Con	Pro	Con
Likability, warmth (codes 301–312)	155	2	26	89
Total responses	1320	789	794	862
	Nixon, 1968		Humphrey	
	Pro	Con	Pro	Con
Likability, warmth (codes 301–312)	28	45	37	41
Total responses	839	855	775	944

Entries are numbers of respondents who mentioned a given trait in their first responses to open-ended questions concerning what they liked or disliked about each candidate.

Hubert Humphrey, although widely known as a "happy warrior," did not wholly succeed in conveying the right impression to voters in 1968. He may have appeared promiscuous by lavishing affection on all audiences, and he occasionally sounded frantic or hysterical. Moreover, Humphrey's determined joyousness could be seen as inappropriate to grave and unhappy times. Nixon cruelly played upon this contrast by running a TV spot which showed arguments at the Democratic convention and flaming riots in the streets, with shots of Humphrey and background music of "Hot Time in the Old Town Tonight." The ad then pictured GIs under fire and a blasted battlefield, and a long close-up of Humphrey laughing; then a poor Appalachian farmer and distorted pictures of Humphrey's face, with the "Hot Time" music again.[17] As table 29 indicates, Humphrey did not make a very positive impression with respect to warmth.

On the other hand, however, when candidates appear cold, they tend to suffer at the polls. George McGovern had a flat, unemotional speaking tone and an undemonstrative manner; he did not project a great deal of warmth. Nor did Adlai Stevenson, with his emotional restraint and urbane wit (see table 29).

The great exception to any claim that warmth is a necessary condition for getting elected president is Richard Nixon; even at his most exuberant, few would accuse him of having a radiant personality. Nixon exemplifies the efforts that can be made to engineer a personal image, but also the limits to success at image making when the raw materials are lacking.

When Nixon's pollsters told him that he was doing poorly on the "warm/cold" semantic differential scale in 1968, his public relations people tried to do something about it. Professional writers injected some humor. Nixon was placed in informal, apparently unstaged situations—such as regional TV shows with carefully selected panels of citizens—where he would answer questions live and achieve a conversational tone in interacting with people. Film clips of spontaneous casualness were sought; "rich, warm advertising," with colored pictures of Nixon's family, was recommended for women's magazines; films of Nixon's motorcade in Chicago (where the Democrats had had their divisive convention and bloody demonstrations) were used to show Nixon as a unifying hero, the man to heal all wounds. But all to little avail. As one of Nixon's PR men remarked, "Let's face it, a lot of people think Nixon is dull. Think he's a bore, a pain in the ass. They look at him as the kind of kid who always carried a bookbag."[18] Nixon got elected, but the voters never saw him as warm, friendly, or likeable (see table 29).

Activity

A president's level of activity and physical energy is a dimension upon which the preferences of the public apparently vary at different times. To be sure, the idea of a completely inert president is absurd, and in the late twentieth century a president even as passive as, say, Harding or Coolidge is scarcely conceivable. Given the huge size of the gov-

ernment, its deep involvement in the economy, and the fast pace of
foreign policy, a president would have to be rather active merely to
ensure peace and quiet. Still, the American people are more eager
for action at some times than at others. Indeed, a case can be made
that there are periods when Americans want an active government
and an active president; they elect one; then—especially if the activity
leads to war abroad or trouble at home—people grow tired and seek
more tranquil times; a relatively passive president is elected; but after
a period of quiet there grows a sense of unease that problems aren't
being solved; so the public seeks an active presidency, and the cycle
begins again.

It is not easy to prove that such cycles occur; if they do, they do not
necessarily have any simple mechanical cause or any uniform peri-
odicity. But observers have long noted ebbs and flows in the activity
of the U.S. government. It is not unreasonable to point to the 1910s,
1930s, 1940s, and the early 1960s—when activists Woodrow Wilson,
Franklin Roosevelt, Harry Truman, John Kennedy, and Lyndon Johnson were winning votes—as times when most Americans wanted action; and to the 1920s, 1950s, and the late 1960s and early 1970s—
represented by the relatively passive Harding, Coolidge, Hoover, Eisenhower, Nixon and Ford—as times when Americans wanted a return to quiet and normalcy. It is particularly striking that an activist
foreign policy and costly wars—World War I, Korea, and Vietnam—
preceded each period of passivity, and that even the relatively successful World War II cut away at the activist majority in 1948.

The argument, in other words, is that this particular characteristic
of presidential candidates resonates (or fails to resonate) with a shifting mood of the public; and that the mood itself shifts in response
to political events which themselves result, in part, from the consequences of a previous mood.

Activism in an individual is partly a matter of psychological and
physiological makeup. It is often found, along with warmth and positivity, in the creative, outgoing personality that Barber calls "active
positive," and is said to blossom when a child receives a judicious mixture of parental affection and ambition. According to Barber, energy
and activism can also take a compulsive or "active negative" form,
in compensation for low self-esteem inflicted by childhood traumas.[19]

At the same time, however, it is obvious that in any translation

from personal energy level to the level of government activity, not
only character but also world view or political philosophy plays a
part. Richard Nixon, whether healthy or compulsive or a little of each,
was undeniably an active personality; the same must be said of Herbert Hoover. Yet each, in office, in accord with a philosophy of individualism and limited government, devoted much energy to *reducing*
government activity. Hoover tried to combat the Depression with min-
imal federal involvement; Nixon attempted to return much domestic
policy-making power to the states and localities, and (through an activist foreign policy) to cut back American involvement in Southeast
Asia and ease the Cold War.

It is also clear that differences in the activist/restraint aspect of
political philosophy are linked to differences between the political
parties. At least since the election of Woodrow Wilson and the de-
fection from the Republicans of Theodore Roosevelt, the Democrats
have tended to greater federal government activism, in both foreign
and domestic affairs, and the Republicans to more limited government.
The presidential candidates of each party (perhaps in personality; certainly in philosophy) have tended to reflect these differences. Thus on
the activity dimension voters have often been presented with rather
clear choices, related to party cleavages on policy.

During much of the twentieth century the party alternations in
power can be understood largely in terms of the ebb and flow of
activism. Often enough to suggest more than coincidence, the Democratic interventionism which led to domestic prosperity, when applied
to foreign affairs led the United States into war; the Republican restraint which was then sought for disengagement and peace abroad,
also led sometimes to recession and depression at home. The popular
image of the Democrats as the "party of war" and the Republicans as
the "party of depression" contained more than a little truth, and left
voters with something less than ideal alternatives. Their response was
to fluctuate between foreign and domestic trouble. The evaluations of
past performance which we discussed in chapter 7 have interlocked,
therefore, with the political philosophies of the parties, the personalities and views of their candidates, and with cycles of activism.

Few candidates try directly to communicate abstract ideas of political philosophy. Instead, the dimension of activism, with its complicated mixture of policy, philosophy, and personality, is usually mani-

fested in slogans, in discussion of particular goals and problems, and in the personal campaign style of the candidate. Harding's front porch campaign, and his refusal to dash about the country—together with the explicit promise of "normalcy"—signaled a relatively passive administration. The energetic whistle-stopping of a Truman or a Kennedy (or, for that matter, of a Bryan or a Wilson) foreshadowed activism. It was the Democrats, after all, who invented active campaigning for the presidency.

A particularly interesting example is that of John Kennedy, who in 1960 projected an image of great vigor and energy. In doing so he turned his youth—which we saw was a handicap on the experience dimension—into an advantage. Kennedy looked and acted young and vigorous. He had a boyish lock of hair and a handsome, youthful face. He moved quickly and spoke rapidly and crisply, making chopping gestures with his arms to accentuate points.

In his rhetoric Kennedy emphasized activity. His speeches were filled with assertions that the country (or "we") must "move ahead," must "move forward," "do better," "get America moving again." On election eve, for example, in Boston's Faneuil Hall, Kennedy summed up his view of the meaning of the election. After invoking Lincoln's 1860 campaign, he said:

> Now, 100 years later, the question is, will the world exist half slave and half free, or will it move in the direction of freedom? Or will it move in the direction of slavery?
>
> I believe it will move in the direction of freedom. And I believe that this is especially true if we here in the United States begin to move again.
>
> The challenge of 1960, of 1961, 1962, 1963 and 1964 is whether or not the people of the United States are determined to move forward again; to build a stronger, more progressive, more vigorous society. . . .
>
> You must make your judgment between sitting and moving.
>
> This is a race . . . between the comfortable and the concerned. Those who are willing to sit and lie at anchor and those who want to go forward.[20]

Kennedy's frequent calls for sacrifice, for help, for us to ask what we could do for our country, contributed to his image as an active leader who would move the country and its people. So did his refer-

ences to the "energy and vitality and purpose" of the Roosevelt and
Wilson administrations; to the need to revive the "zeal" of Democratic legislative pioneers; and to the need for "courage and dedication," "hard work and sacrifice," that would be required on the New
Frontier.

Kennedy's campaign also illustrates the fact that candidates can try
to create or at least accentuate public desires for particular personal
characteristics, by the way in which they articulate goals and point out
problems. Kennedy's talk about foreign threats and domestic drift implied that the United States had not been moving, and was in trouble
as a result. This argument was designed to set the stage for, to create
demand for, a vigorous actor like himself.[21] For analytic convenience
we have treated policy stands, personal characteristics, and the rhetoric of goals, problems, and past performance in separate chapters;
but this should not be allowed to obscure the relations among them.
They are often integrated in coherent packages, so that each appeal
reinforces the others.

Strength

A cluster of traits almost universally desired in leaders is strength, decisiveness, and potency. These seem to be rather fundamental aspects
of personality, which develop early in life; whether for cultural or ge-
netic reasons, they have historically been associated with masculinity.

The desire for strength in presidents is a reasonable one: this is a
hard world, and any leader without strength is likely to get trampled
in the crush and to find himself unable to maintain peace or order, let
alone progress. Both parties try to come up with strong candidates,
and if one is unable to do so, it tends to lose.

Franklin Roosevelt in a unique way epitomized strength. He had
conquered polio, and had risen from paralysis to lead a state and then
the nation. He was sufficiently self-confident in his strength that he
could make public appearances in a wheelchair, and accept the help
of other men in moving about, or getting to the podium, with every
sign of cheerfulness. A man who could overcome such a physical dis-
ability might be expected to overcome the Depression. If he said there
was nothing to fear but fear itself, people could believe it.

Potency takes many forms. With Lyndon Johnson, it was the "John-

son treatment"—overpowering physical presence and pressing of flesh
that cowed senators and underlings into submission; there were ninety-
miles-an-hour beer-drinking automobile chases on the ranch; there
were wild forays in foreign policy. With Nixon, it was lashing out at
enemies abroad, as in the Cambodia invasion designed to avoid seeming a "pitiful, helpless giant"; there were plans to "screw" enemies at
home. With Eisenhower, there was a facade of benign befuddlement
(concealing a determination to get his way), while Joseph McCarthy
ran out of steam, Richard Nixon tried to prove himself, and the Democratic congress writhed in futility. Even the affable Gerald Ford refused to be pushed around by Congress. Whatever the variations in
style, it is hard to name a recent American president who did not try
to dominate all he surveyed.

Not so with some unsuccessful candidates. Adlai Stevenson, his
manner intellectual and urbane, and his shoes in need of repair, could
be seen as somehow flippant and ineffectual; his divorce could be interpreted as showing failure as a husband and father, two roles in
which strength is paramount. In 1968 Hubert Humphrey found it hard
to convince the public of his independence from the authority figure
for whom he was vice-president, Lyndon Johnson.

The clearest case in which Americans perceived lack of strength in
a candidate was in 1972, when George McGovern was widely seen as
weak, indecisive, and inconsistent. One source of this perception was
McGovern's diffident speaking manner. Another was his shifting on
the issues, which fed into a perception of inconsistency. While the
changes were not many or great (see chapter 5), the high expectations
set by his claim of candor, together with other, unrelated evidences
of weakness, made them seem important. It was in the management
of his campaign, however, and particularly in the Eagleton affair, that
McGovern most notably failed to display strength or decisiveness. The
Eagleton matter deserves some detailed attention, because it illustrates
the interplay of reality with behavioral clues, public relations efforts,
and media scrutiny in affecting voters' perceptions of candidates'
character.

Thomas Eagleton had been selected as McGovern's running mate in
a hurry because of convention time pressures and the belatedly abandoned hope that Edward Kennedy would accept the job. Despite some
rumors about alcoholism or mental illness, Eagleton passed a cursory

background check, and did not volunteer any damaging information about himself when asked. Shortly after his nomination, however, (apparently with encouragement from the Nixon campaign) the rumors increased in intensity; when confronted with them, Eagleton eventually acknowledged to McGovern's staff that he had three times been hospitalized (in 1960, 1964, and 1966) for nervous exhaustion and depression, and on two of those occasions had undergone electro-shock therapy.[22]

On Friday, July 21, while on a plane bound for his postconvention vacation at Sylvan Lake Lodge, South Dakota, McGovern learned that Eagleton had confirmed the rumors. Apparently he was little concerned at the time; he reserved decision until the following week, when Eagleton was to come to South Dakota, and in the interim he made friendly references to Eagleton on the television program *Face the Nation.*

Tuesday morning, July 25, the Eagletons breakfasted in the McGovern's cabin, along with Frank Mankiewicz and Richard Dougherty and two members of Eagleton's staff. Eagleton reviewed his medical history and offered to resign from the ticket. McGovern did not accept the resignation, or ask for time to decide, but quickly told Eagleton he would stand by him.

The public received its first clear impression about the matter at a joint news conference held that same day. (Because the Knight newspapers were about to print the facts, something had to be said.) Eagleton made a statement outlining his hospitalizations and, under questioning, mentioned the electro-shock treatments. He claimed to be currently, and for the past six years, in "good, solid, sound health." McGovern spoke up twice, rather extravagantly, on Eagleton's behalf:

> . . . As far as I am concerned, there is no member of that Senate who is any sounder in mind, body and spirit than Tom Eagleton. I am fully satisfied and if I had known every detail that we discussed this morning . . . he still would have been my choice for Vice President. . . .
> Well, I think Tom Eagleton is fully qualified in mind, body and spirit to be the Vice President of the United States and, if necessary, to take on the Presidency at a moment's notice. . . . I know fully the whole case history of his illness . . . nor would I have any hesitance at all trusting the U.S. government to his hands. I

wouldn't have hesitated one moment if I had known everything Senator Eagleton said here today.[23]

Eagleton flew off to Los Angeles and Hawaii, determined to stay on the ticket and confident that McGovern would stand by him. His determination was reinforced by sympathetic crowds and by an unproved (and grudgingly retracted) Jack Anderson column alleging an arrest for drunk driving.

Immediately, however, there was an intensely negative reaction to Eagleton, much greater than McGovern had anticipated, especially among regular Democrats. McGovern's finance chairman complained publicly that contributions were drying up. A flood of alarmed phone calls and telegrams poured in.

On Wednesday, the day following the press conference, McGovern's press secretary, Dougherty—after getting into some trouble over the word "now"—declared for McGovern, "He's standing firm with Eagleton. Period!" But McGovern quickly saw that his initial whole-hearted support for Eagleton had been an error, and on the same day he told an AP reporter that he was waiting to see what the public reaction would be. When that story appeared, however, McGovern switched again; he denied it categorically and insisted that he was "a thousand per cent" behind Tom Eagleton.

The "thousand per cent" statement, besides evoking unfortunate memories of the $1,000 welfare plan, locked McGovern even further into an untenable position. By the next morning, Thursday, McGovern had told his staff that Eagleton would have to go but that he would continue to support him publicly until the matter could be resolved. There followed an agonizing series of hints that Eagleton should go (hoping to prompt a resignation), and denials that any such thing was on his mind. Mankiewicz quipped that Eagleton support had dropped to 400 percent. On Friday McGovern had a private interview with Jules Witcover, who wrote in the *Los Angeles Times* that McGovern had decided Eagleton should leave the ticket. That evening McGovern arranged to drop by the tables of a number of reporters at the Sylvan Lake Lodge, and discussed his worries about Eagleton's health, about possible effects on the autumn election, and about the question of Eagleton's candor at the Miami convention. The reporters' stories naturally contrasted this with the "thousand per cent" of two days before.

Eagleton refused to take the hints, in part, perhaps, because in their
telephone conversations McGovern never directly asked him to withdraw, and kept reassuring him of his support. On Sunday, the same
day that—at McGovern's request—Democratic Chairman Jean West-
wood declared on national television that it would be "the noble
thing" for Eagleton to step down, Eagleton was also on television
asserting his intention to stay and claiming McGovern's backing.

Finally, on Monday, July 31, McGovern flew to Washington and
confronted Eagleton in person, insisting, after some two hours of argument, that Eagleton resign. Even then, McGovern gave in to Eagleton's demand that in their joint statements, McGovern should say,

> I am fully satisfied that his health is excellent. I base that con-
> clusion upon my conversations with his doctors and my close per-
> sonal and political association with him.
> In the joint decision we have reached health was not a factor.[24]

Rather, McGovern said, Eagleton was resigning in order not to divert
national attention from the great issues that needed to be discussed.

One might attribute the whole debacle to a betrayal by Eagleton,
in first concealing his medical history and then clinging to the vice-
presidential nomination despite everything. Or one might attribute it
to McGovern's compassion and (conceivably, as some McGovern staf-
fers claim) to a humane silence if he belatedly learned that Eagleton's
health was less sound than even Eagleton thought. Or perhaps it was
simply miserable luck. But what is certain is that the affair conveyed
an impression that McGovern was indecisive, weak, and incapable of
making a tough decision and sticking to it. The initial decision to back
Eagleton seemed hasty and emotional; the hemming and hawing looked
weak and underhanded; and the final retreat (since "health was not a
factor") looked like simple expediency, so that McGovern's image
of candor and dedication to principle, as well as that of strength,
suffered enormously.

Some voters no doubt remembered Eisenhower's quite different
reaction when Nixon's "secret fund" was revealed in 1952: by silence
and geographical separation he dissociated himself from the problem,
and declared that Nixon would have to prove himself "clean as a
hound's tooth" if he wanted to stay on the ticket. Only after the
Checkers speech won public support did Eisenhower welcome Nixon
back into the fold. Similarly, Fred Dutton is said to have remarked

about Eagleton that "If he'd pulled this on a Kennedy, we'd find his body at the base of a cliff in the morning."

McGovern's reaction to the Eagleton affair seemed to confirm the meaning of several lesser incidents. Doubts about his strength and candor that had arisen with his vacillation over the $1,000 welfare proposal and other issues in the spring were reinforced by his symbolic flirtation with Chicago's Mayor Daley and other regulars while denying change; by the sacrifice of the women's South Carolina challenge, and denials of the sacrifice; by the private offer and then withdrawal of the party chairmanship to Lawrence O'Brien and the abandonment of Pierre Salinger as vice-chairman; and finally by his treatment of Eagleton.

After Eagleton's resignation, the press and opponents were quick to seize upon any further signs of ineffectuality or confusion in the McGovern campaign, and such signs were not lacking. The search for a vice-presidential replacement involved a humiliating sequence of six public refusals by leading Democrats, until Sargent Shriver took up the burden. Shortly thereafter McGovern was trapped into a series of "corrections" after he denied that he had sent Salinger to Paris to talk with North Vietnamese representatives. With morale low the campaign was plagued by staff leaks to the press (calling O'Brien's campaign position "purely honorary," for example, just after McGovern had emphasized its importance), backbiting, and resignations, all contributing to the impression that McGovern could not control even his own staff.

The SRC/CPS open-ended responses for 1972 show frequent, and overwhelmingly negative, perceptions of McGovern as weak, indecisive, and inconsistent. This was unusual; in most elections, neither strength nor its absence is much mentioned. The Eagleton affair, too, was often specifically referred to. Nixon was still seen as "tricky," dishonest, or insincere by a number of voters; but McGovern was thought insincere by nearly as many as cited his much proclaimed candor (see table 30).

Honesty, Dignity, Stability, Religion

A variety of other personal traits and characteristics, many of them interrelated, enter into voters' evaluations of presidential candidates.

We have already touched upon candor and sincerity as they relate to strength: contradictions and indecisiveness suggest dishonesty as well as weakness. Barry Goldwater scored very high on candor, especially at the outset of his campaign. (Why should he say the things he did unless he really believed them?) Similarly, George McGovern began

Table 30	Evaluations of Candidates' Strength and Candor, 1972			
	Nixon		McGovern	
	Pro	Con	Pro	Con
Strength, decisiveness (codes 303, 304)	16	3	8	143
Honesty, sincerity (401, 402)	54	92	65	60
Total responses	877	607	500	885

Entries are numbers of respondents who mentioned a given trait in their first responses to four open-ended questions concerning what they liked or disliked about each candidate.

in January 1971 by stating a lofty purpose: "The kind of campaign I intend to run will rest on candor and reason. . . . For my part, I make one pledge above all others—to seek and speak the truth with all the resources of mind and spirit I command."[25] The last line, pledging to seek and speak the truth, was used as a motto on campaign stationery until about the time of the Democratic convention. McGovern's early policy proposals, detailed and unorthodox, seemed to confirm his forthrightness, but the Eagleton affair virtually destroyed that impression; voters' reactions were all the more harsh because of high hopes.

Personal morality forms a somewhat distinct dimension. Americans obviously don't want venal or corrupt presidents; the problem comes in ferreting out this kind of dishonesty. Lyndon Johnson was mistrusted by some in 1964 because of his association with unsavory characters like Billie Sol Estes and Bobby Baker, as well as the quick fortune he had made in the government-regulated television business. But voters had no idea in 1972 of Nixon's evasion of income taxes or of his extensive abuse of powers. The selling of policy for campaign contributions is particularly difficult to detect or prove. Often morality is a topic of sloganeering, as with Eisenhower's 1952 pledge to "clean up the mess in Washington" and to sweep clean with a new broom. Such appeals are easiest for the outsider not yet tainted by the dirty world of politics.

A modicum of dignity is presumably necessary for election as head of state; yet, as we mentioned in connection with warmth, candidates have varied widely between reserve and folksiness, with little apparent relation to their success at the polls. There was a notable contrast between Truman's and Johnson's earthy language on the one hand, and Roosevelt's and Kennedy's aristocratic demeanor on the other. Eisenhower, without wealth or old family, somehow came across as a natural aristocrat, and managed to combine great personal warmth with an Olympian stance above the mass. Eisenhower's barracks' language, unlike Truman's, was used only in private and never penetrated the national consciousness; Nixon was able to assert in 1960—referring to mothers holding their babies up to see the president—that Eisenhower had "restored dignity and decency and, frankly, good language" to the presidency.

Stability, a quality always desired in presidents, is somewhat akin to strength in that inconsistency is taken as a sign of weakness. But stability also has a further meaning of reliability and predictability. Barry Goldwater, for example, was certainly seen as potent: he offered strong medicine for America's ills, and was not afraid to talk about nuclear weapons. Yet by the same token his off-the-cuff remarks led to an impression of rashness or impulsiveness. Whether Goldwater would actually have been quicker than Johnson to start a war is another question; a respectable argument can even be made that Goldwater, hemmed in by a Democratic Congress, might not have got the United States so deeply into Vietnam. The fact is, however, that—again according to SRC data—large numbers of voters feared Goldwater as rash, impulsive, unstable, and dangerous.

Americans have usually elected white Anglo-Saxon Protestant males to the presidency; to be female or black or Jewish or Catholic has historically been a serious handicap. The role of such personal characteristics has a way of changing, however. John Kennedy's handling of his Catholicism in 1960 illustrates how opposition on one of these grounds, religion, was defused. Together with the case of Jimmy Carter, the Kennedy example also indicates how religious feelings can affect public affairs even in a secular age.

For whatever reasons—simple prejudice, fear of the unknown, or
concern about church interference with politics—many Americans in
1960 were uneasy about or flatly opposed to the idea of a Catholic
president. Some 20 to 24 percent of the voters openly admitted that
if their party "nominated a generally well-qualified man for President, and he happened to be a Catholic," they would not vote for
him.[26] During 1960 more and more Americans became aware of Kennedy's Catholicism, particularly after the Wisconsin primary, in which
Kennedy's "Catholic vote" was much discussed. The increasing awareness had negative effects on his popularity, especially in heavily Protestant and fundamentalist West Virginia, where he was committed to
a primary contest against Hubert Humphrey.[27]

It was difficult for Kennedy to deal with the religion question because it was mostly a subterranean issue, raised in whispering campaigns and pamphlets and sermons rather than in charges by political
opponents. If Kennedy discussed it, he ran the danger of inflaming
the issue or seeming to exploit it.

In West Virginia, however, the dire forecasts of the polls forced
Kennedy to face the problem head on. He used two main tactics.
First, he attempted to transform vague fears about Catholicism into
specific policy questions, on which he took definite and broadly acceptable stands. He opposed opening diplomatic relations with the
Vatican; he would not impose his personal views about birth control
on others; he opposed aid to parochial schools; and, above all, he
"would not take orders from any Pope, Cardinal, Bishop, or priest"
on political matters. Indeed, he asserted that his very religion would
prevent religious interference with his conduct in office:

> . . . when any man stands on the steps of the Capitol and takes
> the oath of office of President, he is swearing to support the sep-
> aration of church and state; he puts one hand on the Bible and
> raises the other hand to God as he takes the oath. And if he breaks
> his oath, he is not only committing a crime against the Constitu-
> tion, for which the Congress can impeach him—and should im-
> peach him—but he is committing a sin against God. (*Pause, raising
> his hand toward the sky.*) A sin against God, for he has sworn on
> the Bible.[28]

Second, having disposed of the policy questions, Kennedy cast the
issue as one of religious tolerance:

Are we to say that a Jew can be elected Mayor of Dublin, a Protestant can be named Foreign Minister of France, a Moslem can
sit in the Israeli Parliament but a Catholic cannot be President of
the United States?[29]

In this he was helped by some Protestant clergy, led by Dean Francis
Sayre of the Washington Episcopal Cathedral, who wrote an "open
letter" to their fellow pastors urging that religious lines should not
be drawn; it would be unjust to discount a candidate because of his
chosen faith.

Kennedy's strategy proved successful in West Virginia and was repeated, on a larger scale, in the general election campaign. The religious issue reemerged with a strong anti-Kennedy statement by the
National Conference of Citizens for Religious Freedom, an organization of Protestant clergymen headed (though later disavowed) by
Norman Vincent Peale. Kennedy agreed to speak, on September 12,
before the Greater Houston Ministerial Association in Texas, where
he skillfully wove together the themes of church-state policy and religious tolerance:

I believe in an America where the separation of church and
state is absolute—where no Catholic prelate would tell the President (should he be Catholic) how to act, and no Protestant
minister would tell his parishioners for whom to vote—where no
church or church school is granted any public funds for political
preferences—and where no man is denied public office merely
because his religion differs from the President who might appoint
him or the people who might elect him.

. . . For while this year it may be a Catholic against whom the
finger of suspicion is pointed, in other years it has been, and may
someday be again, a Jew—or a Quaker—or a Unitarian—or
a Baptist.[30]

Kennedy handled a series of tough questions from the ministers with
aplomb: he explained the obscure Chaplain's Chapel incident of fourteen years before; promised to work for freedom for Protestant mis-
sionaries abroad; rejected the doctrine of mental reservation as to
oaths of office; and repeated his dramatic offer to resign the presidency if he ever had to choose between violating his conscience or
violating the national interest.

Excerpts of the Houston confrontation were distributed by film and transcript throughout the country. Kennedy occasionally echoed its themes later in the campaign—lavishly praising the Mormons for their espousal of religious liberty, for example, when he spoke at the Tabernacle in Salt Lake City—but he did not again explicitly raise the question of Catholicism, and referred questioners to his prior statements.

On election day, as Philip Converse has shown, Kennedy lost some votes because of his religion.[31] It is a reasonable inference that without his skillful portrayal of independence from the church and appeals to tolerance he would have lost many more.

Not unlike Kennedy's problem with Catholicism was Jimmy Carter's with his fundamentalist, "born again" Baptism. On the one hand, Carter had much to gain by appealing to the spiritual longings of the Protestant majority; but on the other hand he could not afford to alienate those of other faiths or those of no faith at all. Carter's solution was to emphasize the importance of God in his life; to mention his conversion, his Sunday school teaching, and his frequent prayers; but at the same time to make clear that he was not intolerant of unbelievers and that he would keep church and state strictly separate.

Beginning in the late spring of 1976, Carter made a special effort to reassure Jews, who played such an important part in the Democratic party. He advertised heavily in Jewish publications, met with Jewish leaders, and collected endorsements and testimonials like that published in the *New York Times* by Morris Abrams. Carter himself spoke of his support for Israel and for Soviet Jews, and his belief in "absolute and total separation" of church and state; others, speaking for him, cited his tolerance toward other religions and his friendship with Jews in Georgia.[32]

Carter's fullest treatment of his religion (partly obscured from public view by the fuss about his comments on "lust") appeared in his interview in the November issue of *Playboy*. In that interview Carter spoke of prayer as a regular part of his life. Asked about victimless crimes, he noted that, according to the Bible, committing adultery and engaging in homosexual activities are sins, just as stealing and lying are.

> But Jesus teaches us not to judge other people. We don't assume the role of judge and say to another human being, "You're condemned because you commit sins." All Christians, all of us, acknowledge that we are sinful and the judgment comes from God, not from another human being.

As governor of Georgia, I tried to shift the emphasis of law
enforcement away from victimless crimes.[33]

Pushed further on this question, Carter declared that you can't legis-
late morality. He expressed some nervousness about homosexuality
but said it should be handled no differently from other sexual acts
outside marriage: as governor he didn't run around breaking down
people's doors to see if they were fornicating.

Rejecting the notion that he would set a "puritanical tone" in the
White House, Carter asserted that

> . . . we don't think we're better than anyone else. We are taught
> not to judge other people. But as to some of the behavior you've
> mentioned, I can't change the teachings of Christ. I can't change the
> teachings of Christ! I believe in them, and a lot of people in this
> country do as well.[34]

Returning to the topic of religion at the end of the interview, Carter
repeated his basic reassurance:

> One thing the Baptists believe in is complete autonomy. I don't
> accept any domination of my life by the Baptist Church, none.
> Every Baptist church is individual and autonomous. We don't
> accept domination of our church from the Southern Baptist Con-
> vention. The reason the Baptist Church was formed in this country
> was because of our belief in absolute and total separation of
> church and state.[35]

Personalistic Democracy:
Selection of a Benevolent Leader

There is more to be learned about exactly how much impact particular
personal characteristics have upon the voters under particular circumstances, but we can be quite certain that perceptions of candidates'
personalities have an enormous effect on the outcome of elections.
Voters consider personality important, feel confident of their judgments, and are prepared to vote on that basis. Moreover, they have
opportunities to do so: opposing candidates, similar and ambiguous
on policy stands, often differ markedly in personal characteristics and
give the voters a real choice. Thus the tremendously positive response
to Eisenhower's personality and the tremendously negative reaction to
Goldwater's made much of the difference between a Republican land-

slide in 1956 and a Republican disaster in 1964. McGovern's defeat in 1972 resulted largely from concern about his character.[36]

As we have suggested, voters who pay attention to the personal characteristics of candidates should not be dismissed as irrational. While the ambiguity of candidates makes it costly to find out in any detail exactly what policies they stand for, information about personal characteristics is relatively cheap and abundant: it can be drawn from memory of candidates' past experience, from observation of major campaign decisions, and from scrutiny of performances in TV news-clips and televised debates, speeches, and interviews.

Moreover, this information is relevant. A flaw like rigidity or impulsiveness in presidential character may affect behavior in foreign policy crises and could conceivably lead to nuclear catastrophe. Experience and competence surely have something to do with whether a candidate will be able to solve unforeseen problems and realize voters' values as the reward and punishment theory dictates. Warmth and activity are related to the general direction which policy is likely to take—how people-oriented, how activist. Even religion and regional and social background can be relevant to some policy choices and to questions of group benefits. In short, these matters bear upon the utility income or benefits which voters can expect to get from alternative electoral outcomes.

By the same token, although the emphasis of voters and parties on matters of candidate personality does not accord well with purely policy-oriented theories of democracy, it is consistent with a sort of democratic control which we can label *selection of a benevolent leader*. This refers to "benevolence" not in any narrow sense, but to the election of a president who embodies whatever personal characteristics the voters want: who represents the most desired character and style.

Such popular control might work in two different ways, analogous to the two types of democratic theory concerning policy stands. On some traits, the major party candidates might differ systematically in ways related to policy cleavages: voters might be able to choose, in a "responsible party" fashion, between Democrats and Republicans. On other traits, electoral competition might drive both parties to put forward men with the desired characteristics so that the winner—whoever he turned out to be—would have just the character that the voters wanted.

The pattern of twentieth-century elections suggests that both these processes work to some extent. Both parties do seek men whose personalities will win votes; both look for experience, warmth, strength. The parties also lean differentially toward certain qualities, such as greater or lesser activity, which fit their distinct philosophies. Party competition and voters' choices ensure a degree of popular control over what personalities are elected president. But here too we must consider certain possible obstacles to the working of democratic control.

The first is the problem of image making and manipulation. What if the man who is elected is not what he seems? What presidential candidates *are*, what images they try to project, and what the voters actually perceive are not necessarily identical. At the same time, however, we would argue that there are limits to manipulation and confusion, and that voters can judge candidates' personalities, just as they can judge the government's past performance, with reasonable accuracy.

Experience, for example, is a fact of a candidate's life history, widely known and not easily counterfeited. Although there is room for argument about military heroes and vice-presidents, experience is probably a fairly good indicator of general competence and knowledge. The methods by which Kennedy and Carter displayed knowledge were not mere fakery but indicated that these candidates had heads for factual detail; their cram sessions continued in the White House. Presidential campaigns, which require running a large, loose organization, and responding to questions on a wide range of topics, provide useful, if imperfect, measures of competence.

Activity and strength are likewise tested by the nomination and election processes, which demand exhausting travel, personal exposure to thousands of people, and quick decisions. (True, candidates can choose not to attend the exam, by running a tightly controlled and inaccessible campaign of the sort that Nixon did in 1968.) When a candidate fails this test—often in the prenomination stage, with the media playing an important part—the results are quite visible. Again, McGovern's indecisiveness and inconsistency may have been overblown by opponents for reasons of their own, but his behavior indicated that there was real reason for concern. John Kennedy's campaign demeanor enabled him to accentuate impressions of vigor, but his later conduct in office indicated that the reality was not far removed.

Perceptions of warmth and positivity are somewhat more problematic. On the one hand, television gives voters a firsthand view of candidates and a good chance to assess how much warmth toward people they display. Not even all the gimmicks chronicled by McGinniss in *The Selling of the President* enabled Nixon to come across as a warm human being; in 1968 and 1972, as in 1960, he was still seen as something of a cold fish. On the other hand, hidden negativity, self-doubt and compulsiveness may be possible to conceal, unless the voters act like psychologists and attend to small behavioral clues and candidates' developmental histories. They have not always done so. Nixon's second term brought some unpleasant surprises. Woodrow Wilson's troubles as president of Princeton did not seem to alarm anyone on the national scene in 1912, although they might do so if he were running now, given increased public sensitivity to rigid behavior. Such mishaps, however, are not inconsistent with learning by voters and eventual convergence to a popular-control equilibrium; a crucial question is whether or not voters' learning is outpaced by new trickery.

The story is much the same for other traits. Perceptions of Goldwater's "impulsiveness," like McGovern's "inconsistency," were no doubt inflated by opposition propaganda, but the public judgment does not seem entirely unreasonable: there were grounds for doubt, if not for the psychiatrists' hasty diagnosis in *Fact* magazine that Goldwater was "unfit" for the presidency. Kennedy did not fool anybody about his Catholicism; for the most part he offered reasoned answers to public doubts, and he continued to bend over backwards on church-state questions while in office. Dishonesty and corruption may be the traits in which the truth is most successfully concealed, but here too there are signs of increased public awareness.

One piece of evidence that image making has limits is the simple fact (apparent in our tables) that the voters perceive so many negative characteristics in candidates so often. Surely the public relations people are not getting their way all the time; all negative perceptions cannot be attributed to professional image destruction.

Still, we have been somewhat tentative in these judgments, because no one knows, for sure, just how effective image making (or image destroying) can be, or just how well the average voter can penetrate the haze and assess the character of aspirants to the presidency. Certainly television helps; perceptions of personality are no longer limited to hearsay. But there is need for vigilance. If perceptions are to be accurate, candidates must be forced into travel and public exposure, especially in spontaneous forums; public awareness of psychological processes (presuming that experts can agree on what they are) and of candidates' life histories should be increased; and Madison Avenue must be watched alertly for new image-making technology, whether it is better TV makeup, or counterfeit "body language," or new methods of subliminal manipulation.

A further problem with the benevolent leader theory of democracy is that the demands of the voters often cannot be satisfied because the supply of suitable candidates is insufficient. No matter how much both parties would like to come up with a Roosevelt or an Eisenhower for every election, such heroic figures aren't always available. The parties and voters have to take what they can get, and sometimes democratic control just means the selection of the lesser evil. This is much like the difficulty with electoral reward and punishment, that politicians aren't always able to avoid war or depression when they try; the point is not that the system is biased or unresponsive to citizens' wishes, but that it is not always possible to fulfill those wishes. Little can be done about the shortage of philosopher kings.

Even if supply were adequate and the theory worked perfectly, so that the electoral process cast up a paragon of benevolent leadership every time, we would still have to ask whether it is not a debasement of language to call this democracy. It has about it a flavor of citizen abdication, of giving up on instrumental benefits of government and settling for the symbolism of a father figure or a dignified elected monarch.

In isolation, certainly, the selection of a benevolent leader is a weak sort of democracy. "Rule by the people" must concern substance as well as style, and the connections between presidential personality and policy and performance, while significant, are not sufficient to dictate in detail what government does. Only in conjunction with other processes of democratic control does the selection of an appropriate presidential personality take on normative importance. It can be an important supplement, helping to ensure the capacity to perform, or rounding out the party program. But even this modest role for candidate personality may conflict with rather than complement other considerations: voters may be forced to decide whether to punish bad past performance, or to choose a favored set of future policy stands, or to pick the most attractive personality.

Leadership and Manipulation

It is the urgent duty of a political leader to lead, to touch if he can the potentials of reason, decency and humanism in man, and not only the strivings that are easier to mobilize.

Adlai E. Stevenson

Leadership in the electoral process implies something more than responsiveness to the policy preferences of the public. It involves the offering of new ideas or information, the initiating of actions, which advance citizens' interests in ways the citizens themselves have not thought of.

In the purest and simplest economic theories of politics there is no space for leadership. Under the assumptions that citizens' policy preferences are complete and fixed, that voting is costless, and that information is perfect, vote-seeking parties and candidates will stand for and enact the most preferred policies (presuming that an optimal social choice exists), just as the entrepeneurs in classical economics produce exactly what the consumers demand. The public's preferences are translated mechanically into policy. Citizen sovereignty prevails, and, according to the economic theory of democracy, this is just as it should be.

As we have seen, however, the relaxation of those assumptions opens a number of ways in which the simple version of citizen sovereignty is modified to permit unequal influence by activists, money givers, and interest groups. The same relaxation of assumptions opens up opportunities for politicians to exert several different types of leadership.

Incomplete preferences, for example, mean that the popular will cannot possibly dictate all details of policy; where preferences do not exist, politicians and other actors have latitude (perhaps subject to later accountability) to influence what government does. Similar leeway is provided when citizens are unable to vote their policy preferences because of uncertainty about the parties' stands: voting based on candidate personality or other factors puts considerably less public constraint on policy making. The same is true, at least in the short run, when citizens vote on the basis of past performance. Politicians can (and indeed must) take action on their own, to be judged later.

Moreover, under conditions of costly and imperfect information, candidates, parties, and others can themselves provide information (or misinformation) of various sorts to the voters. They can thereby affect what policies people think a party or its opponents stand for; what voters know or believe about problems and past performance; and how voters view the personalities of their own or opposing candidates.

Most important, voters' preferences too can be affected by the information provided. Information concerning the effects of alternative policies can influence which policies citizens favor or oppose. Beliefs about the state of the world can help determine what intermediate goals are sought and what kind of presidential personality is desired by voters. Thus there is room for new ideas and new information which can convince and educate and persuade.

We have argued that some of these opportunities for leadership, while inconsistent with the economic theory of democracy, are congruent with other varieties of democratic theory. In the electoral reward and punishment theory, for example, politicians are supposed to have leeway to solve problems as best they can, so long as they eventually satisfy the citizens' basic values. This allows for a kind of creative leadership, which remains totally accountable to the voters. Responsible party theories call for a less constrained kind of leadership, in which the parties are supposed to invent new policies, persuade voters to accept them, and inform citizens about how their interests can be furthered.

A profoundly disturbing possibility, however, is that some of the very features of the electoral process which permit leadership, may by the same token open up opportunities for policians, interest groups, and others to manipulate the public.

The concept of manipulation is rather uncongenial to economists, most of whom emphasize the fixedness of preferences and the smooth working of markets in response to preferences, and most of whom reject the notion of true underlying interests from which wants or preferences might diverge. It is more akin to sociologists' concerns with "false consciousness" and with the use of socialization processes to create, in malleable man, attitudes and behavior opposed to his objective interests.[1]

We are inclined to accept the argument that there exist some fundamental human wants which are highly resistant to change. We also are wary of objective definitions of interest (who does the defining?), and we take the individual's wants as our normative foundation. But our acceptance of these utilitarian cornerstones of economic reasoning and democratic theory does not rule out the possibility of manipulation. Because information is imperfect, citizens may hold incorrect beliefs that lead them to act or express preferences contrary to those they would hold if fully informed; contrary, that is, to the realization of their true wants and values. Manipulation, as we define it, is the influencing of beliefs or preferences by false or misleading information.

There are a number of ways in which citizens might be manipulated within the electoral process as analyzed here. Candidates and parties could—and would appear to have incentives to—misrepresent opponents' policy stands; they could, by using attractive symbols, misrepresent their own stands to the general public, while quietly pleasing special audiences. Candidates could present a false image of their own personal characteristics, or put their opponents in a bad light. They could try to deceive the voters about how good or bad times are by misstating the facts or, if they are the incumbents, by making temporary improvements. They could misrepresent the consequences of alternative policies, overstating the costs of their opponents' proposals or the benefits of their own.

This chapter explores the nature and extent of leadership and manipulation in the electoral process, the providing of true and false ideas and information. The difficult question of what effects this information actually has on the public cannot be answered directly;[2] focusing on the nature of the stimuli, however, we may make some inferences about responses.

Innovation in Elections

Proposing new policy ideas and persuading voters to accept them is the kind of leadership most emphasized in responsible party theories. But it is not in fact a conspicuous feature of U.S. presidential elections. Innovative policy ideas are rarely brought forward. When they are, it is sometimes third parties that do the innovating.

A leading example of third party policy innovation is that of the People's Party, or Populists, of the 1890s. The Populist platform of 1892 called for public ownership of the railroads, telegraph, and telephone; for counteracting deflation by unlimited coinage of both gold and silver; for a graduated income tax; and for reclaiming land held by aliens and excess land held by railroads. The same party in 1896 advocated direct legislation through initiative and referendum; direct election of the president, vice-president, and senators; home rule for the territories and the District of Columbia; and public works in time of depression. It opposed arbitrary court use of indirect contempt and injunctions, as well as the "wholesale system of disfranchisement" being adopted in some states.[3] While the causal impact of third parties is hard to sort out, a number of these ideas were later embraced by the major parties and enacted into law.

Similarly, new policy ideas are sometimes offered by insurgent or outsider candidates who capture major party nominations. Goldwater's proposals to seek victory in the Cold War through threats of military action, and his many proposals to dismantle New Deal programs, were certainly novel in the mid-1960s. Some liberals soon found themselves rethinking the New Deal and Great Society along not totally dissimilar lines. McGovern's detailed proposals for a zero-based defense budget, and for demogrants and tax reform put new policy alternatives before the public. But even Goldwater's and McGovern's ideas were not free from ambiguity, and were somewhat diluted in efforts to shift toward the center.

Only occasionally do regular major party candidates come up with important new ideas. Harry Truman, for example, in 1948 proposed a number of programs which became part of the liberal agenda for years to come. He advocated national health insurance; comprehensive civil rights measures; housing assistance; and large increases in social security, minimum wage, and other social welfare programs. Adlai Stevenson in 1956 suggested ending atmospheric nuclear testing. He also proposed ending the peacetime draft, as, in more concrete terms, did Nixon in 1968. John Kennedy in 1960 suggested a Peace Corps, much as Roosevelt proposed the Civilian Conservation Corps in 1932. Beyond these, however, it is not so easy to find examples. Nor are there many cases in which policy proposals, new or old, were strongly emphasized and backed by detailed factual arguments, as one would expect if they had an educational purpose. The major parties do not, in this respect, live up to responsible party theories.

There are good reasons why innovative policy proposals are not characteristic of American election campaigns. Regular candidates, as opposed to insurgents and third party challengers, tend to be in tune with the vote-winning, middle-of-the-road policies that the government is already pursuing, and are little tempted to suggest bold new directions. The staff resources of candidates are small and time pressure great, so that innovation would be difficult even if the candidates sought it. Most important, as was argued in chapter 6, the competition for votes forces candidates to be ambiguous about policy and to emphasize consensual appeals. Policy leadership is discouraged by the logic of electoral competition.

As we saw in chapter 4, a responsible party process does work, to a degree, in the sense that there are systematic policy differences between candidates on party cleavage issues. But these differences do not usually involve well-articulated proposals, and they are not usually put forward to the public for the first time in campaigns. Instead, the parties do most of their innovating in office, while grappling with concrete problems. The resulting party programs are then reflected, dimly, in subsequent campaign rhetoric, such as Truman's 1948 proposals, which consisted in good part of unfinished business from the Roosevelt administration. To some extent a nonincumbent party can do the same thing; its legislators and other members of its policy subculture can put forth some of their favorite unenacted proposals when they help write the party platform and serve on research "task forces" for the challenging candidate.[4]

Electoral leadership by the major parties more often takes the form of analyzing problems and past performance, and articulating general goals. Parties have incentives to provide citizens with certain kinds of information, in order to bolster the parties' claims of past achievements and their attacks on opponents' failures. Rates of unemployment, inflation, economic growth, and the like are used to praise or condemn past performance. Figures on the size of the federal budget and the cost of particular programs, examples of waste and inefficiency, casualty rates and the monetary costs of wars, are cited for the same purposes.

Some factual discussions of this kind, even if devoid of specific policy suggestions, can illuminate problems of which voters are unaware, with the effect of persuading citizens that government should move in new directions. Many of Adlai Stevenson's campaign addresses from the 1950s, such as those concerning natural resources, inflation, and education, can still be read with profit as reasoned analyses of public problems, although they proposed few solutions. Eisenhower in 1952, Nixon in 1968, and Carter in 1976, in their diverse ways, helped alert people to some of the costs and disadvantages of big government. Kennedy in 1960 pointed out the extent of suffering in depressed areas like Appalachia, as well as in the underdeveloped world; he documented the apparent national shortage of school classrooms. Johnson in 1964 made people aware of the plight of the unfortunate in their midst. Goldwater in that same year drew attention to the problem of urban crime, which liberals were prone to ignore. Humphrey in 1968 set forth the aims of reconciliation with China and the Soviet Union which Nixon later pursued in office. McGovern in 1972 opened, for the first time in decades, the question of redistribution of income and wealth.

A similar type of leadership is that which influences the sort of personal characteristics people want in their presidents. The articulation of goals and problems can demonstrate needs for a particular leadership style, such as an active or a passive one. The portrayal of a given style in an attractive fashion, as with Kennedy's vigorous "get America moving again" activism or Eisenhower's reassuring warmth, can perhaps help to arouse desires for that sort of leader. Reasonable discussion of particular traits, like Kennedy's Catholicism, can reduce fears of the unknown and broaden public tolerance.

A quite different kind of leadership takes place between elections, in the electoral reward and punishment process, when incumbents try to solve problems in accordance with citizens' values. Although it falls largely outside our field of view in this book, there is reason to believe that this is one of the most important types of political leadership in a representative system, and that much of the business of government consists of problem solving. Elected politicians have strong incentives to perform well and avoid punishment. There is room for creativity in devising policies which will have good results. At the same time, the electoral vulnerability of several recent presidents indicates that such efforts at leadership have not always been successful.

Deception

Manipulation of the public, as we construe it, involves providing false or misleading information which changes preferences or beliefs, and diverts voters from their interests. Since there is often room for real doubt about what the truth is, we cannot always identify misinformation; nor can we always tell what effects misinformation actually has on the voters. But we can be certain that falsehood is not uncommon in election campaigns, and that misleading statements are legion.

The policy stands of opposing candidates are sometimes misrepresented by surrogates or by candidates themselves. We saw how McGovern was erroneously tagged as favoring acid, abortion, and amnesty, and how "warmonger" rhetoric was heaped on Goldwater's proposal to delegate nuclear authority to the NATO commander, even though rather similar authority had already been delegated by past presidents.

It is more usual to misrepresent the consequences of an opponent's policy stands than it is to charge that he stands for something he does not. The assertion that Goldwater's voluntary plan would "destroy" Social Security, and Humphrey's grossly inflated estimates of the cost of McGovern's welfare plan, exemplify this type of distortion. Campaigns are filled with unfounded accusations that the opponent's proposals will cost billions of dollars, will cause inflation or recession, will leave the basic problem untouched, and will have a variety of dire consequences.

By the same token, candidates make overblown predictions about the benefits of their own stands, engaging in what Murray Edelman calls "symbolic politics."[5] Who could tell, from the rhetoric of Democrats, whether the "War on Poverty" was a war or a skirmish? How was the voter to know that "urban renewal" meant Negro removal, without replacement of bulldozed housing; that the minimum wage would increase unemployment of the lowest-paid workers; or that home mortgage guarantees would subsidize mortgage bankers and lead to defaults and abandoned houses? Who could tell, from the talk of Republicans, that "trimming waste" in government spending meant cutting social programs; that a "new Attorney General" or the reversal of Supreme Court decisions would have little effect on crime; or that efforts to halt inflation entailed a planned recession?

As we saw in the last chapter, candidates sometimes try to present a deceptively favorable personal image. The opposite side of the coin is character assassination, in which the opponent's personal qualities —such as his sexual morality or financial integrity—are misrepresented in a negative way. Because candidates must be careful that neither they nor their staffs seem to engage in mud-slinging, the preferred technique is to start rumors or plant newspaper stories which cannot easily be traced to the campaign organization, as in the anti-Catholic whisperings about Kennedy in 1960. For the most part rumors are effective only when they contain a germ of truth, like those concerning Grover Cleveland's illegitimate son, or Eagleton's mental health, or Lyndon Johnson's association with the wheeler-dealers Bobby Baker and Billy Sol Estes.

Occasionally campaign staffs resort to outright sabotage, as in the remarkable CREEP campaign for Nixon in 1972, when defamatory letters were forged on Democratic candidates' stationery; Senator Muskie was provoked to emotional outbursts by the spurious "Canuck" letter; and McGovern's campaign was made to seem even more disorganized than it was, by a series of bogus party invitations and merchandise orders and schedule foulups.

It is common for candidates, including incumbent presidents, to conceal or misrepresent facts about the state of the world which are relevant to judging past performance. After the Tonkin Gulf incident of 1964, Lyndon Johnson did not reveal that American ships had been simulating attacks on North Vietnam to test radar defenses, and he neglected to mention the likelihood that the alleged second North Vietnamese attack on a U.S. destroyer was imagined by a panicky U.S. sonar man. Kennedy's "missile gap" of 1960, and for that matter his classroom gap as well, turned out to be mostly fiction. In 1960 both Nixon and Kennedy gave the distinct impression that no invasion of Cuba was in the works, when Nixon certainly and Kennedy probably knew that preparations had been under way for some time.

Foreign affairs are particularly subject to secrecy and deception, in the ordinary course of government as well as during campaigns, since the facts are distant from most citizens. It is hard for ordinary Americans to learn what is happening in the world or what their own government is doing, or to imagine what the effects of alternative policies might be. During the 1950s and 1960s the public was mostly unaware that its government, through the CIA, was meddling in foreign elections, overthrowing governments, and trying to assassinate foreign heads of state in Iran, Guatemala, Cuba, the Dominican Republic, the Congo, Vietnam, and elsewhere.[6]

Although it is harder to conceal what is happening close to home, the effects of particular government programs are often sufficiently obscure to permit the playing of symbolic politics, both with past performance and with future proposals. Incumbent presidents also have opportunities to make things temporarily look better than they are, as in the preelection "liberal hour" of accelerated spending.

Beyond particular instances of misrepresentation, there is a sense in which the political system itself may deceive the voters about policy alternatives by severely limiting the range of possibilities discussed and the depth with which they are explored. The candidate ambiguity which results from competition for votes limits the amount of available information. The two-party system, which restricts the entry of new parties by means of such institutional barriers as single-member plurality-vote districts (and by repression of radical groups), largely limits policy proposals to those agreed upon by one of the major party coalitions. The search for votes, and the reliance upon business and organized labor for money and activists, ordinarily ensures that nothing very unorthodox is considered. Restricted discussion bolsters the status quo. What voters do not consider, they cannot demand.

Certainly campaign rhetoric has not much inspired Americans to think about possibilities of a communal rather than a competitive society, or egalitarianism rather than inequality, or a socialist ordering of the economy, or disarmament and world unity instead of anarchic nationalism. Candidates have mostly repeated the prevailing wisdom that national security must be sought through mutual armament; that "freedom" must be defended abroad against socialism; that welfare-state capitalism maximizes individual happiness. It is hard to make a case that many politicians have touched Stevenson's "potentials of reason, decency and humanism in man."

Our focus here is on the rhetoric and actions of presidents and presidential candidates, but it is plain that a number of nonelectoral institutions, such as schools, advertising, the media, and workplaces, can have similar and, indeed, probably greater effects upon the beliefs and preferences of the populace. If power over those institutions (like power over parties and candidates) is unequally distributed, and if the powerful misrepresent facts in order to mold public opinion in their own interest rather than the public's, then we can speak of a broader and more fundamental kind of manipulation.[7]

Moreover, the economic and social systems themselves, like the political system, can by their structure influence citizens' preferences and beliefs. Considerations of limited information dictate that, short of calamity, most people take these systems as given and look for improvements only within their confines. But once a system is accepted, its workings largely dictate which policy changes are possible or impossible, and which are desirable or undesirable.

This point is particularly clear with respect to the question of redistributing wealth and income in a capitalist society. In order to increase incomes, it is in everyone's interest to have economic growth, and therefore to preserve material incentives for corporations and individuals to work, save, and invest. Thus we find business urging, and labor going along with, investment tax credits and accelerated depreciation allowances and special treatments for capital gains. We find both rich and poor opposing "confiscatory" progressive taxation as threatening economic growth. The capitalist order thereby achieves what Gramsci calls "hegemony," in which all defend it against change, because in the short run any small or moderate change would be harmful to all, even if an altogether different economic system might be superior.[8]

Since democratic ideals are founded upon the wisdom and autonomy of the individual, any distorting influences upon citizens' beliefs and preferences—whether coming from politicians, or powerful groups, or the economic system—are profoundly disquieting to democratic

theory. If citizens are deceived about what candidates stand for or
what government has done, they may vote contrary to their interests.
If people are misled about the consequences of policies, or about what
the alternatives are, they may express (and have government act upon)
preferences which are "inauthentic" and do not accord with what they
would want if they were well informed.

The pervasiveness of imperfect information suggests not only that
democracy is not realized in practice, but also that it may in principle
be impossible of realization, if there is no way to prevent the misleading of voters. A correspondence between public preferences and government action loses its normative attractiveness if it is spurious or if
it reflects reciprocal influence of politicians upon the public, or a response to outside influences merely mediated through the public.

As we have noted, the reaction of some economists to these problems is to dismiss them, on the grounds that imperfections of information cause only short-run disturbances. In the long run, they argue,
voters will penetrate through concealment or deception and find the
facts. There will be a market for information, and voters will pay
anyone who provides the truth which will help them understand politics and vote correctly. There will be movement toward an equilibrium
in which no government dares to deviate from what fully informed
citizens would want, and democracy flourishes.

One possible rejoinder to this argument is that the market for
political information is itself imperfect. Information is hard to sell,
because of its intangible and easily replicable character. He who has
information can spread it at little cost, and no producer can control
distribution well enough to make a profit selling to many small consumers. That is, political information for which many people each
have a small need is a public good and is not produced or distributed
efficiently in the private market. Even when it is for sale, information
is hard to buy intelligently; the consumer needs information in order
to know what information he needs and what is accurate, and so on in
an infinite regress.

Moreover, even if the information market works well, so that
truth will out, it becomes important when and how fast correct information is arrived at. This is so in the sense of Lord Keynes's remark
that in the long run we shall all be dead; a four-year wait to rectify
an electoral error can be painful enough, to say nothing of decades

or centuries of muddling toward equilibrium. But more serious still is the possibility of permanent disequilibrium between policy making and public awareness and control. Perhaps new techniques of deception can be invented faster than voters can catch up. About such long-range properties of the political system we have no evidence at all.

Most important, even if the market for information works well and quickly, the working of such a market alters the distribution of political power by changing the political currency. The political equality essential to democracy rests upon the use of votes as the sole currency, with each citizen given one vote. But information costs mean that money and other resources are needed for producing, conveying and purchasing information about candidates' stands and performance and personalities. Since wealth and income and other resources are distributed unequally, groups and individuals have unequal voices in information dissemination and acquisition, and unequal impacts upon citizens' beliefs and preferences, upon electoral outcomes, and upon policy making. Economic and social inequality is reproduced in the political sphere.

10 Conclusion

Choices, Echoes, and Democracy

We have been concerned with three main questions: what sorts of choices parties and candidates offer in presidential elections, and why; how voters are affected by the nature of these choices; and what light our findings shed upon the workings or nonworkings of electoral democracy.

We found that much of the behavior of candidates and parties can be understood in terms of rational or purposive theories derived from economics. Indeed a central theme of this study is that economic reasoning can account for a broad range of electoral phenomena. At the same time, it is important to distinguish carefully among theories in the economic tradition. The simplest spatial models are inadequate, in two senses: some of their predictions are incorrect, and much goes on that they do not deal with at all.

As the standard spatial models predict, there is some tendency for both parties to offer up candidates who take policy stands near the midpoint of public opinion, so that both candidates echo the public and stand close to each other. Nixon, Humphrey, and even McGovern stood rather close to the public on most issues. But these candidates were by no means in perfect harmony with public opinion: each of them disagreed with a plurality of the public

278

some 20% to 30% of the time, and Humphrey stood outside the second and third quartiles of opinion on about 35% of the issues we examined. The insurgent candidate of the right, Barry Goldwater, actually disagreed with a plurality of the public most of the time, on 68% of the issues.

Many issues upon which candidates diverge from the public and from each other concern matters of party cleavage, on which the activists, convention delegates, money givers, and ordinary identifiers of one party disagree with those of the other. In the post–New Deal period, party cleavage issues have included questions of social welfare, labor-management relations, and (with some variation over time) civil rights for blacks, but not usually foreign policy. We found that on party cleavage issues, the candidates' policy stands almost always followed the opinions of their party coalitions. Democratic candidates generally took more liberal stands than Republican candidates. Often the differences were modest, but sometimes Democratic candidates were substantially more liberal (or Republican candidates substantially more conservative) than the general public.

This finding is important in itself, and also as a test between two broad classes of spatial models. It supports party cleavage theories of electoral competition, which predict systematic party differences, and refutes public opinion theories, which do not allow for such differences.

Contrary to a variety of dynamic theories, candidates' policy stands usually remain constant throughout an election year, at least in the sense that outright inconsistencies or changes are rare. Candidates may tend to shift their stands when the policy preferences of the general public change, but marked changes in public sentiment within the short period of an election campaign are not very common. Candidates do make appeals to special audiences, mainly by choosing low-visibility forums to make statements that are not contradicted elsewhere. The chief exception to the rule of constancy is that insurgent candidates like Goldwater and McGovern tend to shift from their early "extreme" stands toward the midpoint of public opinion; but even these shifts are relatively small.

In contrast to the definite, clear issue stands assumed in most spatial models, candidates' policy proposals are highly ambiguous. They are

infrequent, inconspicuous, and nonspecific. Ambiguity is best understood in terms of the low emphasis that vote-seeking candidates put
on divisive policy stands, and the high emphasis they place on consensual goals and values. There are some variations which depend upon
the candidate, the issue, and the setting in which stands are taken, but
ambiguity is quite pervasive. It extends even to the rhetoric of insurgent candidates and to stands on party cleavage issues.

The great bulk of campaign rhetoric concerns goals, problems, and
past performance. Incumbents boast of their achievements, and paint
a glowing picture of how good times are. Challengers point out problems and failures, especially in times of war or depression or disorder.
All candidates put forth inspiring visions of what their next administration will bring. There are some party differences, with Democratic
candidates emphasizing prosperity and condemning Republican depressions of the past or present, while Republican candidates promise
peace and castigate the Democrats for their wars. While the emphasis
on goals and performance is not easily accommodated in spatial models, it is consistent with rational vote seeking when information is
limited.

Another major aspect of electoral choice not well captured by spatial models concerns the personal characteristics of candidates. Opposing candidates often differ markedly on such dimensions as knowledge
and experience, warmth, activity, and strength. Again there is evidence
of certain party differences, with Democrats putting forward candidates
who are more active in political philosophy and perhaps in personality
as well, but in other respects both parties try to nominate candidates
with the same desirable characteristics. Candidates use a whole arsenal
of techniques to project personal images (or communicate reality) so
as to please voters.

In a variety of ways, electoral stimuli tend to influence the beliefs
and preferences of the public. Sometimes candidates try to exercise
leadership by communicating important facts and inspirational ideals,
but often the "facts" are false or misleading, and there are efforts to
manipulate the citizenry. Leadership and manipulation do not usually
appear in spatial models (or in economic theories of any kind), but
they too are consistent with rational behavior by politicians and
citizens.

Understanding Voting Behavior

We have argued, along with V. O. Key, that voters' decisions necessarily echo the choices they are offered: that the responses of citizens can only be understood in relation to the stimuli which are presented in the electoral process. Many of the familiar findings of voting studies make more sense in the light of what we have learned about the behavior of parties and candidates. The debate about "rationality" or lack thereof in ordinary citizens takes on quite a different appearance.

If Americans have usually perceived only moderate differences between the stands of Republican and Democratic parties and candidates, that need not be taken as evidence of the voters' stupidity or incapacity: often there has *been* rather little difference. If citizens have perceived greater differences between candidates on party cleavage than on noncleavage issues, and more difference on cleavage issues in some periods than in others, and more differences between opposing candidates when one was an insurgent, each of these phenomena can be understood as a reflection of electoral reality.

If perceptions of parties' and candidates' stands are often confused or absent altogether, the reason is not necessarily apathy or lack of cognitive skill on the part of the citizenry. To be sure, voters do not receive or retain every scrap of available information about politics: it would be costly and irrational to do so. But often the information is simply not available. The extreme ambiguity of candidates' policy stands—the low emphasis with which they are taken, and the lack of specificity in even the least ambiguous statements—add greatly to the costs of obtaining such information and sometimes make it altogether unobtainable. Candidate ambiguity is an important cause of misperception and nonperception by voters.

Nor should we be surprised if policy voting is uncommon. Often, especially on noncleavage issues, the opposing candidates' stands are similar to one another, and offer no basis for choice. In addition, ambiguity obscures whatever differences exist; in some cases there exists no candidate's stand at all upon which to cast an issue-oriented vote. It is easy to understand why we find more policy voting when an insurgent or a third party candidate is in the race. When clearer choices are offered, more citizens cast issue-oriented votes.

The systematic differences between opposing candidates on party cleavage issues help to explain the apparent importance of party identification in voting. To some extent, party voting is an illusion created by the fact that Republican and Democratic candidates tend to differ most on precisely the same issues and in the same directions as party identifiers' opinions do; therefore issue voting is easily mistaken for habitual party loyalty. At the same time, the persistence of the same sorts of candidate differences from one election to the next means that party identification can reasonably be used as a cue in voting decisions, thus minimizing the need to investigate candidates' stands fully in each election.

The importance of retrospective voting, or electoral reward and punishment, can be understood in a similar fashion. Candidates' ambiguity about future policy, and their emphasis on past performance, accentuate voters' inclination to attend to the past. In an environment of uncertainty about the future, it is perfectly rational for voters to pay attention to what they can judge through their own experience: the performance of the parties in office.

The great impact of candidate personality on voting reflects the fact that voters have some relatively inexpensive and reliable information about such matters, and also the fact that real choices are frequently offered in terms of personality and style. In some elections the most significant differences between the Republican and Democratic parties are not in policy stands but in the nature of their candidates.

We can speculate that levels of interest and involvement too may respond to the electoral stimuli. When candidates are ambiguous and take similar stands, or when both are seen as deficient personalities, attention to the campaign and concern about the outcome are understandably low. When choices are clearer or more attractive, interest and participation may rise.

No doubt even the public's policy preferences depend to some degree upon what is communicated by politicians. A high level of "don't know" responses or instability in policy opinions is understandable if the public is given few facts upon which to base opinions. The direction of opinions, too, can be affected by what information or misinformation is conveyed. Public opinion is not purely autonomous; to an extent which is unknown but potentially very important, it can be influenced from above.

Beyond the Economic Theory
of Democracy

It would be rash, on the basis of this study, to offer sweeping conclusions about the state of democracy in America, but our evidence does cast some light on the ways in which elections do and do not ensure democratic control of policy making. It suggests a mixed judgment. There are important elements of democratic control in U.S. presidential elections—probably closer control than in the lower-salience, less visible elections for other offices;[1] and possibly (though we cannot tell one way or the other) more democracy than in many other political systems. At the same time, the democratic tendencies are far from perfect. Elections do not guarantee a frictionless translation of public preferences into public policy.

In the perfect-information *economic theory of democracy*, electoral competition is supposed to ensure, under certain conditions, that both parties in a two-party system take the same policy stands, at the positions most preferred by the public, so that whichever party wins, the popular will is carried out. As we have seen, there is a tendency for candidates' stands to echo public opinion; but there is no perfect correspondence between candidates and public, and in fact there are many substantial deviations. The nature of the deviations, especially in connection with our findings on party cleavages, indicates that they result not only from random error or from lack of equilibrium but from the fact that other forces besides the opinions of the general public influence issue stands.

These barriers to the workings of an economic theory of democracy come from within the electoral process itself. In addition there may be slippage between campaign stands and actions in office, depending upon whether politicians are compelled to keep their promises (or are constrained in office by popularity-maximizing considerations), or whether nonpopular factors like organized interest groups or the wealthy hold more sway over policy making once the electoral spotlight is removed. A further possibility is that the public preferences to which parties are supposed to be responding are themselves manipulated by elites or by the state itself.

Just as there is a tendency toward democracy by electoral competition on noncleavage issues, we have seen some evidence of a *responsible party* version of democratic control, on issues of party cleavage.

Republican and Democratic candidates tend to stand for somewhat different policies; voters are enabled to choose between them on policy grounds. Government action follows a zigzag pattern, changing direction with each alternation of the parties in power. To some degree, the simplification of alternatives may help mobilize citizens, especially those of moderate income, to act in their own interest.

Again, however, the functioning of democratic control is by no means perfect, and this is due to more than the inherent conflict or division of labor between the economic and responsible party theories. Not only are party differences modest, but ambiguity blurs the differences which exist, obscures the nature of the choice, and thwarts the educating or informing functions of parties. Discrepancies between campaign stands and policy making may follow, in the legislative if not the executive process, from the decentralized and undisciplined party structure. In addition, a fundamental defect of this theory of democracy is that, to the extent that it operates, it gives the public only the power to choose the party whose policies are seen as the lesser evil. There is no guarantee that either party will stand for policies which are really popular. The content of the choice, and of party cleavages, is determined by elites who have money or organization and the motivation to do political work. In the United States that has meant business and the professions, organized labor, and occasional movements of amateur activists; the very poor and the unorganized tend to be left out.

The *electoral reward and punishment* model of democratic control asks less of voters and politicians than other theories do. Citizens need only judge whether times are good or bad, and vote accordingly. Politicians need not keep promises, but only selfishly seek reelection. As a result, it works more reliably. A party which gets the country into trouble is usually thrown out of office, and there is a strong incentive for those who enjoy positions of authority to learn what results the public wants and to try to achieve them. There can be little doubt that U.S. presidents try to attain peace, progress, and prosperity.

Failure is not unknown, since politicians cannot always be sure of the consequences of their actions; from time to time they blunder into disasters, Democrats being particularly prone to war and Republicans to depressions. This should not be regarded as a failure of democratic control: if the people are uncertain what policies they want and delegate the power to experiment, they cannot expect more than maximum human effort. But the opportunities for deception by misrepresenting the state of the world, or by manipulating events on a temporary basis, certainly do interfere with democracy. In any event, electoral reward and punishment probably exercise only a rough sort of control. The average voter can tell when prices or unemployment are rising, when wages are falling, or when the country is at war; but on other matters, imperfections of information may weaken the accountability of politicians. Many consequences of government action (whether the overthrow of regimes abroad, or policy failures at home) necessarily go unnoticed by the average citizen, so that there may be only limited pressure on politicians to pursue public values.

The model of democracy which we have called *selection of a benevolent leader* shares this advantage of asking little of politicians and voters. We have seen some evidence of the degree to which it functions: citizens do vote heavily on the basis of candidates' personal characteristics; elections have usually annointed the candidate with the more preferred personality; and the parties try to put forward nominees with the most desired traits.

This variety of democracy is sufficiently attenuated that one might be uncomfortable with it, in isolation from other forms of popular control, even if it worked perfectly. But again there are imperfections. Image making, to some (perhaps limited) extent, allows politicians to deceive the public about what kind of president it is getting. More important, parties are by no means always able to find a candidate of the ideal sort; chance plays an important part in which candidates with which characteristics are available, and the voters are often reduced to choosing the less objectionable personality. Since we are ruled by mortals, we have no right to expect anything else. But the individual characteristics of a president are so important that personality factors can come to dominate the electoral outcome, and other forms of democratic control are inhibited.

These theories of electoral democracy, and their many variants, differ in several respects. Some are based on voters' policy preferences, and others on preferred leadership traits, or on more deep-seated wants or values; some look forward in time, and others backward to past performance; in some there is instant responsiveness, and in others delayed accountability; some depend upon competition and similarity, others on choice. Clearly the theories discussed here are not exhaustive. It is possible to elaborate other combinations of behavior by voters and politicians that imply different kinds of connections between citizens and policy. Nor are the theories mutually exclusive. They interact in complicated ways, sometimes complementing and sometimes conflicting with each other. They imply somewhat different conceptions of democracy, each with certain normative advantages and disadvantages.

It has been assumed here, without much explicit discussion, that democracy of one sort or another is a worthy ideal. We do not necessarily urge that democracy ought to be maximized at the expense of all possible conflicting values, but do agree with James Mill that the chief end of government should be to further the interests of its citizens, and that in the end no one but the people can be trusted to know what those interests are or to guarantee that they are attended to.

Moreover, some common objections to democracy are not terribly impressive. The "intensity problem" (whether to give extra weight to strong preferences) is solved, in part, by the fact that populistic democracy can reflect intensity of an intrapersonal kind; it ignores only an interpersonal utilitarian calculus in which some are rewarded for an alleged (probably unmeasurable) greater capacity for pleasure. The question of liberties and minority rights is a more serious one, but there is hope that the nonconflictual aspects of interests, the basic decency of people, and the electoral reflection of intensity together go a long way toward obviating possible threats to individuals from majority rule. It is, in any event, no easy matter to define—or to decide who has the power to define—rights so fundamental that they ought to be upheld against the will of a well-informed citizenry. Finally, concern about the consequences of government by popular whim or error are more appropriately directed at the processes of disseminating political information than at the ideal of democracy, which we have defined in full-information terms.

By the same token, however, this study has offered a number of reasons why democracy may fail to be realized in the electoral process. We have noted the paradox of social choice theory, that under many circumstances no democratic outcome may exist. There is no reason to expect that the conceptions of democracy in terms of basic wants or fully informed preferences would be any more exempt from this problem than is the idea of aggregating policy preferences.

Still more important is the point that even when a democratic outcome can be uniquely specified, it will not necessarily be attained. Information costs and transaction costs interfere with political equality, and give extra weight in policy making to the wealthy and the well organized. Resources which are unequally distributed partially replace votes as the political currency. Unequal influence may extend even to citizens' beliefs and preferences. Thus in this book we have been led by economic reasoning, far from models of perfect voter sovereignty, to discussion of deception and manipulation.

These arguments point toward some ways of reducing political inequality, by cutting transaction costs and information costs to the citizenry, and by weakening the electoral effectiveness of resources other than votes. A number of commonplace reform proposals move in those directions: facilitating or requiring universal voting turnout; eliminating private campaign contributions; requiring parties to provide information and to expose themselves to questioning; increasing the visibility of government and the transmission of political news; and encouraging rather than suppressing minority political movements.

But the same reasoning also suggests that it may be impossible, short of a fundamental transformation of society, altogether to eliminate political inequality. So long as politics involves any privately borne information or transaction costs, money and other resources can be used to defray them and thereby to produce political power. So long as these resources are unequally distributed, political influence will be unequal as well. It is scarcely conceivable that all costs of obtaining and analyzing and acting upon political information could be collectively imposed; and unequally distributed resources are inherent in capitalism and indeed in any system relying upon material incentives for work or investment. If material incentives lie at the root of political inequality, the near-term prospects for complete political equality do not appear bright. The questions become, How far from it are we? And how much movement toward equality is possible, at what cost?

Appendix

Policy Opinion Items, 1967–68

Data based on the opinion items listed below were used in the analysis of candidates' closeness to public opinion (chapter 3), inconsistencies in policy stands (chapter 5), and ambiguity (chapter 6). A subset of items, for which breakdowns of opinion by the party identification of respondents were available, was used in analyzing candidates' responses to party cleavages (chapter 4). Those items are identified as party cleavage ("PC") or noncleavage ("NC") issues, depending on whether they met the criterion of a 6% difference between the opinions of Republican and Democratic party identifiers.

The organizations that originally gathered these data include the Survey Research Center—subsequently the Center for Political Studies—of the University of Michigan (SRC); the American Institute for Public Opinion or the Gallup poll (AIPO); the Opinion Research Corporation (ORC); and the Harris poll. The SRC data were made available through the Inter-University Consortium for Political and Social Research; the AIPO data were published in the monthly *Gallup Opinion Index* (GOI); the ORC data were commissioned by Richard Brody, Sidney Verba, Jerome Laulicht, and the present author; and the Harris data were made available in news releases and published in the *Washington Post* and elsewhere. These public opinion data are discussed further in the text and notes of chapters 3 and 4.

1   Isolationism (NC)
    SRC, October 1968 16:23

2   Foreign aid (NC)
    SRC, October 1968 5:29

3   Amount of foreign aid (PC-12%)
    AIPO, May 1967
    (*GOI*, June 1967, p. 11.)

4   Foreign aid for birth control (PC-6%)
    AIPO, August 1968
    (*GOI*, September 1968, p. 25)

5   Foreign aid to Asia (PC-9%)
    ORC, June 1968

6   Training and supplying Asian troops (NC)
    ORC, June 1968

7   Military intervention (NC)
    ORC, June 1968

8   United Nations membership (NC)
    AIPO, July 1967
    (*GOI*, September 1967, p. 16)

9   United Nations support (PC-7%)
    AIPO, July 1967
    (*GOI*, September 1967, p. 15)

10 Vietnam: escalate or de-escalate militarily
    Harris, September 1968
    (*Washington Post*, 7 October 1968, p. A6)

11 Vietnam: UN role (NC)
    AIPO, October 1967
    (*GOI*, November 1967, p. 14)

12 Vietnam: turning over more fighting to the South
       Vietnamese (NC)
    AIPO, July 1968
    (*GOI*, August 1968, p. 17)

13 Vietnam: U.S. troop level (PC-8%)
    ORC, June 1968

13a Vietnam: invade the North (NC)
AIPO, November 1967
(*GOI*, December 1967, p. 5)

14 Vietnam: bombing level (PC-13%)
ORC, June 1968

14a Vietnam: nuclear weapons (NC)
AIPO, March 1968
(*GOI*, April 1968, p. 18)

15 Vietnam: conditional bombing halt (NC)
AIPO, September 1968
(AIPO release, 6 September 1968);
Item text in *GOI*, July 1968, p. 12)

16 Vietnam: negotiated coalition government
Harris, May 1968
(*Washington Post*, 3 June 1968, p. A13)

17 Vietnam: elected coalition government
Harris
(*Washington Post*, 19 August 1968, p. A2)

18 Vietnam: neutralist government
Harris
(*Washington Post*, 19 August 1968, p. A2)

19 Alliances
Harris, August 1968
(*Washington Post*, 2 September 1968, p. A8)

20 U.S. troops in Germany (NC)
AIPO, October 1968
(*GOI*, November 1968, p. 8)

21 Negotiation with communist countries (PC-6%)
SRC, October 1968 5:31

22 Negotiations with USSR
Harris, August 1968
(*Washington Post*, 2 September 1968, p. A8)

23 Trade with communist countries (NC)
SRC, October 1968 5:33

24 Fighting Communist China (PC-10%)
ORC, June 1968

25   Admission of China to UN (PC-12%)
     SRC, October 1968 5:42

26   Getting the communist government out of Cuba
       (NC)
     SRC, October 1968 5:43

27   Sending U.S. troops to Germany until Russians
       leave Czechoslovakia (PC-7%)
     AIPO, October 1968
     (*GOI*, October 1968, p. 29)

28   Demanding the Russians leave Czechoslovakia
     Harris, August 1968
     (*Washington Post*, 2 September 1968, p. A8)

29   Arab recognition of Israel
     Harris
     (*Washington Post*, 10 July 1967, p. A17)

30   Israel: Use of the Gulf of Aqaba
     Harris
     (*Washington Post*, 10 July 1967, p. A17)

31   Israel: use of the Suez Canal
     Harris
     (*Washington Post*, 10 July 1967, p. A17)

32   Israel: occupation of Arab territory
     Harris
     (*Washington Post*, 10 July 1967, p. A17)

33   Neutralization of Jerusalem
     Harris
     (*Washington Post*, 9 October 1967, p. A6)

34   Arab refugees
     Harris
     (*Washington Post*, 10 July 1967, p. A17)

35   U.S. troops to help the Arabs (NC)
     AIPO, July 1968
     (*GOI*, August 1968, p. 24)

36   U.S. military aid to Arabs (NC)
     AIPO, July 1968
     (*GOI*, August 1968, p. 23)

37   U.S. troops to Help Israel (NC)
     AIPO, July 1968
     (*GOI*, August 1968, p. 22)

38   U.S. military aid to Israel (PC-6%)
     AIPO, July 1968
     (*GOI*, August 1968, p. 21)

39   Federal government power (PC-29%)
     SRC, October 1968 4:56

39a Aid to cities
     Harris
     (*Washington Post*, 3 April 1967, p. A2)

40   War on Poverty
     Harris
     (*Washington Post*, 3 April 1967, p. A2)

40a Revenue sharing (NC)
     AIPO, July 1967
     (*GOI*, August 1967, p. 25)

41   Community Action Program
     AIPO, February 1967
     (Lloyd A. Free and Hadley Cantril, *The Political
        Beliefs of Americans: A Study of Public Opinion*
        [New York: Simon and Shuster, 1968], p. 11)

42   Government job assistance (PC-21%)
     SRC, October 1968

43   Guaranteed work (PC-6%)
     AIPO, June 1968
     (*GOI*, July 1968, p. 24)

44   Job retraining
     AIPO, February 1967
     (Free and Cantril, p. 12)

45   Work projects
     Harris
     (*Washington Post*, 20 November 1967, p. A2;
     Item text given 14 August 1967, p. 1)

46   Guaranteed income (PC-16%)
     AIPO, June 1968
     (*GOI*, July 1968, p. 23)

47   Welfare
     Harris
     (*Washington Post*, 3 April 1967, p. A2)

48   Educational aid (PC-29%)
     SRC, October 1968 4:54

49   College scholarships
     Harris
     (*Washington Post*, 3 April 1967, p. A2)

50   Head Start
     Harris
     (*Washington Post*, 3 April 1967, p. A2)

51   Medical aid (PC-36%)
     SRC, October 1968 4:53

52   Medicare
     Harris
     (*Washington Post*, 3 April 1967, p. A2)

53   Mental clinics
     Harris
     (*Washington Post*, 3 April 1967, p. A2)

54   Medicare for all
     Harris
     (*Washington Post*, 23 January 1967, p. A2)

55   Low-income housing
     Harris
     (*Washington Post*, 3 April 1967, p. A2)

56   Urban renewal
     Harris
     (*Washington Post*, 20 November 1967, p. A2;
     Item text given 14 August 1967, p. 1)

56a Rat control
     Harris
     (*Washington Post*, 20 November 1967, p. A2;
     Item text given 14 August 1967, p. 1)

57   Summer camps
     Harris
     (*Washington Post*, 20 November 1967, p. A2;
     Item text given 14 August 1967, p. 1)

58 Tight money
Harris
(*Washington Post*, 16 October 1967, p. A2)

59 Tax surcharge (NC)
AIPO, January 1968
(*GOI*, February 1968, p. 26)

60 Wage and price controls (NC)
AIPO, November 1967
(*GOI*, January 1968, p. 20)

61 Cutting spending
Harris
(*Washington Post*, 16 October 1967, p. A2)

62 Permit unions for teachers (PC-19%)
AIPO, March 1968
(*GOI*, April 1968, p. 23)

63 Unions for nurses (PC-18%)
AIPO, March 1968
(*GOI*, April 1968, p. 25)

64 Union for farmers (PC-18%)
AIPO, March 1968
(*GOI*, April 1968, p. 26)

65 Taft Hartley 14B
Harris
(*Washington Post*, 28 March 1967, p. A2)

66 Permit right to strike by rubber workers
Harris
(*Washington Post*, 23 October 1967, p. A2)

67 Strike by auto workers
Harris
(*Washington Post*, 23 October 1967, p. A2)

68 Strike by railroad workers
Harris
(*Washington Post*, 23 October 1967, p. A2)

69 Strike by garbage men (PC-18%)
AIPO, March 1968
(*GOI*, April 1968, p. 27)

70   Strike by teachers (PC-21%)
       AIPO, March 1968
       (*GOI*, April 1968, p. 24)

71   Strike by police
       Harris
       (*Washington Post*, 23 October 1967, p. A2)

72   Strike by firemen
       Harris
       (*Washington Post*, 23 October 1967, p. A2)

73   Strike by defense workers
       Harris
       (*Washington Post*, 23 October 1967, p. A2)

74   Strike by nurses (PC-13%)
       AIPO, March 1968
       (*GOI*, April 1968, p. 25)

75   Compulsory arbitration (NC)
       AIPO, January 1968
       (*GOI*, February 1968, p. 27)

76   Pace of integration (PC-12%)
       AIPO, October 1968
       (*GOI*, October 1968, p. 30)

77   Integrated public accommodations (PC-8%)
       SRC, October 1968 5:11

78   Open housing laws (PC-7%)
       AIPO, October 1968
       (*GOI*, October 1968, p. 31)

79   Equal job opportunities for Negroes (PC-17%)
       SRC, October 1968 4:73

80   Integrated schooling for Negroes (PC-16%)
       SRC, October 1968 4:76

81   Drafting protesters
       Harris
       (*Washington Post*, 18 December 1967, p. A2)

82   Shooting looters (NC)
       AIPO, May 1968
       (*GOI*, July 1968, p. 17)

83   Law and order: federal versus local
     Harris
     (*Washington Post*, 9 September 1968, p. A2)

84   Law and order and the courts
     Harris
     (*Washington Post*, 9 September 1968, p. A2)

85   Courts' severity with criminals (PC-8%)
     AIPO, February 1968
     (*GOI*, March 1968, p. 15)

86   Supreme Court appointments (PC-26%)
     AIPO, July 1968
     (*GOI*, August 1968, p. 26)

87   Gun control—registration
     Harris
     (*Washington Post*, 23 April 1967, p. A4)

88   Gun control—permits (NC)
     AIPO, August 1967
     (*GOI*, September 1967, p. 17)

89   Gun control—eighteen-year-olds (PC-11%)
     AIPO, August 1967
     (*GOI*, September 1967, p. 18)

90   Selective service
     Harris
     (*Washington Post*, 13 May 1968, p. A3)

91   Army pay (NC)
     AIPO, November 1967
     (*GOI*, January 1968, p. 25)

92   Volunteer army
     Harris
     (*Washington Post*, 20 February 1967, p. A2)

93   Draft lottery
     Harris
     (*Washington Post*, 13 May 1967, p. A3)

94   Universal service
     Harris
     (*Washington Post*, 20 February 1967, p. A2)

95   Graduate student deferments
     Harris
     (*Washington Post,* 13 May 1968, p. A3)

96   Undergraduate deferments
     Harris
     (*Washington Post*, 20 February 1967, p. A2)

97   Draft resisters
     Harris
     (*Washington Post,* 13 May 1968, p. A3)

98   Air pollution
     Harris
     (*Washington Post*, 3 April 1967, p. A2)

99   Water pollution
     Harris
     (*Washington Post*, 3 April 1967, p. A2)

100 Pollution tax
     Harris
     (*Washington Post*, 24 July 1967, p. A2)

101 Underground wires (NC)
     AIPO, December 1967
     (*GOI*, January 1968, p. 19)

102 Highways
     Harris
     (*Washington Post*, 3 April 1967, p. A2)

103 Commuter trains
     Harris
     (*Washington Post*, 3 April 1967, p. A2)

104 Space program
     Harris
     (*Washington Post*, 3 April 1967, p. A2)

105 Moon landing
     Harris
     (*Washington Post*, 31 July 1967, p. A2)

106 Farm subsidies
     Harris
     (*Washington Post*, 3 April 1967, p. A2)

107   National primary
      AIPO, September 1968
      (Gallup release, 22 September 1968)

108   Campaign spending limit (NC)
      AIPO, June 1968
      (*GOI*, July 1968, p. 26)

109   Voting age (PC-8%)
      AIPO, September 1968
      (Gallup release, 22 September 1968)

110   Earlier presidential elections (NC)
      AIPO, March 1967
      (*GOI*, April 1967, p. 21)

111   Electoral College (NC)
      AIPO, June 1968
      (*GOI*, July 1968, p. 25)

112   Disclosure of congressmen's assets (NC)
      AIPO, May 1967
      (*GOI*, May 1967, p. 9)

113   Disclosure of congressmen's income
      Harris
      (*Washington Post*, 8 May 1967, p. A2)

114   Bribes
      Harris
      (*Washington Post*, 8 May 1967, p. A2)

115   Item veto (NC)
      AIPO, March 1967
      (*GOI*, April 1967, p. 20)

116   Jail for drinking drivers (NC)
      AIPO, January 1968
      (*GOI*, February 1968, p. 29)

117   School prayers (NC)
      SRC, October 1968, 14:53

Notes

Chapter 1

1 Milton Friedman, "The Methodology of Positive Economics," in *Essays in Positive Economics* (Chicago: University of Chicago Press, 1953), pp. 3–43.

2 Anthony Downs, *An Economic Theory of Democracy* (New York: Harper, 1957).

3 For an economic treatment of changes in manifest preferences, however, see George J. Stigler and Gary S. Becker, "De Gustibus Non Est Disputandum," *American Economic Review* 67 (March 1977):76–90.

Chapter 2

1 Joseph A. Schumpeter, *Capitalism, Socialism, and Democracy*, 3d ed. (New York: Harper and Row, Colophon ed, 1975; orig. pub. 1950); pp. 243–73, esp. 269.

2 John Locke, *Two Treatises of Government*, ed. Peter Laslett (Cambridge: Cambridge University Press, 1960; orig. pub. 1690); Jean Jacques Rousseau, *The Social Contract*, ed. Charles Frankel (New York: Hafner, 1957; orig. pub. 1762); Alexander Hamilton, James Madison, and John Jay, *The Federalist Papers*, ed. Clinton Rossiter (New York: New American Library, 1961; orig. pub. 1787–1788). For discussions see Robert A. Dahl, *A Preface to Democratic Theory* (Chicago: University of Chicago Press, 1956), chaps. 1 and 2; and

Brian Barry, *Sociologists, Economists, and Democracy* (London: Collier-Macmillan, 1970).

3 James Mill, *An Essay on Government* (Cambridge: Cambridge University Press, 1937; orig. pub. 1828).

4 Jeremy Bentham's *An Introduction to the Principles of Morals and Legislation* (New York: Hafner, 1948; orig. pub. 1789) is addressed to the ideal legislator, and scarcely mentions democracy. Bentham's *The Constitutional Code*, in John Bowring, ed., *The Works of Jeremy Bentham* (Edinburgh: William Tait, 1843), vol. 9, reflects his later prodemocratic position. John Stuart Mill's *Considerations on Representative Government* (New York: Henry Holt, 1882) displays considerable wariness of the masses, esp. in chap. 6; it suggests limits on representatives' power in chaps. 5 and 14, and limits on suffrage in chap. 8.

5 The early history of the paradox is discussed in Duncan Black, *The Theory of Committees and Elections* (Cambridge: Cambridge University Press, 1958), part 2.

6 Kenneth J. Arrow, *Social Choice and Individual Values*, 2d ed. (New York: Wiley, 1963; orig. pub. 1951). Summary discussions of the paradox can be found in William H. Riker and Peter C. Ordeshook, *An Introduction to Positive Political Theory* (Englewood Cliffs, N.J.: Prentice-Hall, 1973), chap. 4; Steven J. Brams, *Paradoxes in Politics* (New York: The Free Press, 1976); and especially Charles R. Plott, "Axiomatic Social Choice Theory: An Overview and Interpretation," *American Journal of Political Science* 20 (August 1976): 511–96.

7 Black, *The Theory of Committees and Elections*, part 1; Jerome Rothenberg, *The Measurement of Social Welfare* (Englewood Cliffs, N.J.: Prentice-Hall, 1961); Amartya K. Sen, *Collective Choice and Social Welfare* (San Francisco: Holden-Day, 1970); Peter C. Fishburn, *The Theory of Social Choice* (Princeton: Princeton University Press, 1973).

8 Harold Hotelling, "Stability in Competition," *Economic Journal* 39 (March 1929): 41–57.

9   Otto A. Davis and Melvin Hinich, "A Mathematical
    Model of Policy Formation in a Democratic Society,"
    in *Mathematical Applications in Political Science II*,
    ed. Joseph L. Bernd (Dallas: Southern Methodist Uni-
    versity Press, 1966), pp. 175–205.

10 For a chart setting forth predictions and conjectures un-
    der some 56 different combinations of assumptions, see
    Riker and Ordeshook, *An Introduction*, p. 343.

11 Charles R. Plott, "A Notion of Equilibrium and Its
    Possibility Under Majority Rule," *American Economic
    Review* 57 (September 1967): 787–806; Gerald H.
    Kramer, "On a Class of Equilibrium Conditions for
    Majority Rule," *Econometrica* 41 (March, 1973): 285–
    97; Richard D. McKelvey, "Intransitivities in Multidi-
    mensional Voting Models and Some Implications for
    Agenda Control," *Journal of Economic Theory* 12
    (June, 1976): 472–82. See also Peter C. Fishburn,
    "Lotteries and Social Choice," *Journal of Economic
    Theory* 52 (October 1972): 189–207.
        Gerald Kramer and Donald Wittman offer dynamic
    models predicting gradual movement (over a series of
    elections) toward a central set of policies even when no
    equilibrium of the usual sort exists. See Donald Witt-
    man, "Candidates with Policy Preferences: A Dynamic
    Model", *Journal of Economic Theory* 14 (1977):
    180–89; Gerald Kramer, "A Dynamical Model of
    Political Equilibrium", *Journal of Economic Theory*
    (forthcoming).

12 The main features of the work by the Carnegie group
    are summarized in Otto A. Davis, Melvin J. Hinich,
    and Peter C. Ordeshook, "An Expository Development
    of a Mathematical Model of the Electoral Process,"
    American Political Science Review 64 (June 1970):
    426–48, and in Riker and Ordeshook, *An Introduction*
        The early papers by Lerner and Singer and by Smith-
    ies also present public opinion theories. So do numer-
    ous articles by Aranson, Bernholz, Chapman, Gar-
    vey, Hoyer and Mayer, Jackson, Kramer, McKelvey,
    Shepsle, Taylor, Tullock and others. As we will see,

some of these same scholars have also developed party cleavage theories.

13   Otto A. Davis and Melvin Hinich, "A Mathematical Model"; Davis and Hinich, "On the Power and Importance of the Mean Preference in a Mathematical Model of Democratic Choice," *Public Choice* 5 (Fall 1968): 59–72.

14   Woodrow Wilson, *Congressional Government* (Boston: Houghton Mifflin, 1885); E. E. Schattschneider, *Party Government* (New York: Holt, 1942). An excellent discussion is Austin Ranney's *The Doctrine of Responsible Party Government: Its Origins and Present State* (Urbana: University of Illinois Press, 1962; orig. pub. 1954).

15   American Political Science Association, Committee on Political Parties, "Toward a More Responsible Two-Party System," *American Political Science Review* 44 (September 1950): part 2.

16   A. P. Lerner and H. W. Singer, "Some Notes on Duopoly and Spatial Competition," *Journal of Political Economy* 45 (April 1937): 145–86.

17   Arthur Smithies, "Optimum Location in Spatial Competition," *Journal of Political Economy* 49 (June 1941): 423–39.

18   Anthony Downs, *An Economic Theory of Democracy* (New York: Harper, 1957): p. 118.

19   Downs, p. 122; Gerald Garvey, "The Theory of Party Equilibrium," *American Political Science Review* 60 (March 1966): 29–38; Riker and Ordeshook, *An Introduction*, pp. 343, 349–50.

20   Richard A. Brody and Benjamin I. Page, "Indifference, Alienation, and Rational Decisions: The Effects of Candidate Evaluations on Turnout and the Vote," *Public Choice* 15 (Summer 1973): 1–17.

21   Primary elections or nominating conventions are allowed for in one section of Davis and Hinich, "A Mathematical Model"; and in Peter H. Aranson and Peter C. Ordeshook, "Spatial Strategies for Sequential Elections," in *Probability Models of Collective Decision*

Making, ed. Richard G. Niemi and Herbert F. Weisberg (Columbus: Charles Merrill, 1972): pp. 298–331; as well as in James Coleman, "Internal Processes Governing Party Positions in Elections," *Public Choice* 11 (Fall 1971): 35–60. Several such factors are included in John Ferejohn and Roger Noll, "A Dynamic Theory of Political Campaigning," paper delivered at the 1972 annual meeting of the American Political Science Association, Washington, D.C., 5–9 September.

Policy goals of a unitary party are postulated in Donald A. Wittman, "Parties as Utility Maximizers," *American Political Science Review* 67 (June 1973), 490–98, and Wittman, "Candidates with Policy Preferences."

22   Wittman, "Parties as Utility Maximizers" and other papers. Wittman's parsimonious assumption of unitary parties also disposes of the question which could be asked of some party cleavage theories: why are only some actors policy-oriented, but not others?

Chapter 3

1   Even so, this method is subject to measurement error. In practice, for items with three or four response alternatives it is not easy to estimate the location of the quartiles, and there is additional uncertainty in locating candidates' positions relative to the quartiles.

With such data it is not possible to distinguish the mean from the median (assumed to be the same in the symmetrical distributions of many spatial models), or to test propositions which are contingent upon particular shapes of opinion distributions.

2   Louis Hartz, *The Liberal Tradition in America: An Interpretation of American Political Thought since the Revolution* (New York: Harcourt, Brace, 1955).

3   See George H. Gallup, *The Gallup Poll: Public Opinion 1935–71* (New York: Random House, 1972), 3 vols., and the monthly *Gallup Opinion Index*.

4   The Gallup, or American Institute of Public Opinion (AIPO) items were taken from press releases and from the monthly *Gallup Opinion Index* (*GOI*); the Louis

Harris, Inc., items from reports published in the *Washington Post*; and Opinion Research Corporation (ORC) items from surveys conducted for Richard A. Brody, Sidney Verba, Jerome Laulicht, and the present author. Data from the Survey Research Center, University of Michigan (SRC)—and, later, the Center for Political Studies (CPS)—were provided through the Inter-University Consortium for Political and Social Research, which bears no responsibility for analysis or interpretation.

The exact question wordings and the marginal frequencies of responses can be found in Benjamin I. Page, "Presidential Campaigning: The Rhetoric of Electoral Competition" (Ph.D. dissertation, Stanford University, 1973), Appendix A.

5   Humphrey's speeches were kindly provided by the Democratic National Committee, through the good offices of Raymond E. Wolfinger and John Stewart. Nixon's were generously made available by the Republican National Committee, at the request of Representative Charles Gubser. The texts of some of Nixon's speeches are reprinted in *Nixon Speaks Out* (New York: Nixon-Agnew Campaign Committee, 1968), and excerpts of others can be found in *Nixon on the Issues* (New York: Nixon-Agnew Campaign Committee, 1968).

6   In performing this test we take the liberty of treating our set of issues as a sample. Although no sampling procedure was employed (none was possible), we would maintain that the collection of issues has sufficient representative properties to make the binomial test useful. For the same reason we report the results of statistical tests at several other points in the book.

7   The dates and locations of most of the Nixon and Humphrey quotations used in this and other chapters are given in Page, "Presidential Campaigning."

8   Gallup, *The Gallup Poll*, 3:1797–1899. The sources for Goldwater's stands are given in the notes to chapter 5.

Goldwater later moved somewhat from these early stands toward the center of public opinion, but the movement does not substantially affect our findings.

9   *The Gallup Poll*, 3:2282–2332; *Gallup Opinion Index*, December 1971 through November 1972. Sources for McGovern's stands are cited in chapter 5. McGovern's slight movement toward the center does not appreciably affect the extent of his agreement with the public shown in these early stands.

10 See Benjamin I. Page and Richard A. Brody, "Policy Voting and the Electoral Process: The Vietnam War Issue," *American Political Science Review* 66 (September 1972): 979–95.
    The use of medians rather than means reduces the influence of outlying (presumably distorted) perceptions. The single-peakedness of Vietnam preferences, which is presupposed in our treatment of the median as comprising the most popular policy, is supported—though not proven—by the Guttman scalability of preferences in 1967 and 1968.

Chapter 4

1   Alexander Heard, *The Costs of Democracy* (Chapel Hill: University of North Carolina Press, 1960): 95–141, 169–211; John David Greenstone, *Labor in American Politics* (New York: Knopf, 1969).

2   Herbert McClosky, Paul J. Hoffman, and Rosemary O'Hara, "Issue Conflict and Consensus among Party Leaders and Followers," *American Political Science Review* 54 (June 1960): 406–27.

3   John Soule and James Clark, "Issue Conflict and Consensus: A Comparative Study of Democratic and Republican Delegations to the 1968 National Conventions," *Journal of Politics* 33 (February 1971): 72–91; David Nexon, "Asymmetry in the Political System: Occasional Activists in the Republican and Democratic Parties, 1956–1964," *American Political Science Review* 65 (September 1971): 716–30; Samuel J. Eldersveld, *Political Parties: A Behavioral Analysis* (Chicago: Rand McNally, 1964), esp. chaps. 8 and 9; Thomas A. Flinn and Frederick M. Wirt, "Local Party Leaders: Groups

of Like Minded Men," *Midwest Journal of Political Science* 9 (February 1965): 77–98.

4 McClosky et al., "Issue Conflict"; Gerald M. Pomper, "From Confusion to Clarity: Issues and American Voters, 1956–68," *American Political Science Review* 66 (June 1972): 415–28; Everett Carll Ladd, Jr., and Charles D. Hadley, *Political Parties and Political Issues: Patterns in Differentiation Since the New Deal* (Beverly Hills, Calif.: Sage, 1973).

5 V. O. Key, Jr., "A Theory of Critical Elections," *Journal of Politics* 17 (February 1955): 3–18; Kristi Anderson, "Generation, Partisan Shift, and Realignment: A Glance Back to the New Deal," in Norman H. Nie, Sidney Verba, and John R. Petrocik, *The Changing American Voter* (Cambridge: Harvard University Press, 1976), chap. 5.

6 The criterion for a party cleavage issue was a difference of six percent or more between Republicans and Democrats—an amount significantly different from zero at approximately the $p = .05$ level by chi-square test. (The exact significance level varies with sample size and skewness of the marginals.) This rather loose criterion works against the hypothesis upheld in this chapter, and thereby strengthens the argument.

Percentage differences between the opinions of Republicans and Democrats on party cleavage issues are given in parentheses in the Appendix. For the marginal frequencies by party, see Benjamin I. Page, "Presidential Campaigning: The Rhetoric of Electoral Competition" (Ph.D. dissertation, Stanford University, 1973), Appendix B.

7 Roosevelt's major speeches are collected in Franklin D. Roosevelt, *The Public Papers and Addresses of Franklin D. Roosevelt, with a Special Introduction and Explanatory Notes by President Roosevelt* (New York: Random House, 1938), vol. 1, ed. Samuel I. Rosenman. A useful account of the campaign is Roy V. Peel and Thomas C. Donnelly, *The 1932 Campaign: An Analysis* (New York: Farrar and Rinehart, 1935), esp. chap.

6. An insider's view is Rexford G. Tugwell, *The Brains Trust* (New York: Viking, 1968).

8   A prize-winning history of the 1948 campaign and its context is Irwin Ross, *The Loneliest Campaign: The Truman Victory of 1948* (New York: New American Library, 1968). An interesting account by a Democratic director of publicity is Jack Redding, *Inside the Democratic Party* (New York: Bobbs-Merrill, 1958). Both political and social aspects of voters' reactions are discussed in Bernard Berelson, Paul F. Lazarsfeld, and William N. McPhee, *Voting: A Study of Opinion Formation in a Presidential Campaign* (Chicago: University of Chicago Press, 1954).

    Truman's speeches can be found in *Public Papers of the Presidents of the United States*; some of Dewey's are reprinted in *Public Papers of Governor Thomas E. Dewey—1948*.

9   Berelson et al., *Voting*, p. 221. Most voters knew that Truman opposed Taft-Hartley; they were more confused about the ambiguous Dewey (p. 219). Berelson's data were gathered in August, before the autumn campaign, and perceptions may have been more accurate later.

10 Some of Stevenson's 1952 speeches are reprinted in Adlai E. Stevenson, *Major Campaign Speeches, 1952* (New York: Random House, 1953). Stanley Kelley, Jr., in *Professional Public Relations and Political Power* (Baltimore: Johns Hopkins University Press, 1956), offers a brief and lively account of the campaign, emphasizing the use of media and the rhetoric of past performance.

11 Some of Stevenson's major 1956 speeches are reprinted in Adlai E. Stevenson, *The New America* (New York: Harper, 1957). Eisenhower's can be found in the *Public Papers of the Presidents of the United States*.

    Charles A. H. Thomson and Frances M. Shattuck, *The 1956 Presidential Campaign* (Washington, D.C.: Brookings, 1960) is a detailed chronicle of the events and issue stands of the campaign. Stanley Kelley, Jr.,

*Political Campaigning: Problems in Creating an In-
formed Electorate* (Washington, D.C.: Brookings, 1960)
is an excellent treatment of campaign distortions and
ambiguity. Angus Campbell, Philip E. Converse, Warren E. Miller, and Donald E. Stokes, *The American
Voter* (New York: Wiley, 1960) reports voters' responses to the 1956 election (and, to some extent, 1952
as well) with particular emphasis on the role of party
identification.

12   U.S., Congress, Senate, Committee on Commerce, *Freedom of Communications: Final Report Pursuant to S.
Res. 305, 86th Congress*, 4 vols., 87th Cong., 1st sess.,
1961. These volumes include a virtually complete collection of Kennedy's and Nixon's 1960 campaign
speeches, upon which the present analysis is based.

13   Our analysis of the 1976 campaign is based on speech
texts obtained from the Carter and Ford campaign
organizations, and the reports in the *New York Times*.
Some of Carter's early stands are summarized in Robert
W. Turner, *"I'll Never Lie to You": Jimmy Carter in
His Own Words* (New York: Ballantine, 1976) and in
Jimmy Carter, *Why Not the Best?* (New York: Ban-
tam, 1976; orig. pub. Broadman, 1975).

14   The binomial test assumes independence among issues.
Since opinions in the U.S. population tend to be somewhat intercorrelated, the null hypothesis is not that the
candidates took stands corresponding to the opinions of
two randomly selected individuals, but that their stands
on each separate issue were randomly selected.

15   The discussion in this section is based on our collection
of 156 Nixon and 120 Humphrey speeches, described
in chapter 3. For the dates and locations of quoted remarks, see Page, "Presidential Campaigning," chapter 4.

16   We used quartile deviations of public opinion as constant units for measuring the amount of candidate difference comparably across issues. The estimation of
quartiles for items with few response options is inherently difficult, and some errors of measurement undoubtedly occurred; table 8 must therefore be inter-

preted with more caution than table 7, which relies on more precise ordinal judgments.

17   Medians rather than means are used in figure 4 and elsewhere in order to reduce the effects of extremely deviant perceptions. The argument for using means, in John H. Aldrich and Richard D. McKelvey, "A Method of Scaling with Applications to the 1968 and 1972 Presidential Elections," *American Political Science Review* 71 (March 1977): 111–30, depends upon their assumption that misperceptions are random. This ignores both end-point effects (the impossibility of perceptions less than 1 or greater than 7 on seven-point scales) and motivated misperception.

The standard errors of the means—in these distributions—give a rough indication of the confidence limits around the medians. Because of the elastic nature of the scales, the magnitudes of candidate differences on different issues are compared in relation to the dispersion of opinion.

18   James L. Sundquist, *Dynamics of the Party System: Alignment and Realignment of Political Parties in the United States* (Washington, D.C.: Brookings, 1973).

19   The classic treatment of realignment is Key, "A Theory of Critical Elections." The processes of change are probed more deeply in Walter Dean Burnham, *Critical Elections and the Mainsprings of American Politics* (New York: Norton, 1970), and Sundquist, *Dynamics of the Party System*. An account of the realignment process at the level of the individual voter is given in Nie et al., *The Changing American Voter*.

20   Some methodological problems are discussed in Richard A. Brody and Benjamin I. Page, "Comment: The Assessment of Policy Voting," *American Political Science Review* 66 (June 1972): 450–58, and in the September 1976 *APSR* symposium. The appropriate simultaneous equation models are hard to specify convincingly and have rarely been estimated. (An exception is John E. Jackson, "Issues, Party Choices, and Presidential Votes," *American Journal of Political Science* 19 (May 1975): 161–85.)

A leading technique has been Stokes's OLS regression using open-ended responses; it avoids some causal inference problems (while raising others) by lumping preferences and perceptions together, but it cannot distinguish very finely among the importance of different issues. Donald E. Stokes, "Some Dynamic Elements of Contests for the Presidency," *American Political Science Review* 60 (March 1966): 19–28; Gerald M. Pomper, *Voters' Choice: Varieties of American Electoral Behavior* (New York: Dodd, Mead, 1975). Simple cross-tabulation or regression of multiple-issue scale scores with votes may also provide not wholly unreasonable estimates of issue voting; they too reduce the probability that expressed policy preferences are influenced by intended vote, but they both gain and lose by ignoring perceptions. Nie et al., *The Changing American Voter*.

The most influential argument that issue voting is rare avoided methodological quagmires by offering no estimate of the extent of issue voting, but simply cataloguing factors which would make it difficult or impossible for many voters: Campbell et al., *The American Voter*, chap. 8.

21   Benjamin I. Page and Richard A. Brody, "Policy Voting and the Electoral Process: The Vietnam War Issue," *American Political Science Review* 66 (September 1972): 979–95.

22   Pomper, *Voters' Choice*; Nie et al., *The Changing American Voter*.

23   Anthony Downs, *An Economic Theory of Democracy* (New York: Harper, 1957). Downs (pp. 230–34) was actually somewhat ambivalent about the rationality of delegating analysis and evaluation to parties, but voters may have no feasible alternative.

24   Campbell et al., *The American Voter*; Pomper, *Voters' Choice*; Nie et al., *The Changing American Voter*.

25   Julius Turner, *Party and Constituency: Pressure on Congress* (Baltimore: Johns Hopkins University Press, 1951; rev. ed. by Edward B. Schneier, Jr., 1970); James L. Sundquist, *Politics and Policy: The Eisen-*

hower, Kennedy, and Johnson Years (Washington, D.C.: Brookings, 1968); Benjamin Ginsberg, "Elections and Public Policy," *American Political Science Review* 70 (March 1976): 41–49; Douglas A. Hibbs, "The Politics of Macroeconomic Policy," *American Political Science Review* (forthcoming).

Chapter 5

1   Kenneth A. Shepsle, "The Strategy of Ambiguity: Uncertainty and Electoral Competition," *American Political Science Review* 66 (June 1972): 555–68.

2   Anthony Downs, *An Economic Theory of Democracy* (New York: Harper, 1957).

3   John Ferejohn

4   Such a possibility is implicit in Otto A. Davis and Melvin Hinich, "A Mathematical Model of Policy Formation in a Democratic Society," in *Mathematical Applications in Political Science II*, ed. Joseph L. Bernd (Dallas: Southern Methodist University Press, 1966), pp. 175–205, and in several other party cleavage theories.

5   John Ferejohn and Roger Noll, "A Dynamic Theory of Political Campaigning," paper delivered at the 1972 annual meeting of the American Political Science Association, Washington, D.C., 5–9 September.

6   The frequencies are calculated from U.S. Congress, Senate, Committee on Commerce, *Freedom of Communications: Final Report . . . Pursuant to S. Res. 305, 86th Congress*, 4 vols., 87th Cong., 1st sess., 1961, which includes all available texts and transcripts for Kennedy and Nixon, from August 1 through November 7, 1960. We have relied on the editors' categorization of texts.

7   The discussion of Nixon's and Humphrey's 1968 stands in this chapter is based on the collection of 156 Nixon and 120 Humphrey texts described in chapter 3. Since this 1968 speech collection is not complete, it is con-

ceivable that we have missed some inconsistencies. The likelihood of this is reduced, however, by the fact that most of the omitted texts involve informal remarks, in which the policy content was probably low.

8   American Institute of Public Opinion, *Gallup Opinion Index*, April 1968, p. 15, and May 1968, pp. 19–20; surveys carried out for Richard A. Brody, Sidney Verba, Jerome Laulicht and the present author, by the Opinion Research Corporation of Princeton, N.J., in February, June, August, and November 1968. For a general discussion of trends in opinion concerning the Vietnam war, see John E. Mueller, *War, Presidents, and Public Opinion* (New York: Wiley, 1973).

9   The early organizational efforts are chronicled in F. Clifton White, *Suite 3505: The Story of the Draft Goldwater Movement* (New Rochelle, N.Y.: Arlington House, 1967).

Excellent overall accounts of the 1964 campaign are given in John H. Kessel, *The Goldwater Coalition: Republican Strategies in 1964* (Indianapolis: Bobbs-Merrill, 1968); in Theodore H. White, *The Making of the President 1964* (New York: Atheneum, 1965); and— more briefly—in Stanley Kelley, Jr., "The Presidential Campaign," in *The National Election of 1964*, ed. Milton Cummings (Washington, D.C.: Brookings, 1966): 42–81. Stephen Shadegg, *What Happened to Goldwater? The Inside Story of the 1964 Republican Campaign* (New York: Holt, Rinehart, 1965), and Robert D. Novak, *The Agony of the G.O.P. 1964* (New York: Macmillan Co., 1965), are also useful. Kessel disagrees with the argument of this chapter that Goldwater tried to move toward the center.

Some of the analysis in this section relies on the texts of thirty-eight of Goldwater's autumn campaign speeches, which were generously shared by Stanley Kelley, Jr. For his earlier stands Goldwater's own books, *The Conscience of a Conservative* (New York: MacFadden, 1961; orig. pub. 1960), *Why Not Victory? A New Look at American Foreign Policy* (New York: MacFadden, 1963; orig. pub. 1962), and *Where I Stand*

(New York: McGraw Hill, 1964), were helpful, as
were Arthur Frommer, *Goldwater from A to Z: A
Critical Handbook* (New York: Frommer/Pasmantier
Publishing Corp., 1964)—a compilation of quotations
—and Lionel Lokos, *Hysteria 1964: The Fear Campaign against Barry Goldwater* (New Rochelle, N.Y.:
Arlington House, 1967).

10 Frommer, *Goldwater from A to Z*, p. 66.

11 Ibid., p. 41.

12 Lokos, *Hysteria 1964*, p. 124.

13 The objective merits of Goldwater's stands are discussed sympathetically in Lokos, *Hysteria 1964*, and in
White, *The Making of the President 1964*, pp. 294–314.

14 Some twenty-eight of McGovern's most important
speeches, from December 1970 to November 1972, are
reprinted (with minor editing) in *An American Journey: The Presidential Campaign Speeches of George
McGovern* (New York: Random House, 1974). Others
were kindly provided by John Holum. For some of
McGovern's remarks in press conferences, interviews,
and the like, I have relied on clippings from the *New
York Times*, the *Miami Herald*, and the *Wall Street
Journal*.

   Gordon Weil, *The Long Shot: George McGovern
Runs for President* (New York: Norton, 1973), gives
a staff member's account of the development and presentation of issue stands, especially those on taxes and
welfare. Gary Warren Hart, *Right from the Start: A
Chronicle of the McGovern Campaign* (New York:
Quadrangle, 1973) tells of Hart's and others' organizational efforts. Timothy Crouse, *The Boys on the Bus*
(New York: Random House, 1973) describes press
coverage.

   A sympathetic overview of the campaign is given in
Richard Dougherty, *Goodbye, Mr. Christian: A Personal Account of McGovern's Rise and Fall* (Garden
City, N.Y.: Doubleday, 1973); a notably unsympathetic
view, in Theodore H. White, *The Making of the President 1972*; and a fascinating hallucinogenic account in

Hunter S. Thompson, *Fear and Loathing: On the Campaign Trail '72* (San Francisco: Straight Arrow Books, 1973).

15 For a general treatment of the platform, see Benjamin I. Page, "Innovation and Compromise: The Making of a Party Platform," in Denis G. Sullivan, Jeffrey L. Pressman, Benjamin I. Page and John J. Lyons, *The Politics of Representation: The Democratic Convention 1972* (New York: St. Martin's 1974), pp. 71–115.

16 Theodore C. Sorenson, *Kennedy* (New York: Harper, 1965), pp. 215–16.

17 U.S., Congress, House of Representatives, Committee on the Judiciary, *Privileged Report on Impeachment*, 93d Cong., 2d sess., 1974; Theodore H. White, *Breach of Faith: The Fall of Richard Nixon* (New York: Atheneum, 1975); George Thayer, *Who Shakes the Money Tree? American Campaign Finance Practices from 1789 to the Present* (New York: Simon & Schuster, 1973).

18 The effect of imperfect information on political equality is a principal, but often neglected, theme in Downs, *An Economic Theory of Democracy*. Cf. Downs's chap. 6.

Chapter 6

1 The analysis of Nixon and Humphrey in this chapter is based on the collection of speeches described in chapter 3. The sources for other campaigns are described in chapters 4 and 5.

   Nixon's acceptance speech was reprinted in Richard M. Nixon, *Nixon Speaks Out* (New York: Nixon-Agnew Campaign Committee, 1968), pp. 277–91.

2 Rexford G. Tugwell, *The Brains Trust* (New York: Viking, 1968).

3 A readable brief history of campaigning is Marvin R. Weisbord, *Campaigning for President: A New Look at the Road to the White House* (Washington, D.C.: Public Affairs Press, 1964).

4   Anthony Downs, *An Economic Theory of Democracy* (New York: Harper, 1957) advocates use of past performance in calculating the expected party differential, pp. 39–40.

5   Kenneth A. Shepsle, "The Strategy of Ambiguity: Uncertainty and Electoral Competition," *American Political Science Review* 66 (June 1972): 555–68.

6   Peter C. Fishburn, "Lotteries and Social Choice," *Journal of Economic Theory* 52 (October 1972): 189–207; Richard Zeckhauser, "Majority Rule with Lotteries on Alternatives," *Quarterly Journal of Economics* 83 (November 1969): 696–703.

7   Benjamin I. Page, "The Theory of Political Ambiguity," *American Political Science Review* 70 (September 1976): 742–52.

8   Richard M. Nixon, *Nixon on the Issues* (New York: Nixon-Agnew Campaign Committee, 1968).

9   Benjamin I. Page and Richard A. Brody, "Policy Voting and the Electoral Process: The Vietnam War Issue," *American Political Science Review* 66 (September 1972): 979–95.

10 Bernard B. Berelson, Paul F. Lazarsfeld, and William N. McPhee, *Voting: A Study of Opinion Formation in a Presidential Campaign* (Chicago: University of Chicago Press, 1954), chap. 10.

11 Page and Brody, "Policy Voting." The effect of ambiguity must be distinguished in principle (though it is not always easy to do so in practice) from the effects of candidate similarity discussed in chapters 4 and 5, above, and emphasized in Norman H. Nie, Sidney Verba, and John R. Petrocik, *The Changing American Voter* (Cambridge: Harvard University Press, 1976).

12 V. O. Key, Jr., with the assistance of Milton C. Cummings, Jr., *The Responsible Electorate: Rationality in Presidential Voting 1936–1960* (Cambridge: Harvard University Press, 1966): 1–8.

13 Zeckhauser, "Majority Rule."

14 Page, "The Theory of Political Ambiguity."

15 This is a major theme, though often neglected, in Downs, *Economic Theory*. See especially pp. 93–94 and 238–59.

16 Stanley Kelley, Jr., *Political Campaigning: Problems in Creating an Informed Electorate* (Washington, D.C.: Brookings, 1960): 62–83.

Chapter 7

1 Donald E. Stokes, "Spatial Models of Party Competition," in Angus Campbell, Philip E. Converse, Warren E. Miller, and Donald E. Stokes, *Elections and the Political Order* (New York: Wiley, 1966), pp. 161–79.

2 A theory of cognitive psychology could be based upon assumptions of limited-information rationality. Elements of such a theory are present in the work of Downs, Simon, Abelson, and Axelrod, among others.

3 Franklin D. Roosevelt, *The Public Papers and Addresses of Franklin D. Roosevelt, with a Special Introduction and Explanatory Notes by President Roosevelt*, ed. Samuel I. Rosenman, 5 vols. (New York: Random House, 1938), 1:624–27.

4 Roosevelt, *Public Papers*, pp. 627–39.

5 Ibid., pp. 647–59.

6 Ibid., pp. 659–69.

7 Stanley Kelley, Jr., *Professional Public Relations and Political Power* (Baltimore: Johns Hopkins Press, 1966; orig. pub. 1956), p. 147. Our account of Eisenhower's 1952 campaign relies largely on Kelley, pp. 144–201.

8 Ibid., p. 174.

9 Ibid., p. 176.

10 Ibid., p. 189.

11 Ibid., p. 190.

12 Nixon's acceptance speech is reprinted in Richard M. Nixon, *Nixon Speaks Out* (New York: Nixon-Agnew Campaign Committee, 1968), pp. 277–91.

13   Joe McGinniss, *The Selling of the President 1968* (New York: Trident, 1969), pp. 92–95. McGinniss gives the scripts of a number of Nixon commercials, along with a fascinating view of their production.

14   Ibid., pp. 242–43.

15   Ibid., pp. 240–41.

16   This and subsequent Wallace quotations are from a nationally distributed tape recording of a speech made in Charlotte, North Carolina, in (June?) 1968. Wallace repeated much of the same language elsewhere, with local references changed; this is an early version of The Speech.

17   U.S., Congress, Senate, Committee on Commerce, *Freedom of Communications: Final Report Pursuant to S. Res. 305*, 86th Congress, 4 vols., 87th Cong., 1st sess., 1961, 1:347.

18   Ibid., p. 679.

19   Ibid., p. 1156.

20   Ibid., p. 1072.

21   Ibid., p. 1125.

22   *New York Times*, 16 July 1976, p. A10. In addition to a file of newspaper accounts, our materials on Carter include some texts provided by Carol Nackenoff and the Carter presidential campaign staff.

23   George McGovern, *An American Journey: The Presidential Campaign Speeches of George McGovern* (New York: Random House, 1974), pp. 51–58, 59–64, 65–73, 74–83.

24   Irwin Ross, *The Loneliest Campaign: The Truman Victory of 1948* (New York: New American Library, Signet ed., 1969; orig. pub. 1968), pp. 172, 176, 177, 192, 193, 200.

25   *Chicago Tribune*, 20 August 1976, p. 10. Our newspaper file on Ford is supplemented by some campaign materials provided by Philip Jackson.

26   U.S., President, *Public Papers of the Presidents of the United States: Dwight D. Eisenhower, 1956*, pp. 702–15.

27   U.S., President, *Public Papers of the Presidents of the United States: Lyndon B. Johnson, 1963–1964*, 2 vols., 2:1009–13.

28   *Chicago Tribune*, 20 August 1976, p. 10.

29   U.S., *Freedom of Communications*, 1:389.

30   Ibid., p. 1261.

31   *New York Times*, 16 July 1976, p. A10.

32   Such use of past performance to judge *results* must be distinguished from its less reliable use to judge future *policy*. Our argument is similar to Downs's advocacy of using the past to estimate future utility incomes, in *An Economic Theory of Democracy*, pp. 39–40. As Downs points out, evaluations of the incumbents' performance could enter into voting decisions in several different ways: they could be contrasted with the challengers' promises, or with projections from the challengers' past achievements, or with some standard of ideal performance. See also Morris P. Fiorina, "An Outline for a Model of Party Choice," *American Journal of Political Science* 21 (August, 1977): 601–25.

33   Elements of this theory appear in V. O. Key, Jr., *Public Opinion and American Democracy* (New York: Knopf, 1961), pp. 267–68, 272–76, 472–80, and in the work of Carl Friedrich, who is generally credited with formulating the "rule of anticipated reactions." It is a matter of conjecture whether or not matters of performance are more likely than policy alternatives to escape. Arrow's paradox: that is, whether or not an optimal line of action exists.

34   On this and several other points I am indebted to Denis Sullivan.

35   John Stuart Mill, *Considerations on Representative Government* (New York: Henry Hold, 1882; orig. pub. 1861).

36   V. O. Key, Jr., *Public Opinion and American Democracy* (New York: Knopf, 1961); and V. O. Key, Jr., and Milton C. Cummings, Jr., *The Responsible Elec-*

torate: Rationality in Presidential Voting, 1936–1968
(New York: Random House, 1968).

37   For some evidence of this, based on panel data, see
     Richard A. Brody, "Stability and Change in Party Iden-
     tification: Presidential to Off-Years," paper delivered
     at the 1977 annual meeting of the American Political
     Science Association, Washington, D.C., 1–4 September.

38   Gerald Kramer, "Short-Term Fluctuations in U.S. Vot-
     ing Behavior, 1896–1964," *American Political Science
     Review* 65 (March 1971): 131–43; Edward R. Tufte,
     "Determinants of the Outcomes of Midterm Congres-
     sional Elections," *American Political Science Review*
     69 (September 1975): 812–26; Saul Goodman and
     Gerald H. Kramer, "Comment on Arcelus and Meltzer,
     The Effect of Aggregate Economic Conditions on Con-
     gressional Elections," *American Political Science Re-
     view* 69 (December 1975): 1254–65; Edward R. Tufte,
     Political Control of the Economy (forthcoming).

39   Richard A. Brody and Benjamin I. Page, "The Impact
     of Events on Presidential Popularity: The Johnson and
     Nixon Administrations," in *Perspectives on the Presi-
     dency*, ed. Aaron Wildavsky (Boston: Little, Brown,
     1975), pp. 136–48.

40   Tufte, *Political Control of the Economy.*

Chapter 8

1   Donald E. Stokes, "Some Dynamic Elements of Con-
    tests for the Presidency," *American Political Science
    Review* 60 (March 1966): 19–28; Herbert B. Asher,
    *Presidential Elections and American Politics: Voters,
    Candidates, and Campaigns since 1952* (Homewood,
    Ill.: Dorsey, 1976), chaps. 5, 6, esp. p. 126.

2   Similar arguments are made in Samuel Popkin, John
    W. Gorman, Charles Phillips, and Jeffrey A. Smith,
    "Comment: What Have You Done for Me Lately:
    Toward an Investment Theory of Voting," *American
    Political Science Review* 70 (September 1976): 779–
    805.

3   Herbert A. Hyman and Paul B. Sheatsley, "The Political Appeal of President Eisenhower," *Public Opinion Quarterly* 17 (Winter 1953–54): 443–60; Philip E. Converse and Georges Dupeux, "De Gaulle and Eisenhower: The Public Image of the Victorious General," in Angus Campbell, Philip E. Converse, Warren E. Miller, and Donald E. Stokes, *Elections and the Political Order* (New York: Wiley, 1966), pp. 292–345. Using data on MacArthur, Hyman and Sheatsley point out that military stature alone is not sufficient to guarantee political appeal.

4   U.S., Congress, Senate, Committee on Commerce, *Freedom of Communications: Final Report Pursuant to S. Res. 305, 86th Congress*, 4 vols., 87th Cong., 1st sess., 1961, 2:341. See also 2:384–85.

5   Ibid., 2:521.

6   Ibid., 2:533–34.

7   George H. Gallup, *The Gallup Poll: Public Opinion 1935–1971*, 3 vols. (New York: Random House, 1972), 3:1669, 1672.

8   U.S., *Freedom of Communications*, 1:1125.

9   Theodore H. White, *The Making of the President 1960* (New York: Atheneum, 1961; Cardinal Pocket Books ed.), pp. 340–42.

10   Sidney Kraus, ed., *The Great Debates: Background—Perspective—Effects* (Bloomington: Indiana University Press, 1962), see esp. pp. 262, 276, 278; and Elihu Katz and Jacob J. Feldman, "The Debates in the Light of Research: A Survey of Surveys," at pp. 173–223.

11   Jimmy Carter, *Why Not the Best?* (New York: Bantam, 1976; orig. pub. Broadman, 1975), chap. 2, esp. pp. 19–28.

12   *New York Times*, 25 September 1976, p. 8.

13   Ibid., p. 9.

14   Charles E. Osgood, G. J. Suci, and Percy H. Tannenbaum, *The Measurement of Meaning* (Urbana: Univer-

sity of Illinois Press, 1957); Renata Tagiuri, "Person
Perception," in Gardner Lindzey and Elliot Aronson,
eds., *The Handbook of Social Psychology*, 2d ed. (Reading, Mass.: Addison-Wesley, 1968), 3:395–449.

15   James David Barber, *The Presidential Character: Predicting Performance in the White House* (Englewood
Cliffs, N.J.: Prentice-Hall, 1972) builds his typology
upon dichotomized versions of two of these three dimensions, positivity and activity. For a critique, see
Alexander L. George, "Assessing Presidential Character," in *Perspectives on the Presidency*, ed. Aaron Wil-
davsky (Boston: Little, Brown, 1975), pp. 91–134; and,
for a rebuttal, James David Barber, "Strategies for
Understanding Politicians," *American Journal of Political Science* 18 (May 1974): 443–67.

16   Alexander L. George and Juliette L. George, *Woodrow
Wilson and Colonel House: A Personality Study* (New
York: Dover, 1964; orig. pub. 1956); Barber, *Presi-
dential Character.*

17   Joe McGinniss, *The Selling of the President 1968* (New
York: Trident, 1969): 139–40.

18   Ibid. The quote appears on p. 103.

19   Barber, *Presidential Character.* On this point Barber's
argument closely resembles those of Freud, Lasswell,
and George.

20   U.S., *Freedom of Communications*, 1:958.

21   Stanley Kelley, Jr., "The Presidential Campaign," in
The Presidential Election and Transition 1960–61, ed.
Paul T. David (Washington, D.C.: Brookings, 1961):
57–87, at pp. 66–68.

22   For accounts of the Eagleton affair, see Richard Dough-
erty, *Goodbye, Mr. Christian: A Personal Account of
McGovern's Rise and Fall* (Garden City, New York:
Doubleday, 1973), pp. 171–202; Gordon Weil, *The
Long Shot: George McGovern Runs for President* (New
York: Norton, 1973), pp. 156–94; and Theodore H.
White, *The Making of the President 1972* (New York:
Atheneum, 1973; Bantam ed.), pp. 256–89.

23 *New York Times*, 26 July 1972, p. 20.

24 Dougherty, *Goodbye, Mr. Christian*, p. 201.

25 George McGovern, *An American Journey: The Presidential Campaign Speeches of George McGovern* (New York: Random House, 1974), p. 5.

26 Gallup, *The Gallup Poll*, 3:1605, 1690. The 24% figure is from April 1959, and the 20% figure from May 1960.

27 Accounts of Kennedy's handling of his Catholicism are given in Theodore C. Sorenson, *Kennedy* (New York: Harper and Row, 1965), pp. 108–13, 142–47, and 188–95; and in White, *The Making of the President 1960*.

28 White, pp. 128–29.

29 Sorenson, *Kennedy*, pp. 142–43.

30 U.S., *Freedom of Communications*, 1:208.

31 Philip E. Converse, "Religion and Politics: The 1960 Election," in Campbell et al., *Elections and the Political Order*, pp. 96–124.

32 *New York Times*, 5 June 1976, p. 23; 6 June 1976, p. 1; 7 June 1976, p. 22.

33 *Playboy*, November 1976, p. 68.

34 Ibid., pp. 69–70.

35 Ibid., p. 86.

36 Stokes, "Some Dynamic Elements"; Asher, *Presidential Elections*; Popkin et al., "Comment: What Have You Done for Me Lately?"; Arthur H. Miller and Warren E. Miller, "Ideology in the 1972 Election: Myth or Reality—A Rejoinder," *American Political Science Review* 70 (September 1976): 832–49; Warren E. Miller and Teresa F. Levitan, *Leadership and Change: Presidential Elections from 1952 to 1976* (Cambridge, Mass.: Winthrop, 1977).

Chapter 9

1 For a discussion of want satisfaction versus need satisfaction, see Brian Barry, *Political Argument* (London: Routledge and Kegan Paul, 1965).

2   On the effects of certain campaign events, see Sidney
    Kraus, ed., *The Great Debates: Background—Perspec-
    tive—Effects* (Bloomington, Indiana University Press,
    1962).

3   Donald Bruce Johnson and Kirk H. Porter, *National
    Party Platforms 1840–1972* (Urbana: University of Il-
    linois Press, 1973), pp. 89–91, 104–6.

4   Benjamin I. Page, "Innovation and Compromise: The
    Making of a Party Platform," in Denis Sullivan et al.,
    The Politics of Representation (New York: St. Mar-
    tin's, 1974), pp. 71–115; James L. Sundquist, *Politics
    and Policy* (Washington, D.C.: Brookings, 1968).

5   Murray Edelman, *The Symbolic Uses of Politics* (Ur-
    bana: University of Illinois Press, 1964).

6   A remarkable catalogue of government secrecy and de-
    ception from the U-2 to Watergate is David Wise, *The
    Politics of Lying: Government Deception, Secrecy, and
    Power* (New York: Random House, 1973).

7   Ralph Miliband, *The State in Capitalist Society* (New
    York: Basic Books, 1969), pp. 179–264.

8   Antonio Gramsci, *Selections from the Prison Notebooks*,
    ed. and trans. Quintin Hoare and Geoffrey Nowell
    Smith (New York: International Publishers, 1971).
    Gramsci's Aesopian language permits a variety of read-
    ings; mine emphasizes the structuralist side of his
    thought.

Chapter 10

1   Grant McConnell, *Private Power and American De-
    mocracy* (New York: Knopf, 1966). A similar analy-
    sis of effects of the scope of conflict (and, implicitly,
    of the importance of information) is given in E. E.
    Schattschneider, *The Semisovereign People: A Realist's
    View of Democracy in America* (New York: Holt,
    1960).

Index

Abelson, Robert, 318
Activity (in candidates' personalities), 246–50; party differences in, 247–49; Kennedy (1960) and, 249–50, 263
Agnew, Spiro T., 174
Agriculture: Eisenhower on (1952), 71; Goldwater on (1964), 120, 128, 148, 167; Humphrey on (1968), 44, 145–46, 157–59; Nixon on (1968), 44, 157–59; public opinion on (1968), 35, 298; Stevenson on (1952), 71
Aid, foreign. *See* Foreign aid
Aldrich, John H., 311
Alker, Hayward R., Jr., xvii
Alliance. *See* NATO
Ambiguity, 152–91; and democracy, 187–91; infrequency and inconspicuousness, 153–62; and issue voting, 186–88; and perceptions of candidates' stands, 179–86; "real" stands and, 172–76; lack of specificity, 162–65; variations in, 165–72; why politicians are vague, 176–79
Amnesty for Vietnam resisters, 55, 134
Anderson, Kristi, 308
Aranson, Peter H., 303, 304
Arms control, Goldwater on (1964), 122

Arrow, Kenneth, 13, 14, 19, 302, 320
Arrow's paradox, 12–14, 18–19, 177
Asher, Herbert B., 321, 324
Assumptions, 6–9, 18, 20, 26–27, 266–67
Axelrod, Robert, 318

Barber, James David, xvii, 243, 247, 323
Barry, Brian, xvii, 302, 324
Becker, Gary, 301
Bentham, Jeremy, 12, 302
Berelson, Bernard, 185, 309, 317
Bernholz, Peter, 303
Black, Duncan, 13, 302
Blacks, rights of. *See* Civil rights
Borda, Charles-Jean de, 12
Brams, Steven J., 302
Brody, Richard A., xvii, 289, 304, 306, 307, 311, 312, 314, 317, 321
Bryan, William Jennings, 99, 101, 170, 249
Burnham, Walter Dean, 311

Campaigning, development of, 170–71
Campaign rhetoric, types of, 110–13; and ambiguity, 171–72
Campaigns, presidential election. *See specific years and candidates*
Campbell, Angus, 310, 312, 318, 322, 324

Foreign aid: Goldwater on (1964), 53,
120, 122; Humphrey on (1968), 42,
51, 84, 86, 157–59; Nixon on
(1968), 42, 84, 86, 157–59; public
opinion on (1964), 53; (1968), 35,
68, 290
Foreign policy: party differences in
candidates' stands on (1968), 83–88;
party differences in public opinion
on, 66–67, 68. *See also specific
topics*
Frankel, Charles, 301
Friedman, Milton, 6, 301
Friedrich, Carl J., 320
Frommer, Arthur, 315
Future, visions of, 209–19. *See also*
Goals; Past performance

Gallup, George H., 305 and passim
Garvey, Gerald, 303, 304
Gay liberation, McGovern on (1972),
134
George, Alexander, xvii, 323
George, Juliette L., 323
Ginsberg, Benjamin, 313
Goals, 154–56, 192–94, 209–31; Carter
on (1976), 218–19; Eisenhower on
(1956), 210–13; Ford on (1976),
215–16; Johnson on (1964), 213–15;
John Kennedy on (1960), 217–18.
See also Past performance
Goldwater, Barry, 142, 269; ambiguity
of, 153, 167–68, 169, 171, 173;
character of, 235–36, 256, 257,
261–62; 264; and clear choice, v,
4, 21; and movement toward the
center, 118–32, 150; policy stands
of, and party cleavages, 91, 100–
103; policy stands of, and public
opinion, 52–54, 57, 118–32, 136,
150; speeches of, sources for, 314;
unfriendly forums, choice of, 148
Goodman, Saul, 321
Gorman, John W., 321
Gramsci, Antonio, 275, 325
Grant, Ulysses S., 234
Greenstone, J. David, 307
Gubser, Charles, 306
Gun control. *See* Law and order

Hadley, Charles D., 308
Hamilton, Alexander, 195, 301
Harding, Warren G., 170, 246, 247,
249
Harris, Louis, 305, 306, and passim
Harrison, William Henry, 234
Hart, Gary Warren, 133, 315

Hartz, Louis, 305
Health. *See* Medical care
Heard, Alexander, 307
Hibbs, Douglas A., 313
Hierarchies of means and ends, 193–94,
206–8
Hinich, Melvin, 18, 89, 303, 304, 313
Hobbes, Thomas, 11
Hoffman, Paul J., 307
Holum, John, xvii, 135, 315
Homosexual rights, McGovern on
(1972), 134
Honesty, 255–57, 273. *See also* Infor-
mation; Manipulation of opinion
Hoover, Herbert: activity of, 247, 248;
past performance and, 194, 196,
222; policy stands of, 69
Hotelling, Harold, 15–17, 19, 21, 56,
302
Housing: Goldwater on (1964), 120,
122; Humphrey on (1968), 46, 157–
59; Nixon on (1968), 46, 157–59;
public opinion on (1968), 34, 294
Hoyer, Robert, 303
Humphrey, Hubert: ambiguity of,
153–54, 156–65, 173; ambiguity and
perceptions of, 181, 183;
ambiguity and votes for, 187, 188;
appeals to special audiences by,
145–47; character of, 245–46, 251;
constancy and change of, 110–13,
113–18; and Goldwater, 130–31; and
McGovern, 133, 136, 137, 138; past
performance and votes for, 223, 224;
policy stands of and party cleavages,
76–89; policy stands of and public
opinion, 37–52, 57–59; speeches of,
sources for, 306; Vietnam and votes
for, 103
Humphreys, Robert, 198
Hyman, Herbert A., 322

Imports: Humphrey on (1968), 146;
Nixon on (1968), 146
Income maintenance: Goldwater on
(1964), 120, 121, 123, 130, 148;
Humphrey on (1968), 45, 50, 78–
79, 147, 157–59; McGovern on
(1972), 55, 91–94, 134–35, 138–39,
148; Nixon on (1968), 45, 78–79,
157–59; (1972), 91–94; public
opinion on (1968), 34, 67, 293–94;
Truman on (1948), 70
Income tax: Carter on (1976), 95–98,
167; Ford on (1976), 95–98; Goldwater on (1964), 53, 120, 122, 128;
Johnson on (1964), 173; John Ken-

336   **Index**